Praise for *The Lean Product Playbook*

"If you want to create successful, innovative products that customers love, Dan's playbook is a must-read."

—Hiten Shah, co-founder of KISSmetrics and Crazy Egg

"Dan's product expertise was incredibly helpful in the early days of building and growing Box. I found his advice incredibly valuable—and if you want to build a successful product, you will too."

—Aaron Levie, CEO, Box

"A great, detailed guide on how to find product-market fit and make things people will love. This book should be required reading for everybody building products."

—Laura Klein, author of *UX for Lean Startups*

"Dan Olsen makes product development simple and logical. If you want to create kick-ass products, you need to read this book."

—Dave McClure, founding partner
and troublemaker, 500 Startups

"Dan's playbook is the missing manual on how to apply Lean Startup principles. This comprehensive, straightforward book guides you through everything you need to know to build a winning product."

—Sean Ellis, CEO of Qualaroo and GrowthHackers.com

"Dan takes Lean Startup to a new level with his step-by-step playbook for creating great products! This book truly is for everyone—from designers to business people to engineers."

—Kaaren Hanson, VP design, Medallia and
former VP design innovation, Intuit

"Dan Olsen is an established Lean product black belt in Silicon Valley. His book gives product teams a simple and straightforward way to identify product-market fit, launch an MVP, and then improve it systematically over time."

—Ken Fine, chief customer officer, Medallia

"*The Lean Product Playbook* is the first book I've seen that truly explains how to apply Lean Startup concepts in a practical, step-by-step manner. Dan's product work with so many companies makes him an authority on the subject. Whether you're creating a product at a startup or a larger company, this book will prove invaluable."

—Jim Scheinman, founder and CEO, Maven Ventures

"Unlike many product gurus who are long on theory but short on practice, Dan Olsen has battle-tested his approach across many companies, many products, and many years of being a player-coach. Dan's simple but complete playbook gives teams the best chance to create not just great products, but great companies."

—Jeff Maggioncalda, former CEO and first employee,
Financial Engines

"Dan is an exceptionally skilled product leader who was instrumental to our product's success at my first startup. He has distilled his expertise and advice into an easy-to-follow guide to creating products that deliver real customer value. I highly recommend this book to anyone leading, building, or marketing any product or service."

—Christian Pirkner, angel investor and
co-founder, MoodLogic

"Dan transformed our product development process from chaos into a well-oiled machine. Now anyone who reads this book can benefit from his brilliant, practical approach. If you want to improve your organization's ability to innovate, this book is a must-read."

—Jack Lynch, co-founder and co-CEO, PresenceLearning

"This book is a valuable blueprint for those who want to effectively apply Lean Startup concepts to build successful products. Dan knows what he's talking about—and deftly shares his knowledge and experience to bring Lean principles to life."

—Michael J. Nolan, author and former senior editor,
New Riders Voices That Matter series

"Dan is a rare breed in that he's able to blend business and customer needs with thoughtful process and product design. His guidance on best practices was helpful for us at One Medical and for other like-minded companies in Silicon Valley."

—Tom Lee, CEO, One Medical

"For those that are looking for a more structured approach to coming up with winning products, Dan combines modern techniques with experience to step you through the process."

—Marty Cagan, author of
Inspired: How To Create Products Customers Love
and founder, Silicon Valley Product Group

"Dan Olsen takes the mystery out of how to *consistently* create great products using Lean Startup principles. His framework and step-by-step guidance are easy to follow and can be applied by large and small teams alike. This book is a must-read for anyone involved in new product development."

—Greg Cohen, author of
Agile Excellence for Product Managers

"Dan Olsen's *The Lean Product Playbook* is wonderfully thorough and practical. It provides invaluable step-by-step guidance to help you make sure that your product is *The Right It,* and also gives great advice on how to build *It* right. A must-read for any innovator and entrepreneur."

—Alberto Savoia, author of *Pretotype It,*
co-founder of Pretotype Labs LLC and
former Innovation Agitator at Google

"I wish I had this book when I started my business! Following Dan's advice on how to validate ideas before you build them can save you valuable time and money. This must-have playbook really paints a clear picture of the whole process and is filled with eureka insights."

—Sam Crisco, founder, piZap

"Dan helped YouSendIt (now Hightail) launch our first subscription product shortly after we raised our first round of venture financing. His product expertise, which he shares in this book, really got our product management engine going. The result was a well-monetized product that customers loved."

—Ranjith Kumaran, co-founder and CEO, Hightail

"Everyone aspires to increase their speed of innovation, reduce risk, and build products customers love. But it's challenging to do so without the right techniques. *The Lean Product Playbook* gives you the tactical how-to plan to actually achieve those goals."

—Steven Cohn, founder and CEO, Validately

"As a client, we directly benefited from Dan's product expertise. Now that he's documented all this valuable knowledge, anyone who wants to build a successful product should read this book."

—Jeff Tangney, founding CEO of Doximity and Epocrates

THE
LEAN
PRODUCT
PLAYBOOK

THE
LEAN
PRODUCT
PLAYBOOK

HOW TO INNOVATE WITH MINIMUM VIABLE PRODUCTS AND RAPID CUSTOMER FEEDBACK

DAN OLSEN

WILEY

Published by John Wiley & Sons, Inc., Hoboken, New Jersey
Published simultaneously in Canada

For general information about our other products and services, please contact our Customer Care Department within the United States at (800) 762-2974, outside the United States at (317) 572-3993 or fax (317) 572-4002.

Wiley publishes in a variety of print and electronic formats and by print-on-demand. Some material included with standard print versions of this book may not be included in e-books or in print-on-demand. If this book refers to media such as a CD or DVD that is not included in the version you purchased, you may download this material at http://booksupport.wiley.com. For more information about Wiley products, visit www.wiley.com.

Cover Design: C. Wallace
Cover Photograph: Whiteboard © iStock.com/dalton00;
              Whiteboard © iStock.com/cscredon

Library of Congress Cataloging-in-Publication Data is Available:

ISBN 978-1-118-96087-5 (hardback)
ISBN 978-1-118-96102-5 (ePDF)
ISBN 978-1-118-96096-7 (ePub)

Printed in the United States of America

10 9 8 7 6 5 4 3 2 1

For my mom and dad, who taught me to learn and dream,
For Vanessa, my cofounder in life, who amazes me more each day,
And for Sofia and Xavier, may you learn twice as much and dream twice as big.

Contents

PART III   Building and Optimizing Your Product

Introduction: Why Products Fail and How Lean Changes the Game

Building great products is *hard*. We're all familiar with the sobering statistics about the high percentage of new products that fail. For every Apple, Google, Facebook, and other success story you hear, there are countless failed products causing companies to shutter their doors.

Think of all the products you've used in the last year. How many of those products do you love? How many do you hate? How many can you even remember? If you're like most people, you actually *love* a very small number of the products you use.

If you've been on a team that has built a product that customers love, you know how great that feels. Passionate users can't stop raving about your product. Your business metrics are growing up and to the right exponentially. You're struggling to keep up with the high demand. Customers *want* and *value* your product.

But the unfortunate reality is that very few products are like that. Why is it so hard to build a product that customers love? Why do so many products fail?

WHY PRODUCTS FAIL

Throughout my career, I've worked on and studied many different products. When I analyze the root causes of why products fail, a common pattern emerges. The main reason products fail is because they don't meet customer needs in a way that is better than other alternatives. This is the essence of product-market fit. Marc Andreessen of Netscape fame coined the term in 2007. In the same blog post he also contends, as I do, that startups "fail because they never get to product-market fit."

The Lean Startup movement begun by Eric Ries has helped popularize the idea of product-market fit and the importance of achieving it. One reason Lean Startup has such wide appeal is because people know how difficult it is to build successful products. I am a strong advocate of Lean Startup principles.

Many people get excited when they first hear Lean Startup ideas and are eager to try them out. However, I've spoken with many of these enthusiasts who struggle to figure out exactly what they should be doing. They understand the high-level concepts, but don't know how to apply them.

This reminds me of many people who decide they want to get in better physical shape. They are highly motivated to start working out more. They join a gym. They buy new workout clothes. They show up to the gym raring to go—but realize that they have no idea what to do when they get there. What exercises should I be doing? What equipment should I be using? What's the right way to work out? They have plenty of motivation, but lack the specific knowledge about what exactly to do.

WHY THIS BOOK?

I wrote *The Lean Product Playbook* to fill the knowledge gaps faced by many people who want to create a product using Lean Startup principles. This book provides clear, step-by-step guidance to help you build successful products. In working with so many product teams, I have witnessed the various challenges they faced and seen numerous examples of what worked well and what didn't. Over the course of this experience, I developed a framework and process for how to achieve product-market fit.

The Product-Market Fit Pyramid

The framework, which I call the Product-Market Fit Pyramid, breaks product-market fit down into five key components: your target customer, your customer's underserved needs, your value proposition, your feature set, and your user experience (UX). Each of these is actually a testable hypothesis. There is a logical sequence to the five hypotheses based on how they relate to each other, resulting in the hierarchy shown in the pyramid (see Figure I.1).

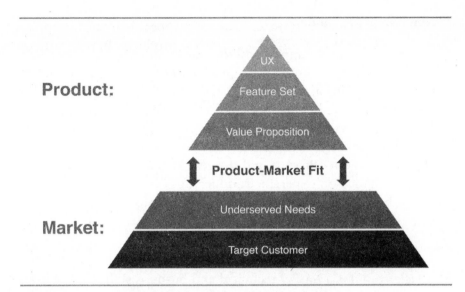

FIGURE I.1   The Product-Market Fit Pyramid

The Lean Product Process

After developing the Product-Market Fit Pyramid, I designed a simple, iterative process to take advantage of it, called the Lean Product Process. This process guides you through each layer of the pyramid from the bottom up. It helps you articulate and test your key hypotheses for each of the five key components of product-market fit. The Lean Product Process consists of six steps:

1. Determine your target customers
2. Identify underserved customer needs
3. Define your value proposition
4. Specify your minimum viable product (MVP) feature set
5. Create your MVP prototype
6. Test your MVP with customers

This book describes each step of the process in detail with relevant real-world examples. I also devote a chapter to share an in-depth, end-to-end case study of the process being applied.

A Comprehensive Guide

I wrote this book as a comprehensive guide because you have to get so many things right to build a great product. I cover a range of important topics in addition to the Lean Product Process. The book walks you through detailed explanations of UX design and Agile development. It also provides in-depth coverage of analytics and how to use metrics to optimize your product.

The Lean Product Process and the rest of the advice in this book come from hands-on experience and lessons learned throughout my career of building high-tech products—both successes and failures.

About Me

My background is a mix of technical and business skills that I began to develop when my parents gave me my first computer at the age of 10. I started my first business a few years later. I studied electrical engineering at Northwestern University and then started my high-tech career designing nuclear-powered submarines. While working, I earned a Master's degree in industrial engineering from Virginia Tech at night, where I learned about the Lean manufacturing principles that inspired the Lean Startup movement.

I moved to Silicon Valley to attend Stanford Business School and then joined Intuit, which provided an incredible post-MBA training ground in product management, product development, customer research, user experience design, and marketing. I led and grew the Quicken product team to record sales and profit. As I learned more, I had a growing desire to take what I had learned and apply it at startups. Since leaving Intuit, I've spent a lot of time working at and with startups.

For years now, I have consulted to numerous companies, helping them apply Lean principles to create successful products. I take a hands-on approach in my consulting: I work closely with CEOs and their management teams and also get in the trenches with product managers, designers, and developers. I usually serve as interim VP of Product for my clients and am often the first product person on their team.

I've tested and refined the advice in this book while working with a wide range of companies. My client list includes Facebook, Box,

YouSendIt (now Hightail), Microsoft, Epocrates, Medallia, Chartboost, XING, Financial Engines, and One Medical Group. I've found these ideas applicable to all my clients, even though they vary in size from small early stage startups to large public companies and span a variety of vertical industries, target customers, product types, and business models.

I enjoy sharing and discussing my Lean Product ideas with as many people as I can. I regularly give talks and workshops and post my slides on SlideShare at http://slideshare.net/dan_o/presentations. I also host a monthly Lean Product meetup in Silicon Valley, which I invite you to check out at http://meetup.com/lean-product. The audiences in those forums have also helped me hone the guidance provided in this book with their questions, suggestions, and feedback.

WHO IS THIS BOOK FOR?

If you are interested in Lean Startup, Customer Development, Lean UX, Design Thinking, product management, user experience design, Agile development, or analytics, then this book is for you. It will equip you with the "how-to" manual you need, and provide a step-by-step process you can follow to ensure you're building a product that customers will find valuable.

This book is for:

- Anyone trying to build a new product or service
- Anyone trying to improve their existing product or service
- Entrepreneurs
- Product managers, designers, and developers
- Marketers, analysts, and program managers
- CEOs and other executives
- People working in companies of any size
- Anyone who is passionate about building great products

The guidance in this book is most valuable for software products. However, it is also relevant to other product categories such as hardware and wearables, and even nontechnical products. The guidance in this book is also applicable to a wide range of business contexts, including business-to-consumer (B2C) and business-to-business (B2B).

HOW THIS BOOK IS ORGANIZED

The book is organized in three parts. Part I, "Core Concepts," explains the foundational ideas of product-market fit and problem space versus solution space.

Part II of this book, "The Lean Product Process," describes each of the six steps of the process in detail, devoting a chapter to each step. Part II also includes chapters on:

- The principles of great UX design
- How to iteratively improve your product-market fit
- A detailed, end-to-end case study using the Lean Product Process

Part III, "Building and Optimizing Your Product," provides guidance that applies after you have validated product-market fit with your MVP prototype. It includes a chapter on how to build your product using Agile development, which also covers testing, continuous integration, and continuous deployment. In addition, it contains two chapters on analytics, which describe a methodology for using metrics to optimize your product and include another in-depth, real-world case study.

Writing this book has given me the opportunity to share the ideas, lessons learned, and advice accumulated over my career with a broader audience. My experience has been informed and influenced by my mentors, colleagues, and many other people passionate about sharing ideas and comparing notes on the discipline of building great products. Our field continues to evolve, with new ideas emerging all the time. That's why I'll use the companion website for this book, http://leanproductplaybook.com, as a place to share and discuss those new ideas. I invite you to visit the website to read the latest information and contribute to the conversation.

Part I

Core Concepts

Chapter 1

Achieving Product-Market Fit with the Lean Product Process

Product-market fit is a wonderful term because it captures the essence of what it means to build a great product. The concept nicely encapsulates all the factors that are critical to achieving product success. Product-market fit is one of the most important Lean Startup ideas, and this playbook will show you how to achieve it.

Given the number of people who have written about product-market fit, you can find a range of interpretations. Real-world examples are a great way to help explain such concepts—throughout this book, I walk through many examples of products that did or didn't achieve product-market fit. But let's start out by clarifying what product-market fit means.

WHAT IS PRODUCT-MARKET FIT?

As I mention in the introduction, Marc Andreessen coined the term *product-market fit* in a well-known blog post titled "The only thing that matters." In that post he writes, "Product-market fit means being in a good market with a product that can satisfy that market." My definition of product-market fit—which is consistent with his—is that you have built a product that creates significant customer value. This means that your product meets real customer needs and does so in a way that is better than the alternatives.

Some people interpret product-market fit much more broadly, going beyond the core definition to also include having a validated revenue model—that is, that you can successfully monetize your product. For others, product-market fit also includes having a cost-effective customer acquisition model. Such definitions basically equate product-market fit with having a profitable business. I believe using "product-market fit" as another way of saying "profitable" glosses over the essential aspects of the idea, which can stand on its own.

In this book, I use the core definition above. In business, there is a distinction between *creating* value and *capturing* value. In order to capture value, you must first create it. To be clear, topics such as business model, customer acquisition, marketing, and pricing are critical to a successful business. Each is also worthy of its own book. This book touches on those subjects, and you can use the qualitative and quantitative techniques in it to improve those aspects of your business. In fact, Chapters 13 and 14 discuss how to optimize your business metrics, but the majority of this book focuses on the core definition of product-market fit and gives you a playbook for how to achieve it.

THE PRODUCT-MARKET FIT PYRAMID

If you're trying to achieve product-market fit, a definition alone doesn't give you enough guidance. That's why I created an actionable framework called the Product-Market Fit Pyramid, shown in Figure 1.1. This hierarchical model decomposes product-market

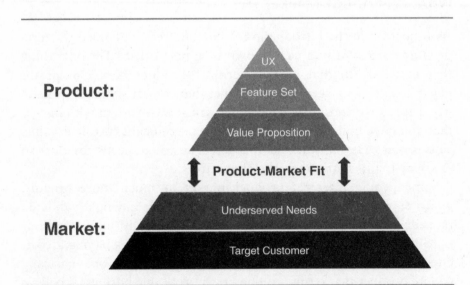

FIGURE 1.1 The Product-Market Fit Pyramid

into its five key components, each a layer of the pyramid. Your product is the top section, consisting of three layers. The market is the bottom section of the pyramid, consisting of two layers. Within the product and market sections, each layer depends on the layer immediately beneath it. Product-market fit lies between the top and bottom sections of the pyramid.

The Market

Given the pyramid's hierarchy, let's start with the bottom section, which is the market. A market consists of all the existing and potential customers that share a particular customer need or set of related needs. For example, all the people in the United States who need to prepare their income taxes are in the U.S. tax preparation market. You can describe the size of a market by the total number of customers in the market or the total revenue generated by those customers. For either of those two measures, you can refer to the current size or the potential future size of the market.

Different customers within a market choose different solutions to meet their needs. For example, some customers in the tax preparation market may use a professional service such as H&R Block. Others may choose to prepare their taxes themselves, either by hand or by using software such as TurboTax.

Within a given market, you can analyze the market share of each competing product—that is, what percentage of the market each product has. For example, you could compare the smartphone market share of Apple versus Samsung. Or you could segment the smartphone market by operating system (iOS, Android, and so forth). Browsers are another example where the market shares of each different product are closely watched.

As you walk down the aisles of a supermarket, you see products in many different market categories: toothpaste, shampoo, laundry detergent, cereal, yogurt, and beer, to name a few. The life cycle stage of a market can vary. Many of the products you see—such as milk, eggs, and bread—are in relatively mature markets, with little innovation or change. That being said, new markets do emerge. For example, Febreze basically created its own market with a new product that eliminates odors from fabrics without washing them.

Prior to its launch, that market didn't exist. You also see active competition in many markets, with companies trying to gain market share through product innovation.

The Product-Market Fit Pyramid separates the market into its two distinct components: the target customers and their needs. The needs layer is above the target customers layer in the model because it's *their* needs that are relevant to achieving product-market fit.

As you try to create value for customers, you want to identify the specific needs that correspond to a good market opportunity. For example, you probably don't want to enter a market where customers are extremely happy with how the existing solutions meet their needs. When you develop a new product or improve an existing product, you want to address customer needs that aren't adequately met. That's why I use "underserved needs" as the label for this layer. Customers are going to judge your product in relation to the alternatives. So the relative degree to which your product meets their needs depends on the competitive landscape. Let's move now to the product section of the pyramid.

Your Product

A product is a specific offering intended to meet a set of customer needs. From this definition, it's clear that the concept of product-market fit applies to *services* as well as products. The typical distinction between a product and service is that a product is a physical good while a service is intangible. However, with products delivered via the web and mobile devices, the distinction between product and service has been blurred, as indicated by the popular term *software as a service* (SaaS).

For software, the product itself is intangible code, often running on servers that the customer never sees. The real-world manifestation of software products that customers see and use is the user experience (UX), which is the top layer of the Product-Market Fit Pyramid. Beyond software, this is also true for any product with which the customer interacts. The UX is what brings a product's functionality to life for the user.

The functionality that a product provides consists of multiple features, each built to meet a customer need. Taken together, they form the product's feature set, which is the layer just below the UX layer.

To decide which features to build, you need to identify the specific customer needs your product should address. In doing so, you want to determine how your product will be better than the others in the market. This is the essence of product strategy. The set of needs that you aspire to meet with your product forms your value proposition, which is the layer just below "feature set" in the Product-Market Fit Pyramid. Your value proposition is also the layer just above customer needs, and fundamentally determines how well the needs addressed by your product match up with the customer's.

Taken together, the three layers of value proposition, feature set, and UX define your product. As shown in Figure 1.1, your product and the market are separate sections of the Product-Market Fit Pyramid. Your goal in creating customer value is to make them fit nicely together.

Product-Market Fit

Viewing product-market fit in light of this model, it is the measure of how well your product (the top three layers of the pyramid) satisfies the market (the bottom two layers of the pyramid). Your target customers determine how well your product fits their needs. Again, customers will judge your product's fit in relation to the other products in the market. To achieve product-market fit, your product should meet underserved needs better than the competition. Let's discuss a product that managed to do that.

QUICKEN: FROM #47 TO #1

A great example of a product that achieved product-market fit while entering an already crowded market is Intuit's Quicken personal finance software. Scott Cook and Tom Proulx practiced Lean principles even though they founded Intuit years before Lean Startup ideas were put forth. When they launched Quicken, there were already 46 personal finance products in the market. However, after conducting customer research, the cofounders concluded that none of the existing products had achieved product-market fit.

The products didn't meet customer needs and were difficult to use. The cofounders had a hypothesis that a checkbook-based design would do well, since everyone at the time was familiar with writing checks. Their hypothesis proved right: the UX they built using the checkbook conceptual design resonated with customers and Quicken rapidly became the leading personal finance software.

A large part of Quicken's success was the fact that Intuit adopted principles that would be called Lean today. The company pioneered the use of customer research and user testing to inform software development. They routinely conducted usability testing of each version before launching it and organized public betas years before those ideas became mainstream. They invented the "follow me home" concept, where Intuit employees would go to retail stores, wait for customers to buy a copy of Quicken, and then ask to follow them home to see how they used the software. This helped immensely in understanding the customer's initial impressions of the product.

Let's assess Quicken using the Product-Market Fit Pyramid. There were many customers in its market, and the product definitely addressed real customer needs: People needed help balancing their checkbook, tracking their balances, and seeing where their money was going. Computer software was well suited to help on that front, but despite 46 products in the market, customer needs were still underserved. By talking with customers, the cofounders ensured Quicken's feature set addressed those needs. Their design insights led to an innovative UX that customers found much easier to use. This dramatic improvement in ease of use was, in fact, the main differentiator in Quicken's value proposition. By achieving product-market fit, Quicken succeeded in the face of stiff competition, which led the founders to joke about having "47th mover advantage."

THE LEAN PRODUCT PROCESS

Now that we have a detailed model for product-market fit, how do we go about achieving it? Based on my experience using the Product-Market Fit Pyramid with many teams on numerous products, I designed a simple, iterative process for achieving product-market fit. The Lean Product Process, shown in Figure 1.2, guides you through each layer of the pyramid from the bottom up.

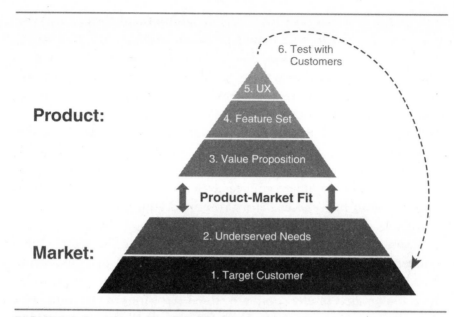

FIGURE 1.2   The Lean Product Process

It helps you articulate and test your key hypotheses for each of the five components of product-market fit.

I describe the six steps of the Lean Product Process in detail in Part II of this book, with a chapter devoted to each one:

1. Determine your target customers
2. Identify underserved customer needs
3. Define your value proposition
4. Specify your minimum viable product (MVP) feature set
5. Create your MVP prototype
6. Test your MVP with customers

The last three steps reference the important Lean concept of a minimum viable product (MVP). I discuss MVP in detail in Chapters 6 and 7, but it's basically the minimum amount of functionality that your target customer considers viable, that is, providing enough value. When you are building a new product, you want to avoid building more than is required to test your hypotheses with customers. The term MVP clearly applies when you're building a completely new version 1 product (v1 for short). In addition, the idea of an MVP makes sense if you are redesigning an existing product or building v2.

The Lean Product Process *also* applies when you are not building a whole product, such as when you add functionality to or improve an existing product. In those situations, you can think of the process steps applying to a "minimum viable feature" instead, if that's clearer.

Step 5 also refers to your MVP *prototype*. I intentionally use this broad term to capture the wide range of product-related artifacts you can test with customers. While the first "prototype" you test *could* be your live product, you can gain faster learning with fewer resources by testing your hypotheses *before* you build your product.

Not all six steps are required for every product or feature. Certain steps are required only when you're building a completely new product. Take, for example, determining your target customers, identifying underserved needs, and defining your value proposition. Once you've successfully completed those steps for your product, you may not need to revisit those areas for a while. But after launching your v1 product, you would continue to improve and add functionality by looping through the three remaining steps: specifying which features to pursue, creating the features, and testing the features with customers.

To increase your chances of achieving product-market fit, the process is designed to encourage a certain amount of rigor in product thinking. In a sense, the process is a checklist to help make sure you've thought about the key assumptions and decisions to be made when creating a product. If you are not making these assumptions or decisions explicitly, then you are making them implicitly. The Lean Product Process helps you articulate the assumptions and hypotheses in your head (which you can revise later as you iterate). If you skip these critical thinking steps, you leave important elements—such as target customer and product strategy—to chance.

A key concept in Lean manufacturing, which inspired Lean Startup, is the concept of *rework*: having to spend time fixing something that you did not build correctly the first time. Minimizing rework is a key tactic for eliminating waste. In addition to helping you achieve product-market fit, the Lean Product Process also enables you to do so more quickly by reducing rework.

To be clear, you *will* have some rework with the Lean Product Process. It is an iterative process that requires you to revise your hypotheses, designs, and product as you make progress—all of which could be considered rework. The goal of the process is to achieve product-market fit as quickly as possible. Quick but rigorous thinking that avoids or reduces rework helps achieve that goal.

You can think of the Lean Product Process like the drills that karate students learn and practice as they make progress earning higher and higher belts. After mastering the core techniques from their drills and becoming black belts, students are able to mix, match, and modify what they have learned to create their own custom style. Martial arts master Bruce Lee eloquently said, "Obey the principles without being bound by them." He also said, "Adapt what is useful, reject what is useless, and add what is specifically your own." I encourage you to heed his advice as you read and practice the ideas and guidance in this book.

Along those lines, I would enjoy hearing any questions or feedback you have, as well as your experiences applying the ideas in this book. Please feel free to share them at the companion website for this book: http://leanproductplaybook.com. There, you can also see the latest information related to the book and contribute to the conversation about how to build great products.

Before jumping to the first step of the Lean Product Process, I discuss in the next chapter the important concept of problem space versus solution space. Understanding this fundamental idea will help clarify our thinking as we work our way up the Product-Market Fit Pyramid.

Chapter 2

Problem Space versus Solution Space

The Lean Product Process will guide you through the critical thinking steps required to achieve product-market fit. In the next chapter, I begin describing the details of the process, but before I do, I want to share an important high-level concept: separating *problem space* from *solution space*. I have been discussing this concept in my talks for years and am glad to see those terms used more frequently these days.

Any product that you actually build exists in solution space, as do any product designs that you create—such as mockups, wireframes, or prototypes. Solution space includes any product or representation of a product that is used by or intended for use by a customer. It is the opposite of a blank slate. When you build a product, you have chosen a specific implementation. Whether you've done so explicitly or not, you've determined how the product looks, what it does, and how it works.

In contrast, there is no product or design that exists in problem space. Instead, problem space is where all the customer needs that you'd like your product to deliver live. You shouldn't interpret the word "needs" too narrowly: Whether it's a customer pain point, a desire, a job to be done, or a user story, it lives in problem space.

THE SPACE PEN

My favorite story to illustrate the concept of problem space versus solution space is the space pen. When NASA was preparing to send astronauts into space, they knew that ballpoint pens would not work because they rely on gravity in order for the ink to flow. One of NASA's contractors, Fisher Pen Company, decided to pursue a research and development program to create a pen that would work in the zero gravity of space. After spending $1 million of his own money, the company's president, Paul Fisher, invented the Space Pen in 1965: a wonderful piece of technology that works great in zero gravity.

Faced with the same challenge, the Russian space agency equipped their astronauts with pencils. You can actually buy a "Russian space pen" (which is just a cleverly packaged red pencil).

This story shows the risk of jumping into the solution space prematurely and the advantage of starting in the problem space. If we constrain our thinking to "a pen that works in zero gravity," we may not consider creative, less-expensive solutions such as a pencil. In contrast, having a clear understanding of the problem space (devoid of any solution space ideas), allows for a wider range of creative solutions that potentially offer a higher return-on-investment. If the pencil and space pen were equally adequate solutions, then avoiding one million dollars of research and development cost would clearly be the preferable alternative.

To avoid fixating on pen-based solutions, we could rephrase the problem space as: "a writing instrument that works in zero gravity." That would allow for a pencil as a solution. But that's still anchored on "a writing instrument" solution. We can do even better than that: "a way to record notes in zero gravity for later reference that is easy to use." That problem space statement would allow for more creative solutions such as voice recording with playback. In fact, considering out-of-the-box solution ideas can help you refine your problem space definition, even if they *aren't* feasible. In this case, a voice recorder would probably not be as good a solution as a Space Pen. It would need a power source and would require playback to refer to the notes again, which would be less convenient than being able to scan and read them. But undergoing this thought exercise would allow us to further refine our problem space definition to: "a way to record notes in zero gravity for convenient reference later on that is easy to use, is inexpensive, and does not require an external power source."

I always like to clarify that this example is by no means an attempt to make fun of NASA. I tell the story a certain way to highlight the point I want to make. Indeed, the conclusion that NASA came to turned out to be the best one. There are good reasons not to use pencils in space: the lead tips can break off and float into an astronaut's eye or cause a short in an electrical connection. After the tragic

Apollo 1 fire in 1967, NASA required all objects in the cabin to be nonflammable, including the writing instruments. So the Space Pen actually *was* a useful innovation, which the Russian space agency also adopted.

When I mention the space pen in my talks, there is often someone who claims that the story is an urban legend. However, it isn't, as NASA explains at http://history.nasa.gov/spacepen.html, and the Fisher Space Pen Company confirms at http://fisherspacepen.com/pages/company-overview. The key point of debate usually is, who spent the money on research and development: NASA or Fisher? Fisher did, as I pointed out above.

PROBLEMS DEFINE MARKETS

Early in my product career, Intuit's founder Scott Cook helped me solidify the concept of problem space versus solution space when I heard him talk about TurboTax. Speaking to a group of product managers, Scott asked us, "Who is TurboTax's biggest competitor?" Multiple hands shot up. At the time, the other major tax preparation software in the market was TaxCut by H&R Block. After someone confidently answered, "TaxCut," Scott surprised us all by saying that the biggest competitor to TurboTax was actually pen and paper. He pointed out that, at the time, more Americans were still preparing their taxes by hand using IRS forms than all tax software combined.

This example highlights another advantage of clear problem space thinking: having a more accurate understanding of the market in which your product is *really* competing. Those of us in the audience were narrowly thinking in solution space of the "tax preparation software" market, as defined by the two main software products. Scott was thinking in problem space of the broader "tax preparation" market—one that would also include tax accountants to whom customers delegate their tax preparation. As the previous chapter discusses, a market is a set of related customer needs, which rests squarely in problem space. A market is not tied to any specific solutions that meet those needs. That is why you see "market disruptions": when a new type of product (solution space) better meets the market needs (problem space). New technology can often enable a market disruption to deliver similar benefits at a much lower cost. Voice-over-Internet-Protocol (VOIP) is a great example of a disruptive technology that has replaced traditional telephone service. At first, the sound quality of VOIP calls couldn't compare to that of traditional phone lines, but the cost was so much lower that it offered a superior solution for much of the telephone market.

THE WHAT AND THE HOW

As a product manager at Intuit, I learned to write detailed product requirements that stayed in the problem space without getting into the solution space. We were trained to first focus on "what" the product needed to accomplish for customers before getting into "how" the product would accomplish it. You often hear strong product teams distinguishing between the "what" versus the "how." The "what" describes the benefits that the product should give the customer—what the product will accomplish for the user or allow the user to accomplish. The "how" is the way in which the product delivers the "what" to the customer. The "how" is the design of the product and the specific technology used to implement the product. "What" is problem space and "how" is solution space.

OUTSIDE-IN PRODUCT DEVELOPMENT

A failure to gain a clear understanding of the problem space before proceeding to the solution space is prevalent in companies and teams that practice "inside-out" product development, where "inside" refers to the company and "outside" refers to customers and the market. In such teams, the genesis of product ideas is what one or more employees think would be good to build. They don't test the ideas with customers to verify if the product would solve actual customer needs. The best way to mitigate the risk of an "inside-out" mindset is to ensure your team is talking with customers. That's why Steve Blank urges product teams to "get out of the building" (GOOB for short).

In contrast, "outside-in" product development starts with an understanding of the customer's problem space. By talking with customers to understand their needs, as well as what they like and don't like about existing solutions, outside-in product teams can form a robust problem-space definition before starting product design. Lean product teams articulate the hypotheses they have made and solicit customer feedback on early design ideas to test those hypotheses. This approach is the essence of Lean—and was actually first advocated for years ago by practitioners of user-centered design.

SHOULD YOU LISTEN TO CUSTOMERS?

Some people criticize user-centered design by saying that talking with users will not lead you to come up with new, breakthrough solutions. Those critics like to quote Henry Ford, who famously said: "If I had asked people what they wanted, they would have said a faster horse." They also like to point out the example of Steve Jobs and how Apple has launched many successful products using what seems to be a very "inside-out" product development process. In fact, Steve Jobs cited the same Henry Ford quote in a 2008 interview with Forbes.

It is true that customers are not likely to identify the next breakthrough solution in your product category. But why would anyone expect them to? They are not product designers, product managers, or technologists. The fallacious thinking comes in when people use this argument to rationalize why it's not important to talk with customers or to understand their needs and preferences. Most people who make that argument are really using it as an excuse to not talk with customers because they want to adopt an "inside-out" philosophy. They think that they have all the answers and that talking with customers is a waste of time. They don't understand problem space versus solution space.

It's likely true that customers won't *invent* a breakthrough product for you; but that doesn't mean it's a waste of time to understand their needs and preferences. On the contrary, a good understanding of customer needs and preferences helps product teams explore new potential solutions and estimate how valuable customers are likely to find each one to be.

Critics of user-centered design like to justify their views by saying, "Apple doesn't talk to customers." At Apple's 1997 Worldwide Developers Conference, Steve Jobs shared a more enlightened perspective that is consistent with the Lean Product Process when he said:

> You've got to start with the customer experience and work backwards to the technology. You can't start with the technology and try to figure out where you're going to try to sell it.... As we have tried to come up with a strategy and a vision for Apple, it started with: What incredible benefits can we give to the customer? ...Not starting with: Let's sit down with the engineers and figure out what awesome technology we have and then how we're going to market that. And I think that's the right path to take.

A TALE OF TWO APPLE FEATURES

Even though Apple does indeed have a reputation for not soliciting customer feedback on products before they're launched, a large part of why their products are so successful is because, despite that, they have an in-depth understanding of customer needs. Consider the Touch ID fingerprint sensor that Apple introduced with the iPhone 5S. Touch ID utilizes advanced technology: the high-resolution sensor is only 170 microns thick and captures 500 dots per inch. The button is made of sapphire crystal—one of the clearest, hardest materials available—to protect the sensor. The button also acts as a lens to precisely focus the sensor on the user's finger. Touch ID maps out individual details in the ridges of fingerprints that are smaller than the human eye can see and can recognize multiple fingerprints in any orientation.

It's unlikely that any iPhone customer would have come up with such a solution. I would guess that Apple didn't test the solution with many customers before launching it. Despite that, I argue that the iPhone team had a good understanding of the problem space and could be confident that customers would consider Touch ID valuable. Touch ID offered a new alternative to the traditional way of unlocking your iPhone and logging in to the App Store to make a purchase. Touch ID is better because what matters to customers when they're authenticating is how convenient and how secure it is. Usually, there is a tension between those two customer benefits, with more convenient authentication mechanisms being less secure (and vice versa).

Most iPhone users will tell you that they unlock their phones quite frequently, often multiple times per day. Because people value their time, reducing the time it takes to unlock is a clear benefit. iPhone users value security, too. They don't want unauthorized people to be able to access their phone, especially if it is lost or stolen. With a four-digit passcode, the odds of someone guessing your passcode are 1 in 10,000. According to Apple, the odds that two fingerprints are similar enough for Touch ID to consider them the same is 1 in 50,000 (and it's much harder to try different fingers than it is to type in different numbers).

Touch ID makes authenticating much quicker than having to enter an unlock passcode or App Store password. It's also more convenient because users no longer have to worry about forgetting these passcodes.

Because Touch ID clearly saves time, is more convenient, and is more secure than the previous solution, the iPhone team could be confident that customers would consider the feature valuable, even without explicitly validating it with them. However, if Apple didn't test Touch ID with customers, it still ran the risk of some unforeseen negative consequence. It's worth pointing out that Apple does test their products internally with their employees (who are often a good proxy for customers). This internal testing tactic where you use your own product is called "dogfooding."

That being said, Apple isn't perfect. For example, customers were not happy with a product "improvement" that Apple made with the power button on the 2013 MacBook Pro. In the prior version of the laptop, the power button was located away from the keyboard keys, was smaller, had a different color, and was inset, all of which made it difficult to press by accident. When users pressed the button in the prior version, a dialog window would appear, providing options to restart, sleep, or shut down their laptop, along with the option to cancel any action. But Apple decided to change the power button design for the 2013 version: they made it look like the other keys and incorporated it into the keyboard (in the upper right, where the eject key used to be). The new power button was placed right next to the "delete" key as well as the key that increases the sound volume, both of which are used frequently. As a result, users started accidentally pressing the power button (and then had to click the cancel button).

To add insult to injury, Apple's subsequent operating system update—OS X Mavericks—changed the behavior of the power button. When the power button is pressed in Mavericks, you no longer get the dialog window with its various choices; instead your computer goes right to sleep. The combined effect of those two changes (moving the power button and changing its behavior) resulted in frustrated users whose laptops would suddenly go to sleep unexpectedly. Usability issues such as this are easy to identify through customer testing—even with a small number of testers.

Let's compare these two Apple examples. In the case of the Touch ID, there were clear benefits and no unforeseen risks arose. In the case of the power button changes, what were the intended customer benefits? It's unclear what they were. Perhaps the new power button design addressed internal company objectives related to aesthetics or reduced cost. Regardless, the button's new design and behavior resulted in dissatisfaction for customers. It's true that customers aren't going to lead you to the Promised Land of a break-through innovative product, but customer feedback is like a flashlight in the night: it keeps you from falling off a cliff as you try to find your way there.

USING THE SOLUTION SPACE TO DISCOVER THE PROBLEM SPACE

Customers are also not likely to serve you their problem space needs on a silver platter. It's hard for them to talk about abstract benefits and the relative importance of each—and when they do, it's often fraught with inaccuracies. It's therefore the product team's job to unearth these needs and define the problem space. One way is to interview customers and observe them using existing products. Such techniques are called "contextual inquiry" or "customer discovery." You can observe what pain points they run into even if they don't explicitly mention them to you. You can ask them what they like and don't like about the current solutions. As you form hypotheses about the customer needs and their relative importance, you can validate and improve your hypotheses using these techniques.

The reality is that customers are much better at giving you feedback in the solution space. If you show them a new product or design, they can tell you what they like and don't like. They can compare it to other solutions and identify pros and cons. Having solution space discussions with customers is much more fruitful than trying to explicitly discuss the problem space with them. The feedback you gather in the solution space actually helps you test and improve your problem space hypotheses. The best problem space learning often comes from feedback you receive from customers on the solution space artifacts you have created.

Problem space and solution space are an integral part of the Product-Market Fit Pyramid, as shown in Figure 2.1. Your product's feature set and UX live in solution space—they're what customers can see and react to. The other three layers of the pyramid live in problem space. The important interface between problem space and solution space occurs between your value proposition and your feature set. It is, of course, within your control to change your feature set and UX as you like. Unlike customers and their needs, which you can target but can't change, value proposition is the problem space layer over which you have the most control.

As Dave McClure of 500 Startups said, "Customers don't care about your solution. They care about their problems." Keeping problem space and solution space separate and alternating between them as you iteratively test and improve your hypotheses is the best way to achieve product-market fit. The Lean Product Process gives you step-by-step guidance on how to do that. Let's jump into the first step of the process: identifying your target customer.

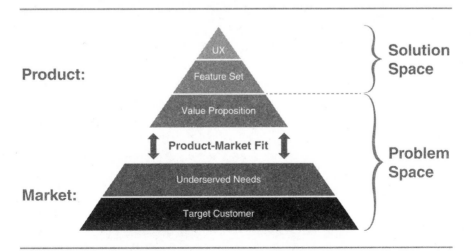

FIGURE 2.1   Problem Space versus Solution Space

Part II
The Lean Product Process

Chapter 3

Determine Your Target
Customer (Step 1)

You begin the Lean Product Process by identifying your target customer, which is the bottom layer of the Product-Market Fit Pyramid. The problem space benefits you're going to identify pertain to a specific customer segment. Different customers will have different needs—and even those who have the same needs can have distinct views on their relative importance.

FISHING FOR CUSTOMERS

Many companies have launched products without any explicit discussion of the target customer. Sometimes, a company will introduce a product with one target customer in mind but end up attracting a somewhat different customer segment. Matching a product with its target customer is like fishing. Your product is the bait that you put out there and the fish that you catch is your target customer. Sometimes you catch the type of fish you were going after and sometimes you catch a different type of fish. You can develop hypotheses about your target market, but you won't truly know who your customers actually are until you throw your hook into the water and see what kind of fish bite. Once you have a product or a prototype to show customers, then you can gain clarity about the target market you're attracting.

Of course, your bait can attract more than one type of customer. For example, Quicken was designed so that individual consumers could easily manage their household finances. But it was so easy to use that small business owners started using it to manage their companies' finances. To the Quicken team's surprise, they had caught a second type of fish with the same bait. Through customer research, Intuit discovered that almost a third of Quicken users were using it to track the finances for their business. So Intuit developed a new Quicken Home and Business version of their software to better address the distinct needs of small business owners. This discovery about their target market also led Intuit to launch QuickBooks, an accounting software application designed exclusively for managing business finances.

Companies often want to expand or change their target market. Some are looking to move "up market." For example, they are currently selling to small businesses and want to sell to larger businesses. Some start out selling to large enterprises and then want to move "down market." A company that has achieved success in one industry vertical may want to expand into adjacent vertical markets. For example, if you've built some course management software that has achieved product-market fit with college professors, you might try to expand into the professional training market. If the needs of the adjacent market are similar, your product may need only minor changes to be a good fit.

HOW TO SEGMENT YOUR TARGET MARKET

You define your target customer by capturing all of the relevant customer attributes that identify someone as being in your target market. These attributes can be demographic, psychographic, behavioral, or based on needs. Dividing a broad market into specific subsets based on attributes is called *market segmentation*.

Demographic Segmentation

Demographics are quantifiable statistics of a group of people, such as age, gender, marital status, income, and education level. Say you were developing an app for moms to easily share photos of their babies with friends and family. You could describe your target customers demographically as women 20 to 40 years old who have one or more children under the age of three.

If you are targeting businesses, you'll use firmographics instead; these are to organizations what demographics are to people, and include traits such as company size and industry. Two well-known systems used to identify industries are the Standard Industrial Classification (SIC) codes and the North American Industry Classification System (NAICS).

Psychographic Segmentation

Psychographics are statistics that classify a group of people according to psychological variables such as attitudes, opinions, values, and interests. For the same app, you might describe your target customers as moms who enjoy using social media and like sharing pictures of their babies with friends and family. Looking back on the demographic description, you'll see that it didn't say anything about whether or not the 20- to 40-year-old women wanted to share photos or not.

Psychographic attributes are more useful than demographics for many products. Rather than being the primary reason why someone is in your target market, demographics are often incidental. In this case, your app is targeted at moms with babies who want to share pictures. The fact that you're targeting moms drives the "women" part, and the statistical data on the age at which women give birth determines the "20 to 40 years old" range.

Behavioral Segmentation

You can also use relevant behavioral attributes to describe your target customer: whether or not someone takes a particular action or how frequently they do. You might define your target market as moms who currently share an average of three or more baby pictures per week on social media (e.g., Facebook, Instagram, etc.). If you were working on a stock trading app for active investors, you might define your target market as investors who place 10 or more stock trades per week.

Needs-Based Segmentation

Another powerful market segmentation technique is needs-based segmentation. With this approach, you divide the market into customer segments that each have distinct needs. Let's take Dropcam, for example, which offers an affordable, easy-to-use wireless camera. As a parent, I use Dropcam to monitor my children while they sleep: I can conveniently see and hear them on my smartphone app without having to go into their rooms. Others use Dropcam as a security camera for their home. Pet owners use it to check on their pets while they're away. Businesses use it as a security camera while they're closed and also while they're open, to catch any dishonest behavior such as shoplifting.

You couldn't come up with a single, tidy demographic or psychographic description to accommodate all four of those disparate customer segments. But when viewed through the lens of needs-based segmentation, they appear as a unified group of customers that have the need to easily capture and view video remotely.

Even though they share that common high-level need, each of these customer segments has different detailed needs. Dropcam understands this and tailors how they market their product to each segment. Under the "Uses" tab on their website, they have dedicated pages for "Home Security," "Baby Monitor," "Pets," and "Business." And Dropcam provides different product features tailored to different segments. For example, they offer cloud recording of the video stream for playback later. Because I use Dropcam only for real-time monitoring while my children sleep, that feature isn't valuable to me. But it's critical for security-minded customers, who are willing to pay Dropcam a monthly service fee on top of the cost of the camera. This example is a brief snapshot of what I discuss in the next chapter—connecting your target customers with what you believe their needs are.

USERS VERSUS BUYERS

In some cases, especially for business-to-business products, the customer who will use your product (the user) is not the same person who makes the purchase decision (the buyer). For example, Salesforce.com is an application used by salespeople in a company. The VP of Sales is often the buyer. But in a particular company, the Chief Technology Officer may be who makes the purchase decision instead. There may be multiple stakeholders in a company who have to agree to a particular purchase decision: the Chief Financial Officer, the General Manager of a business unit, the General Counsel, the Chief Security Officer, and so forth. In such cases, it is useful to distinguish the economic buyer—the decision-maker who controls the budget and writes the check—from the other stakeholders involved in the decision-making process. The others are often potential "blockers" who have the ability to veto your product if they object to unmet requirements. The buyer often has distinct needs from the end user that need to be addressed to achieve product-market fit, and you should define your target buyer in addition to your target customer when warranted.

TECHNOLOGY ADOPTION LIFE CYCLE

You may have heard of *Crossing the Chasm*, Geoffrey Moore's classic book on how to market high-tech products. In his book, Moore helped popularize another important concept to consider when defining your target market—the technology adoption life cycle, which divides a market into five distinct customer segments based on their risk aversion towards adopting new technologies.

Here are descriptions of the five customer segments:

1. **Innovators** are technology enthusiasts who pride themselves on being familiar with the latest and greatest innovation. They enjoy fiddling with new products and exploring their intricacies. They are more willing to use an unpolished product that may have some shortcomings or tradeoffs, and are fine with the fact that many of these products will ultimately fail.
2. **Early Adopters** are visionaries who want to exploit new innovations to gain an advantage over the status quo. Unlike innovators, their interest in being first is not driven by an intrinsic love of technology but rather the opportunity to gain an edge.
3. The **Early Majority** are pragmatists that have no interest in technology for its own sake. These individuals adopt new products only *after* a proven track record of delivering value. Because they are more risk averse than the first two segments, they feel more comfortable having strong references from trusted sources and tend to buy from the leading company in the product category.
4. The **Late Majority** are risk-averse conservatives who are doubtful that innovations will deliver value and only adopt them when pressured to do so, for example, for financial reasons, due to competitive threats, or for fear of being reliant on an older, dying technology that will no longer be supported.
5. **Laggards** are skeptics who are very wary of innovation. They hate change and have a bias for criticizing new technologies even after they have become mainstream.

Moore noted that for many disruptive products that innovators and early adopters have embraced, it is very difficult to gain traction with the early majority. Therefore, he added a gap—or chasm—between early adopters and the early majority, hence the name of his book, which gives advice on how to successfully make that transition.

When you are defining your target customer, it is important to understand the current stage of your product market in the technology adoption life cycle. You may initially target innovators for a new market, since they embrace new solutions, are willing to pay a premium to have them, and are willing to overlook product shortcomings outside the core area of innovation. As you try to gain adoption by additional segments over time, you will discover that they have different needs and preferences—such as increased ease of use, higher reliability, and lower price—that require you to change your product before they will adopt it.

PERSONAS

The persona is a useful tool for describing your target customer. Alan Cooper championed the use of personas as part of his "Goal-Directed Design" process. In his book *The Inmates are Running the Asylum*, he describes personas as "a precise definition of our user and what he wishes to accomplish." Cooper explains, "personas are not real people" but rather "hypothetical archetypes of actual users." Personas have become quite prevalent and are used by many UX designers and product teams that embrace user-centered design. While personas are mainly used during the design phase, I advocate using them earlier in your product process because they are a good way to capture your hypotheses about your target customer. You will put your personas to work again a few steps later in the Lean Product Process when you start to create your initial designs; by starting your personas now, you'll be well prepared.

Personas also help to ensure that everyone in your company who's involved with the product is aligned on the same customer. As with most endeavors involving a large number of people, if you don't write it down, share it, and discuss it, chances are that everyone won't be on the same page. At the end of the day, personas help people on the product team make decisions about which features are important and about how to design the user experience. A good persona empowers everyone on the team with the same solid foundation of information and reasoning. It should facilitate alignment when you're making product decisions as a group. In addition, as each person works on their own, independently making lots of little product decisions, personas should make the results more congruous and additive instead of discordant and counterproductive.

What Info Should a Persona Provide?

Good personas convey the relevant demographic, psychographic, behavioral, and needs-based attributes of your target customer. Personas should fit on a single page and provide a snapshot of the customer archetype that's quick to digest, and usually include the following information:

- Name
- Representative photograph
- Quote that conveys what they most care about
- Job title
- Demographics
- Needs/goals
- Relevant motivations and attitudes
- Related tasks and behaviors
- Frustrations/pain points with current solution
- Level of expertise/knowledge (in the relevant domain, e.g., level of computer savvy)
- Product usage context/environment (e.g., laptop in a loud, busy office or tablet on the couch at home)
- Technology adoption life cycle segment (for your product category)
- Any other salient attributes

The two things on this list that really bring a persona to life are the photograph of the hypothetical person and the quote expressing what's most important to them. Your team members will usually remember the name, photograph, and quote the most, especially when they are not looking at the persona. See Figure 3.1 for a

The Busy Mom
Lisa Bennett

Age: 32
Gender: Female
Marital Status: Married
Education: Bachelor's degree
Job: Teacher
Income: $55,000

"My children's health is my top priority, but raising two kids is a full-time job, so I need an easy way to stay on top of their prescriptions and medical appointments."

Lisa is an elementary school teacher. She lives with her hard-working husband Dave and their two children Addison (12) and Caleb (9). Because Dave often works late, Lisa is the primary caregiver to her children.

Although her children are generally healthy, they both have to take important prescriptions. Addison has asthma and must always have her inhaler by her side. Lisa worries that she might forget to refill a prescription for the inhaler and potentially put Addison in danger.

Life never stops for Lisa, and she rarely has a moment to herself. Therefore, she needs an easy way to keep track of her children's prescriptions and medical appointments.

Goals
- Be reminded of children's medical appointments
- Be able to keep track of children's health info
- Have the ability to refill prescriptions easily

Technology Use
- Average
- Owns an iPhone
- Uses desktop PC
- Uses Facebook to keep up with family and friends

Interests
- Spending time with family
- Being involved with her children's extracurricular activities
- Tennis

FIGURE 3.1 Persona

sample persona. I adapted this example from a persona created by talented UX designer Becca Tetzlaff. You can see other examples of Tetzlaff's work at http://beccatetzlaff.com.

How to Create Personas

So how do you obtain the information to create your persona? If you have customers, you can use interviews and surveys. Talking to customers in one-on-one interviews is the best way to build this knowledge. Once you know the right questions to ask, surveys can help you collect data from many customers at once.

When you use survey data, it is critical that you not use averages of the collected data to populate your persona. You want your persona to represent a real person and should not design your product for some nonexistent "average" customer. As Cooper illustrates, "The average person in my community has 2.3 children, but not a single person in my community has exactly 2.3 children." Clearly, it would be better to specify a persona that has either two or three children. You can use the aggregate survey data to help ensure your persona represents a meaningful portion of your customer base. Reading through the individual survey responses from people who match your target customer profile can be enlightening.

Of course, if you are launching a new product or trying to expand to a new target market, you won't have existing customers. You can always use your judgment to make initial hypotheses about your target customer's attributes, and then test those hypotheses by talking to prospective customers who match that profile. Before you have any designs or product on which to solicit feedback, you will mainly talk with prospective customers to gain a deeper understanding of their needs, usage of current solutions, and pain points so you can identify potential product opportunities.

I and other Lean practitioners call these "customer discovery" interviews. In user-centered design, they are often called "contextual inquiry" or "ethnographic research." As with all steps in the Lean Product Process, you should adopt an iterative approach. As you talk with more customers, you learn more and revise your persona to make it more accurate and robust. Your goal is to iterate until you feel confident that you have identified a target customer with an underserved customer need that you believe you can address. The next chapter covers customer needs in depth.

Potential Problems with Personas

Many product teams have experienced success with personas. However, personas have a bad rap with some people. Those people usually haven't seen high quality personas used in a strong user-centered design process. Like any tool, personas can be misused. Weak personas can lack key information, be poorly written, or be based purely on speculation versus grounded in real customer data. At the other extreme are personas that contain too many superfluous details that don't add value. To be useful, a persona should be pragmatic and provide useful information that can help inform product design decisions.

Developing a persona should not slow down your product process, and you should not spend an inordinate amount of time trying to perfect your initial persona. Instead, you should view it as a first draft that you will revise as you iterate through the process. No one starts out with a persona as robust and as honed as the one shown in Figure 3.1; that is the result of numerous rounds of iterative customer discovery. You will improve the fidelity of your persona over time as you learn more.

Even if a persona is well written, the rest of the product team might ignore it. They should be referring to the persona as they make various design decisions and evaluate proposed designs. If your team members aren't using the persona, you should try providing some education about personas, the benefits they provide, and how the team should use them.

I have also seen companies develop a set of personas and then stop talking with customers. Over time, the company loses touch with its customers, especially as new product team members join. Personas are a great tool; however, they are no substitute for talking to customers on an ongoing basis.

It's good to talk to prospective customers early in your process. But once you have a product or prototype ready, you can gain a more accurate view of your target customer by putting your bait out there to see which kind of fish you actually catch. Like Quicken or Dropcam, you may find that you are attracting more than one distinct type of customer, in which case you should create a new persona for each type.

Some people within your customer base will like your product more than others. Those people likely use it more frequently and recommend it to others, which you can see on social media. Talking with those passionate customers can especially help sharpen your hypotheses about your target market and gain insights into what underserved needs your product is meeting for them.

Now that you have determined—or at least have a set of hypotheses about—your target customer, you are ready to move on to the next step in the Lean Product Process, which focuses on understanding customer needs. As I discuss in the next chapter, you care most about *underserved* needs, which form the next layer of the Product-Market Fit Pyramid.

Chapter 4

Identify Underserved Customer Needs (Step 2)

Now that you have determined your target customers—or at least have a set of hypotheses about them—you should focus on identifying what needs they have that your product could satisfy. The goal is to build and validate your knowledge of the problem space before you set out to design a solution. Since customer needs can seem somewhat fuzzy when we talk about them, let's start off by clarifying our terminology.

A CUSTOMER NEED BY ANY OTHER NAME

I use the word "needs" to refer to what customers want or value. I also use the term *customer benefits* interchangeably with needs. Sometimes customers can tell you what they want, but a need does not have to be something about which the user literally says, "I need [_____]." There are unarticulated needs—those that the customer has but doesn't express in an interview. Unknown needs can arise as well; this happens when a customer doesn't even realize they value something until you interview them about it, or expose them to some new breakthrough product. Customers are generally not skilled at discussing the problem space; they are better at telling you what they like and dislike about a particular solution. Good interviewers excel at listening closely to what customers say, repeating statements back to ensure understanding, and asking additional probing questions to illuminate the problem space.

You've probably heard some people speak of customer *desires* or *wants* as distinct from needs. Though all three terms represent customer value, some people perceive a need as critical, whereas desires and wants are just "nice-to-haves." However, that distinction doesn't add much value and results in confusion. In order to talk about needs, we don't really need multiple terms that differ in importance—especially since I will be describing a framework for quantifying how important different needs are.

When discussing user-centered design or persona development, people frequently use the term *user goal*. A user goal is no different from a customer need. In Agile development, user stories are used to convey what the customer wants. A well-written user story follows the format "As a [type of user], I want to [do something], so that I can [desired benefit]." For example: "As a Dropcam user worried about the security of my business, I want to quickly view only the suspicious activity that took place without having to watch the whole video, so that I can know what's going on in my store without spending too much time watching security videos." Good user stories reflect customer needs.

Customer *pain point* is another frequently used term that also fits under the umbrella of "customer needs." A pain point is just a customer need that is not adequately met, resulting in customer dissatisfaction. I'll be discussing customer satisfaction as part of my framework.

CUSTOMER NEEDS EXAMPLE: TURBOTAX

Let's discuss an example of customer needs. In the United States, most working adults are required to file their personal income taxes each year—not something that most people enjoy. It can take a long time and feel overwhelming for most people since they don't have in-depth knowledge about taxes. Because the rules are complex and change frequently, people often lack confidence that they have prepared their taxes accurately. If the Internal Revenue Service audits your tax return and finds it inaccurate, you have to pay a fine; you could face jail time in cases considered to be tax fraud. So customers clearly have a need to prepare their taxes. As discussed in Chapter 1, they can meet that need in various ways: by manually filling out the IRS forms, hiring a professional accountant, or using tax preparation software such as TurboTax.

One thing to know about customer needs is that they are like onions: they have multiple layers, each with a deeper layer just below it. To fully grasp the problem space that TurboTax addresses requires getting much more detailed than "prepare my tax return."

Tax preparation software can go well beyond the IRS tax forms, which are just instructions for how to prepare your tax return. Tax software can check the accuracy of your return. TurboTax can also file your taxes for you electronically, which is more convenient than having to print out and mail your return. It can help you maximize your deductions and reduce your audit risk. It can even download your tax information from your employer, banks, and brokerages so that you don't have to enter it manually. Each of those items is a distinct customer benefit. Let's list them explicitly:

1. Help me prepare my tax return
2. Check the accuracy of my tax return
3. Reduce my audit risk
4. Reduce the time it takes me to enter my tax information
5. Reduce the time it takes me to file my taxes
6. Maximize my tax deductions

This is by no means an exhaustive list of the customer benefits that TurboTax provides. We could easily keep peeling the onion and identify many more benefits. For example, state tax returns are completely separate from federal returns. Also, TurboTax offers a service that lets you receive your tax refund more quickly. But for the purposes of this discussion, let's focus on the six benefits listed above.

Hopefully the way I've written them strikes you as sounding like customer benefits. One of the easiest ways to tell that a product team is starting with the solution space is that instead of articulating customer benefits, they list *product features*. As with well-written Agile user stories, benefits should be written from the customer's perspective (using "I" and "my"). You'll also notice that each benefit begins with a verb: help, check, reduce, maximize. A benefit conveys value, which means it's doing something for the customer. Finally, many of the benefits speak to increasing something that's desired (tax deductions) or decreasing something that is not desired (audit risk, time required to accomplish a task). You should strive to state your benefits in such a precise manner whenever possible. This makes the benefit very clear and often enables you to objectively measure the performance improvement your product is providing.

As with everything in the Lean Product Process, customer benefits start out as hypotheses. You are saying, "I think that target customer

X would find customer benefit Y valuable." Once you have an initial set of hypothetical customer benefits you feel good about, it's time to test them with users. The best way to do so is via one-on-one, in-person customer discovery interviews.

CUSTOMER DISCOVERY INTERVIEWS

You should share each of your customer benefit hypotheses with the customer during the interviews. You should ask a set of questions about each benefit statement, such as:

- What does this statement mean to you? (to check their understanding)
- How might this help you?
- If a product delivered this benefit, how valuable would that be to you?

(Possible responses: no value, low value, medium value, high value, or very high value)

- For a response of high or very high value: Why would this be of value to you?
- For a response of low or no value: Why wouldn't this be of value to you?

These questions help you to see if the way you're describing the benefit is clear to users. They also help you learn how valuable the benefit is and why. The reasons why customers find certain benefits valuable are the gold nuggets you want to mine, since those comments help you gain a better understanding of how customers think and what's important to them.

If we asked customers in TurboTax's target market about the six benefits we listed, they might respond with comments such as those in Table 4.1.

You'll find when conducting customer discovery interviews that different customers can use different words to describe the same idea. You will also find that statements made by customers can vary quite a bit in how high-level or specific they are. For example, if you asked

TABLE 4.1 Customer Benefits and Related Comments

Customer Benefit	Typical Customer Comment
1. Help me prepare my tax return	"I don't really know much about taxes. I try to follow the instructions but they're confusing. I'm not sure which forms I should be filling out."
2. Check the accuracy of my tax return	"I'm not that great at math, so I know I'm probably making several mistakes when I'm adding and subtracting all those numbers on my tax forms."
3. Reduce my audit risk	"I'm worried about being audited but don't really know how risky my tax return is. It would be great to know if it would raise any yellow flags with the IRS so I could fix those parts."
4. Reduce the time it takes me to enter my tax information	"I spend lots of time each year entering data from all the tax forms I receive from my employer, bank, and brokerages."
5. Reduce the time it takes me to file my taxes	"I normally print my tax return and then go to the post office, wait in line, and mail it so I can get delivery confirmation. It would be great if I could avoid that hassle."
6. Maximize my tax deductions	"I don't know about all the deductions that I'm eligible to take. I'm probably leaving some money on the table."

two customers why they like TurboTax, one may say, "Because it makes taxes much less of a hassle," whereas the other may say, "I like how it checks my return for errors before I e-file it."

CUSTOMER BENEFIT LADDERS

As you talk with customers, you can keep asking them, "Why is that important to you?" until it doesn't lead to any new answers. This helps elevate the discussion from more granular, detailed benefits to higher-level benefits. This market research technique is called "laddering"; as you ask more questions, you are climbing up rungs on a ladder of related benefits. As you move up, ladders can converge, until you eventually reach the top of that particular benefit ladder.

Let's walk through an example of a benefit ladder. Say we're trying to understand why some drivers prefer a sports utility vehicle (SUV) to a minivan. We interview a customer and start by asking him that very question. He answers that he prefers SUVs because he doesn't like sliding doors. When we ask why, he tells us that he prefers vehicles that have a stylish design. When we ask why again, he says, "Because I want to feel trendy." When we ask why again, we learn that the ultimate motivation is that he wants to be accepted by his peers.

When I look at the six benefits in Table 4.1, I see three distinct benefits ladders. The three benefits "help me prepare my tax return," "check the accuracy of my tax return," and "reduce my audit risk" all ladder up to making you feel confident in your taxes. The two benefits "reduce the time it takes me to enter my tax information" and "reduce the time it take me to file my taxes" both have to do with saving time. Finally, the benefit "maximize my tax deductions" ladders up to a higher level "save money" benefit. Table 4.2 shows how each of the detailed benefits maps to the corresponding benefit ladder.

The laddering interview technique is similar to the "Five Whys" tool promoted by Eric Ries. Originally developed by Toyota, the Five Whys is an iterative question-asking technique to explore the root cause of a problem.

TABLE 4.2 Customer Benefit Ladders

Benefit at Top of Ladder	Detailed Customer Benefit
Feel confident	1. Help me prepare my tax return 2. Check the accuracy of my tax return 3. Reduce my audit risk
Save time	4. Reduce the time it takes me to enter my tax information 5. Reduce the time it takes me to file my taxes
Save money	6. Maximize my tax deductions

HIERARCHIES OF NEEDS

In addition to ladders, another complexity you will often encounter in the problem space is that customer needs can have hierarchies. These hierarchies create dependencies between needs, where the value created by addressing one need is a function of how much another need is being met.

Maslow's Hierarchy of Human Needs

Let's discuss a well-known example of this phenomenon: Maslow's hierarchy of human needs, shown in Figure 4.1. Abraham Maslow was a famous twentieth-century American psychologist.

In Maslow's five-level hierarchy, physiological needs such as eating, drinking, and sleeping come first, forming the base. The second tier is safety and security needs. The third tier is love and belonging needs such as family, friends, and intimacy. The fourth level is

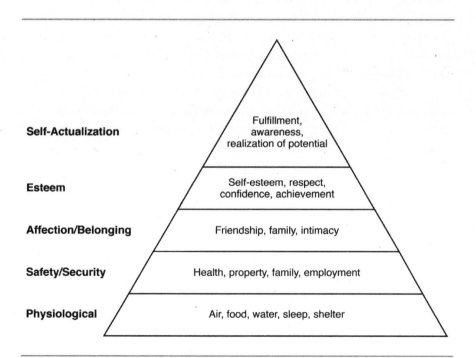

FIGURE 4.1   Maslow's Hierarchy of Human Needs

esteem needs: achievement and respect. The top level of the pyramid is self-actualization needs: fulfillment through realizing your potential.

The implication of the hierarchy is that a higher-level need doesn't really matter unless the more basic needs below it are met. As you explore the problem space for your product, you will likely encounter similar hierarchies. You'll find situations where customer benefit B doesn't matter if benefit A—which is at a lower level on the needs hierarchy—hasn't yet been met.

My Hierarchy of Web User Needs

When I led product management at Friendster, I learned about such hierarchies the hard way. Friendster was the first popular social networking site. Social networking sites (and social products in general) are known for the explosive viral growth they can experience. Friendster experienced a rapid growth in users, so much so that the volume of usage began to outstrip the ability of our web servers to keep up with traffic. Many Friendster users loved our product; however, they didn't like it when our website was loading slowly or just not available due to these technical performance issues. To help our team prioritize its work, I created a hierarchy of web user needs—with a tip of the hat to Maslow—shown in Figure 4.2.

The left side of Figure 4.2 shows the five-level hierarchy from the customer's perspective. To the right of each tier is what it means to us at the company. As entrepreneurs, product managers, developers, and designers, we love to spend our time coming up with cool new feature ideas and designing great user experiences. However, those items sit at the top two levels of the pyramid of user needs. First and foremost, the product needs to be available when the user wants to use it. After that, the product's response time needs to be fast enough to be deemed adequate. The next tier pertains to the product's quality: Does it work as it is supposed to? We then arrive at the feature set tier, which deals with functionality. At the top, we have user experience (UX) design, which governs how easy—and hopefully how enjoyable—your product is to use. As with Maslow's hierarchy, lower-level needs have to be met before higher-level needs matter.

How your product stacks up against this hierarchy of needs is not static, it changes over time. Let's assume you are fortunate enough to have a highly available, fast, bug-free product at a certain point

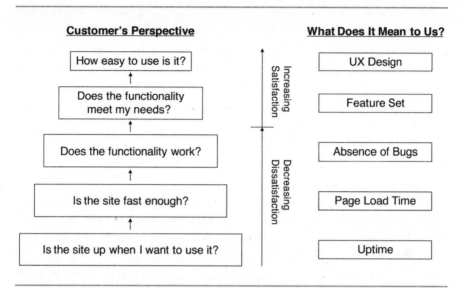

FIGURE 4.2   Olsen's Hierarchy of Web User Needs

in time. You then launch a new feature. It will probably have some bugs, reducing your product's quality. The new feature may place higher demands on your database, degrading your product's performance. Or it may be so popular that your usage spikes, overloading your servers and causing a slowdown. As you work on features and UX design, it's important to keep this hierarchy in mind and proactively "dip down" to address deficiencies at lower levels when they occur.

THE IMPORTANCE VERSUS SATISFACTION FRAMEWORK

Once you've explored the problem space and identified the various customer needs that your product could meet, you have to decide which ones you want to address. So you need a good way to prioritize among the different needs—and prioritizing based on customer value is a good approach. That begs the question: How do you determine customer value? I faced that question when I led product management for Quicken. We launched a new version of Quicken every year, and I had to determine the plan for the next version of the product. Intuit excels at customer research, so I had the opportunity to design both quantitative and qualitative research to capture the information I wanted from customers. I used the results of this research to create a framework based on importance and satisfaction. I've found this framework provides the best way to think about how to create customer value in a rigorous, analytical manner. My framework worked well in prioritizing opportunities to create customer value for that version of Quicken, which achieved new records for sales volume, revenue, and profit. Since then, I've been excited to discover other frameworks that are also based on importance and satisfaction (which I'll discuss later).

Not surprisingly, importance is a measure of how important a particular customer need is to a customer. Importance is a problem space concept, separate from any specific solution space implementation. For a given customer, different needs will have different levels of importance. For example, some people consider the need for privacy more important than the need to share updates and pictures with their friends. I know several people who don't use social media for this reason. The same need will have different levels of importance across different customers. Among my friends, there is a range of how important they consider sharing updates and pictures with their friends. For some, it's so important that they post multiple updates a day. Others post updates very rarely. Differences in the importance of needs influence a customer's decisions and preferences.

Satisfaction is a measure of how satisfied a customer is with a particular solution that provides a certain customer benefit. It indicates how well that solution meets their needs. Different products will have different levels of satisfaction for the same customer, and the same product can provide different levels of satisfaction to different customers.

The power of the framework comes when you look at importance and satisfaction together, as shown in Figure 4.3. Importance is on the vertical axis (from low to high) and satisfaction is on the horizontal axis (from low to high). Let's divide the graph into four quadrants. You can use this framework to evaluate potential product opportunities, either for new products or for additions or improvements to an existing product.

Let's start with the bottom two quadrants. The bottom left quadrant represents low satisfaction and the bottom right represents high satisfaction, but both represent low importance. There is not much point in pursuing low importance ideas, regardless of the satisfaction

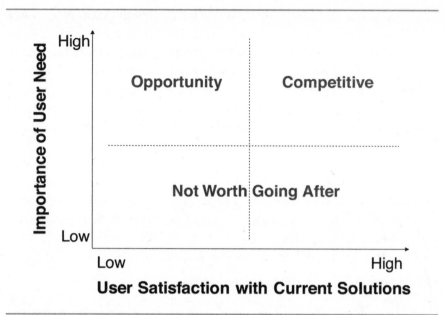

FIGURE 4.3   The Importance versus Satisfaction Framework

level, since they just won't create enough customer value. You want to address high importance customer needs. Later in this chapter, I will show you an importance versus satisfaction chart populated with actual data for a real product.

The upper right quadrant is high importance as well as high satisfaction. This would be the case in a market where the leading products are robust and do a good job of meeting customer needs. Microsoft Excel comes to mind as a relevant example, since it does pretty much everything people expect a spreadsheet application to do. Wikipedia refers to the program as "the industry standard for spreadsheets." The feature set and user interface stabilized years ago with no major innovations in a while—so much so that Excel hasn't had any competition from other desktop spreadsheet applications in a long time. The top competitive threat is from cloud-based application providers, some of which provide a subset of Excel's functionality for free.

It's important to note that it doesn't always have to be the case that markets in the upper right quadrant have a single, dominant product. A market could have several, quite similar products. The leading all-in-one printers fit the bill of high importance and high satisfaction; however, there are comparable models from many manufacturers including Hewlett Packard, Epson, Canon, Brother, and Lexmark.

If you are using the framework to assess a product's features, the upper right quadrant represents a feature that is performing well. It is addressing a high importance need and customers are very satisfied with it. For example, in a user survey for one of my products, I discovered such a feature that scored 100 percent on importance and 98 percent on satisfaction.

The upper left quadrant is high importance of need but low satisfaction with current solutions. Customer needs in this quadrant are important but underserved. As a result, they offer excellent opportunities to create customer value. A good example of this quadrant is the ride service app Uber.

Uber's Success: Meeting Underserved Needs

Uber has experienced spectacular success and growth. Achieving such results clearly requires great execution, and the company has an attractive business model. But looking at Uber through the lens of the importance versus satisfaction framework provides insight into another fundamental reason for the company's success.

Many people have an important need to be driven from one place to another, whether it's on short notice or scheduled in advance. Taxis are a very common and traditional solution for this need. But few taxi riders would say they are very satisfied with their customer experience. Common complaints include dirty cars, rude drivers, problems communicating with drivers, concerns about unsafe driving, uncertainty about the cost of trips, and the hassle of payment and tipping. People also complain about taxis that arrive late or never at all. While taxis (usually) meet the basic overall need of getting people from point A to point B, these complaints reveal many important underserved needs related to safety, comfort, convenience, affordability, and reliability. The needs of taxi customers are clearly in the upper left quadrant. The combination of the high importance of this set of needs, the low satisfaction with existing solutions such as taxis, and the large number of people with these needs points to a substantial market opportunity—one that Uber saw and acted upon.

Uber used technology to capitalize on the opportunity with a mobile app that allows you to easily hail a car on your smartphone.

The app starts with a map of your local area that shows the location of nearby Uber cars. It then matches you with a specific driver, showing you his or her name, photo, rating, car model, and license plate number. The app tells you the estimated time that the driver will take to arrive and shows you the car's location on a map in real-time. This increased transparency compared to calling a taxi or trying to hail one significantly reduces the anxiety about arriving at your destination on time. Uber includes a feedback system that requires riders to rate their drivers. This ratings data empowers riders to be informed about their prospective drivers, and Uber uses it to weed out drivers that aren't up to snuff.

Uber also improves the financial aspects of the customer experience. The app lets riders check the estimated fare before a trip, which helps avoid surprises at the end of their trip. The app stores your credit card information so that it can automatically handle payment at the end of your ride without any effort required. In contrast, dealing with payment at the end of a traditional taxi ride can be a hassle. Having to wait for the driver to run your credit card and print out the credit slip and receipt causes delays. Some drivers accept only cash, which can cause a problem if you don't have enough on hand. With Uber, at the end of your trip you just leave the car and don't have to worry about any of that.

It's clear that Uber addressed multiple underserved needs that were in the upper left quadrant of high importance and low satisfaction. As a result, Uber has seen incredible success since starting in 2009. Though it is a privately held company, financial data leaked in December 2013 showed that Uber had over 400,000 active clients taking over 800,000 rides per week. The gross revenue run rate at the time exceeded $1 billion per year, of which Uber keeps 20 percent. In December 2014, Uber raised $1.2 billion in investment at a valuation of $40 billion. You might not achieve the same level of success as Uber, but the high importance, low satisfaction quadrant is the best place to pursue opportunities.

Disruptive Innovation versus Incremental Innovation

When discussing innovation, it's common to distinguish between disruptive innovation and incremental innovation. Incremental innovation occurs when you make minor improvements that add small amounts of customer value with each new version of your product. You can do so, for example, by increasing satisfaction for the established set of benefits or addressing additional benefits.

It's clear that Uber is disrupting the mature and well-established taxi market. Most people would consider the app an example of disruptive innovation. Their product offering provides significantly more customer value than the alternative solutions that existed when it was launched. People often refer to a "10×" improvement as disruptive innovation. When a new product enables such a better way of doing something that people can't imagine going back to the old way, that's disruptive innovation.

A disruptive innovation such as Uber can emerge from an upper left quadrant opportunity where there was low satisfaction with a high importance need. Disruptive innovations can also redefine the existing satisfaction scale for their market. Consider the example of a mature, competitive market with one or more leading products in the upper right corner of the importance versus satisfaction framework. A disruptive innovation can come along and push all of those leading products to the left by offering a higher level of satisfaction that wasn't available before. In doing so, it changes the scale of the satisfaction axis.

Disruptive Innovation: Music on the Go

Let's discuss a string of innovations where disruption occurred in the market for portable music listening. The high-level customer benefit could be stated as: "Allow me to listen to music on the go." The first product that addressed this benefit was the transistor radio in the 1950s. Prior to that, radios relied on vacuum tubes, which were larger, required more power, and were fragile, making portability infeasible. But while portable radios allowed you to listen to music, you couldn't select the songs you wanted. That changed in 1979 when Sony introduced the first portable cassette audio player, the Walkman. Listeners could now listen to the music they wanted to hear by playing tapes. The Walkman was a disruptive innovation that shifted the satisfaction scale, displacing portable radios in the upper right quadrant and pushing them to the left.

Several years later, Sony launched the first portable CD player, the Discman, which offered additional benefits: higher sound quality and the ability to easily and quickly jump from one song to the next versus having to fast-forward or rewind a cassette tape. Although it was eventually solved later, one negative of the earlier Discman models is that the CD would skip when jostled. I would consider the portable CD player an incremental innovation over the portable cassette player. For some target customers, the portable CD player would be located slightly to the right of the Walkman in my framework, but it didn't change the satisfaction scale.

The next portable music innovation was the MP3 player, first launched in 1998. The first models didn't have a large capacity to store songs, but that changed over time. Apple entered the MP3 player market with the iPod in 2001. It wasn't a runaway hit at first, but the company made major improvements in subsequent models. The combination of its large storage capacity, intuitive user interface, and integration with the iTunes jukebox software and digital music store led it to become the leading MP3 player, with over 70 percent market share. The iPod was a disruptive innovation that yet again redefined the satisfaction scale for portable music listening.

Reflecting on this example, the scale for the satisfaction axis is defined by the solutions that exist in the market—more specifically, by the "high water mark" of current solutions. When better solutions that deliver more customer value come out, the upper value on the right side of the scale gets redefined, shifting everything to the left. In contrast, the importance axis is more stable. The customer need to listen to music on the go was a constant throughout the four waves of new technical solutions across over 50 years. The importance of that need may have changed slowly over time with societal and cultural trends, increasing as more people are on the go—but nowhere near as drastically as the satisfaction scale.

That being said, the iPod and other MP3 players have been on the decline. So who is eating the iPod's lunch? It's the iPhone and other smartphones, which have incorporated everything an MP3 player can do (and more) into their feature set. Interestingly, the need to listen to music on the go has morphed from a stand-alone benefit and has become subsumed by a set of many related needs that customers have when they're on the go—making phone calls, sending text messages, browsing the web, playing games, using apps, and so forth—all of which are addressed by a single solution: the smartphone.

Measuring Importance and Satisfaction

In my workshops, most people see the value that the importance versus satisfaction framework provides. However, one area that I receive a lot of questions about is how to *measure* values for importance and satisfaction. The easiest way to think about this is a question that you ask your customers (or prospective customers). You can ask the question in person or in a survey. Let's pretend we're on the Uber product team. Imagine we survey a thousand of our target customers and ask them: "When you take a ride in a taxi or other hired car, how important is it to you that the driver is polite?" We could use a five-point response scale:

1. Not at all important
2. Slightly important
3. Moderately important
4. Very important
5. Extremely important

We could use the average of all the scores as the importance rating. If we wanted to, we could map this five-point scale to a scale from 0 to 100 (or 0 to 10) for easier interpretation. We would then ask similar questions about the importance of car cleanliness, car comfort, driver punctuality, safe driving, and so forth.

For satisfaction, we could ask: "How satisfied are you with how polite your driver was during the taxi rides you've taken in the past six months?" We could use a seven-point response scale:

1. Completely dissatisfied
2. Mostly dissatisfied
3. Somewhat dissatisfied
4. Neither satisfied nor dissatisfied
5. Somewhat satisfied
6. Mostly satisfied
7. Completely satisfied

We could use the average of the scores as the satisfaction rating. If we wanted to, we could map this seven-point scale to a scale from 0 to 100 (or 0 to 10) for easier interpretation. We would ask similar questions about their satisfaction with car cleanliness, car comfort, driver punctuality, safe driving, and so forth.

In addition to prospective customers, we could also survey current Uber users—and ask the same exact importance questions. We would ask them similar satisfaction questions, but they would instead be in reference to Uber (as opposed to about traditional taxis). Comparing satisfaction ratings with competitive products is a good way to identify where your product is perceived as better or worse.

You might wonder why I used different rating scales for importance and satisfaction. Part of the reason is that there are two types of rating scales: unipolar and bipolar. A bipolar scale goes from negative to positive, whereas a unipolar scale goes from 0 to 100 percent of an attribute. It's usually best to measure satisfaction using a bipolar scale; since people can be satisfied or dissatisfied, a negative score makes sense. In contrast, importance is just a matter of degree—without any negative value—and therefore better measured with a unipolar scale.

You could choose to use different scales with customers, for example, 1 to 10 or 0 to 10. Using more than 11 choices will overwhelm customers, while using fewer than 5 won't achieve enough granularity. For any bipolar scale, I recommend using an odd number of choices so that there is a neutral option in the middle. Significant research has been performed on the reliability and validity of various scales, and it is generally agreed that 5-point scales are best for unipolar and 7-point scales are best for bipolar—which explains why I recommend the choices above.

As I mentioned, you can map the scale you use with customers to another scale to make interpretation and calculations easier. For example, you could map the values of a 5-point scale to 0, 25, 50, 75, and 100. Or to 0, 2.5, 5, 7.5, and 10. Likewise, you could map the values of a 7-point scale to 0, 16.7, 33.3, 50, 66.7, 83.3, and 100. Since you can easily transform the scores, you should use a scale with customers that is easy for them to understand and that doesn't try to ask them for more precision than they can realistically provide.

An Importance and Satisfaction Example with Real Data

To make these concepts more tangible, let's look at some real data from a real product. For one of the products I worked on, we surveyed our users periodically to have them rate the key product features. In one such survey, we asked users to rate the importance of and their satisfaction with 13 key features. We averaged the ratings for each feature and plotted them, as seen in Figure 4.4. Each of the 13 points you see is one of the key features. The number plotted next to each point is the satisfaction rating for that feature. In the upper right corner, you can see the feature I mentioned earlier, with 100 percent importance and 98 percent satisfaction. As a product manager, I was very happy with that result. Because the feature was already doing so well, I didn't want to expend any of our team's precious resources on trying to improve that feature further. Instead, I focused on improving the feature that is closest to the upper left corner of high importance and low satisfaction. See the point labeled "55": that feature had 82 percent importance and only 55 percent satisfaction. There was only one other feature with lower satisfaction (of 41 percent).

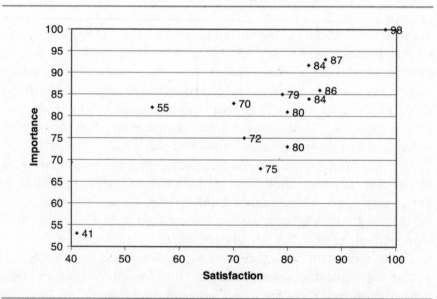

FIGURE 4.4   Real Data for Importance versus Satisfaction

However, that feature was much less important (only 53 percent). It's worth pointing out that customers can only rate the satisfaction of a solution if they've used it.

I often hear people say that they're building a new product and don't yet have a customer base that they can survey. They're concerned about not being able to reach enough customers to achieve statistical significance. But even if you can't easily reach thousands of people, you can still obtain meaningful results.

A Sample Size of Zero Is Okay

Let's return to Uber. Assume we conduct one-on-one interviews with 25 people who frequently use taxis and ask them our importance and satisfaction survey questions. What percentage of them would you expect to be "completely satisfied" with their taxi experiences? It's easy to envision that few or even none of the 25 would say that. In our discovery interviews, we would uncover the more detailed needs of comfort, convenience, safety, reliability, and so forth. Imagine we asked the 25 customers to rate the importance of each of those benefits, along with the corresponding satisfaction level when they've taken taxis. Meaningful patterns could emerge in the results—even though we haven't surveyed thousands of people. For example, if a very large percentage of people you interview rate something high or low, there's a decent chance you've uncovered something that will be proven out as you gain more data points. I call this technique "doing quant on qual"—quantitative analysis on qualitative data. While you must use it with care, it is an underutilized tool. Statistical analysis is a powerful tool that has its place; but too many product people have convinced themselves that they need to prove things beyond a shadow of a doubt. That's just not the case—and often, especially in the early stages of working on a v1 product, not even possible. Statistical significance is great when you have the sample size to achieve it, but it isn't an all or nothing proposition.

I would go one step further and say that you can even use the importance versus satisfaction framework *before you talk to a single customer*. That's right; you can make progress with a sample size of *zero*. How? By using the framework to formulate and clarify your hypotheses. The Lean approach is all about articulating clear hypotheses and then designing tests to determine if they are valid. Before you do your first customer interview, you can form hypotheses about what needs are most important to your target customers. You can also hypothesize about what they like and don't like about current solutions and their level of satisfaction. You could lay out each of your hypotheses on the four-quadrant framework—either digitally or with Post-it notes—and then move them around, revise them, and add new ones as you learn and iterate.

RELATED FRAMEWORKS

I mentioned that I was excited to discover other frameworks that were also based on importance and satisfaction after I came up with my framework at Intuit. *Gap analysis* and *jobs to be done* both use importance and satisfaction to quantify the size of different product opportunities to inform your prioritization.

Gap Analysis

The first related framework is "gap analysis." Now, you will find more than one definition of gap analysis if you search online. The version to which I'm referring is based on calculating the "gap" between importance and satisfaction. So you simply take the rating for importance and subtract from it the rating for satisfaction.

$$\text{Gap} = \text{Importance} - \text{Satisfaction}$$

The bigger the gap, the more underserved the need. With this framework, situations where the satisfaction is greater than the importance will result in a negative gap.

The strength of gap analysis is that it produces a single number that is very easy to calculate. However, its biggest shortcoming is that it treats all gaps of equal size the same. For example, using a 0 to 10 scale, if a need had an importance of 10 and a satisfaction of 5, the gap would be 5. If another need had an importance of 6 and a satisfaction of 1, the gap would also be 5. But this doesn't make intuitive sense because a gap of 5 on a need with an importance of 10 should be more important than the same size gap on a need with an importance of 6. Let's move on to another framework based on importance and satisfaction that addresses this deficiency.

Jobs to Be Done

I was delighted to discover Anthony Ulwick's book *What Customers Want*. In it, he describes his outcome-driven innovation approach, which also uses importance and satisfaction to quantify opportunities. Ulwick utilizes a slightly more complex calculation for his opportunity score that addresses the problem with the gap analysis calculation:

Opportunity Score = Importance + Maximum (Importance − Satisfaction, 0)

His calculation subtracts satisfaction from importance, as in gap analysis. However, he does not allow that difference to become negative; it can only go as low as zero. To that difference he adds importance so that it becomes a tiebreaker for gaps with the same size. Using 0 to 10 for each rating, the resulting score can vary from 0 (when importance is zero) to 20 (when importance is 10 and satisfaction is 0). Ulwick considers opportunities with scores greater than 15 to be very attractive, and those below 10 to be unattractive.

Let's calculate the opportunity score using the same two needs from the previous example. The first need with an importance of 10 and a satisfaction of 5 would have an opportunity score of 10 + Maximum (10 − 5, 0) = 10 + 5 = 15. For the second need with an importance of 6 and a satisfaction of 1, the opportunity score would be 6 + Maximum (6 − 1, 0) = 6 + 5 = 11. Using Ulwick's formula, even though the gap in importance and satisfaction is the same between the two needs, the first need with the higher importance has the higher opportunity score.

Central to Ulwick's methodology is the idea that customers buy products and services to help them get a task or job done. Customers decide which product to buy based on how well it delivers their "desired outcomes" for the "job to be done." Clayton Christensen and others have also promoted this approach, commonly referred to as "jobs to be done."

Ulwick explains why he considers outcomes to be superior to customer needs or benefits. His main criticism of needs and benefits is that they are usually stated imprecisely. He warns against a "customer-driven" approach that relies too heavily on the "voice of the customer," since customers are often imprecise or ambiguous in their language. I agree that customer needs and benefits should be precisely defined—and it is the job of the product team, not customers, to define them. In order to identify innovative solutions, the product team needs to create a rich definition of the problem space. I share Ulwick's concern that all too often, product objectives or requirements are far too "fuzzy"—too high-level or vague.

He explains that "For most jobs, even those that may seem somewhat trivial, there are typically 50 to 150 or more desired outcomes—not just a handful." That sentence resonated strongly with my own belief that it is possible—and actually *essential* to successful innovation—for product teams to create a detailed and precise definition of their problem space. What Ulwick calls outcomes, I would call well-defined customer benefits. Rather than just scratching the surface, good product teams are able to iteratively peel the onion to gain deeper and deeper insights. Steve Jobs shared a similar view, saying:

> When you first start off trying to solve a problem, the first solutions you come up with are very complex, and most people stop there. But if you keep going, and live with the problem and peel more layers of the onion off, you can oftentimes arrive at some very elegant and simple solutions. Most people just don't put in the time or energy to get there.

VISUALIZING CUSTOMER VALUE

If the idea of quantifying product opportunities by using measurements of importance and satisfaction resonates with you, I recommend you read *What Customers Want* by Anthony Ulwick. Using my importance versus satisfaction framework, I have developed my own quantitative approach that I find a bit more visually intuitive. My approach goes beyond just quantifying opportunities;

it provides a broader view that visually explains customer value and how it is created.

Customer Value Delivered by a Product or Feature

Let's return to the importance versus satisfaction framework introduced in Figure 4.3 and get more precise about the values on the axes. Instead of going from low to high, think of importance and satisfaction as ranging from 0 to 100 percent, as shown in Figure 4.5. That way, whether you measure values using a 5-point, 7-point, 10-point, or 100-point scale, you can always be consistent.

Each point that can be plotted on the graph represents a need with a certain importance and level of customer satisfaction with the product or feature addressing that need. Consider the point at the lower left corner of the graph where importance and satisfaction are both zero. A product or feature at that point would not be delivering any customer value. In contrast, a product or feature at the upper right corner where importance and satisfaction are both 100 percent would deliver the maximum amount of customer value for that need.

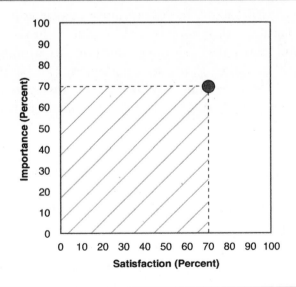

FIGURE 4.5   Visualizing Customer Value

The higher the importance of the need that a product or feature meets, the more customer value it delivers. And the higher the satisfaction with the product, the more customer value it provides. When a product or feature is plotted as a point on the graph, the amount of customer value it provides is the area of the rectangle the point creates with the origin. So you can calculate the customer value delivered with the equation:

$$\text{Customer Value Delivered} = \text{Importance} \times \text{Satisfaction}$$

Consider the product shown in the Figure 4.5 plot. The need has an importance of 70 percent, and the product addressing that need has a satisfaction of 70 percent. Therefore, the customer value this product delivers in meeting that need is $0.7 \times 0.7 = 0.49$.

This approach is visually intuitive. If you plot multiple products or features on the same chart, as shown in Figure 4.4, it's pretty easy to see which delivers the most value. The larger the area of the rectangle, the more customer value the product or feature creates.

Opportunity to Add Customer Value

You can also easily assess the opportunity associated with a given product or feature that is represented by a point in the importance versus satisfaction space. The opportunity for each point is simply the maximum amount of customer value that can be added to it. Customer value can be added by increasing satisfaction, up to the maximum value of 100 percent (or 1). This can be expressed quantitatively as:

$$\text{Opportunity to Add Value} = \text{Importance} \times (1 - \text{Satisfaction})$$

This approach makes it easy to visually assess the opportunity to create additional customer value that is associated with a given product or feature. The opportunity for a product or feature represented by a point is just the area of the rectangle to the right of it, which is the maximum customer value that can be added to better address that need.

Figure 4.6 shows two different product opportunities. Opportunity A (corresponding to the product shown in Figure 4.5) has an importance of 70 percent and a satisfaction of 70 percent, so its opportunity score is:

$$\text{Opportunity A} = 0.7 \times (1 - 0.7) = 0.7 \times 0.3 = 0.21$$

Opportunity B has an importance of 90 percent and a satisfaction of 30 percent, so its opportunity score is:

$$\text{Opportunity B} = 0.9 \times (1 - 0.3) = 0.9 \times 0.7 = 0.63$$

Opportunity B offers the potential to create three times as much customer value as Opportunity A. When you are evaluating opportunities to pursue, you should pursue the ones with the highest opportunity scores. As a reminder, they occur in the upper left quadrant, as did the opportunity that Uber pursued.

If you refer back to Figure 4.4, which shows real data from an actual product, you'll recall that I gave the highest priority to the feature that had an importance of 82 percent and a satisfaction of

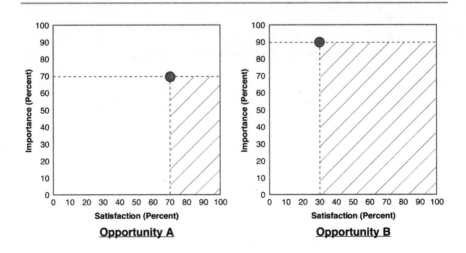

FIGURE 4.6 Measuring Opportunity

55 percent; let's call it "Feature X." Take a look at all the points plotted in the figure. Once you know how to assess opportunity, it's easy to see that Feature X offers the greatest opportunity. The Feature X opportunity score is:

Feature X Opportunity $= 0.82 \times (1 - 0.55) = 0.82 \times 0.45 = 0.37$

All 11 of the features to the right of Feature X in the chart have opportunity scores less than 0.25. And the feature with an importance of 53 percent and a satisfaction of 41 percent only offers an opportunity score of 0.32. Note that although that last feature appears in the bottom left corner of Figure 4.4, that's only because the axes weren't shown going all the way to zero. If they did, that feature would be located near the center of the graph.

The customer value that a product delivers varies with the satisfaction level (the width of the rectangle), but the *maximum* customer value it can deliver (the area of the widest rectangle) is fundamentally determined by the importance of the need (the height). This reinforces why it's best to focus on high importance needs, where you can create the greatest value. So another way to express the opportunity is:

Opportunity = Importance − Current Value Delivered

Customer Value Created by Product Improvements

You can also visualize the *actual* customer value created by product improvements that you make. If an improvement increases satisfaction from the current level (Sat_{before}) to a higher level (Sat_{after}), then the customer value it creates is the area of the incremental rectangle, given by:

Customer Value Created = Importance $\times$ ($Sat_{after} - Sat_{before}$)

Figure 4.7 illustrates the creation of customer value by making a product improvement that increases satisfaction (sticking with the example product from Figure 4.5). The importance of the need is 70 percent and the satisfaction before making the product improvement was 70 percent. The satisfaction increases to 90 percent after

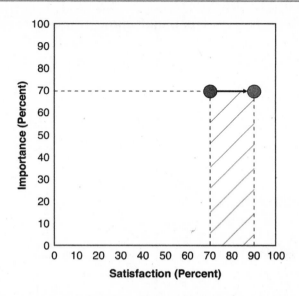

FIGURE 4.7   Creating Customer Value

improving the product. Applying the above formula, the amount of customer value created was 0.14.

$$\text{Customer Value Created} = 0.7 \times (0.9 - 0.7) = 0.7 \times 0.2 = 0.14$$

As I've discussed, a product usually addresses many related customer needs—not just one. So, in addition to increasing satisfaction, another way to create more customer value with your product is to improve it so that it addresses additional, related customer needs—ideally, those with higher importance.

THE KANO MODEL

Another excellent framework for understanding customer needs and satisfaction is the Kano model developed by quality management expert Noriaki Kano. I first studied this model in my industrial engineering graduate program. As shown in Figure 4.8, the Kano model also plots a set of two parameters on horizontal and vertical axes: (1) how fully a given customer need is met (horizontal axis),

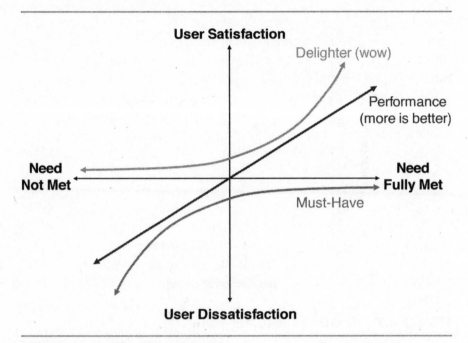

FIGURE 4.8 The Kano Model

and (2) the resulting level of customer satisfaction (vertical axis). The horizontal axis ranges from the need not being met at all on the left to the need being fully met on the right. The vertical axis ranges from complete customer dissatisfaction at the bottom to complete satisfaction at the top—consistent with the bipolar scale discussed earlier.

I won't go into the details of how you generate the data by asking customers questions and the six possible results for a given need. The utility of the model is that it breaks customer needs into three relevant categories that you can use: performance needs, must-have needs, and delighters. With performance needs, more is better. As the need is more fully met, the resulting customer satisfaction increases. Say you were shopping for a car and considering two different models. If they were identical in all aspects but Car A had twice the fuel efficiency (e.g., miles per gallon) of Car B, you would have a preference for Car A. Fuel efficiency is a performance benefit for cars.

Must-have needs don't create satisfaction by being met. Instead, the need *not* being met causes customer dissatisfaction. Must-have features are "table stakes" or "cost of entry"—boxes that must be checked for customers to be satisfied with your product. Sticking with the car example, seat belts would be a must-have feature. If you were interested in a car but realized it had no seat belts, you wouldn't buy it for fear of getting hurt if you were in an accident. Your must-have need for a reasonable level of safety is not being met. That being said, if Car A had five seat belts and Car B had 100 seat belts, you wouldn't say that Car B is 20 times better than Car A. Once you have one seat belt per passenger, your must-have need has been met.

Delighters provide unexpected benefits that exceed customer expectations, resulting in very high customer satisfaction. The absence of a delighter doesn't cause any dissatisfaction because customers aren't expecting it. Returning again to cars, GPS navigation systems were a delighter when the first car models came out with that new technology in the mid-1990s. They meant no longer having to print out directions from your computer and no more getting lost. This feature fundamentally changed how people drove from point A to point B, resulting in customer delight.

Going further back in time, cars did not always have built-in cup holders. Chrysler changed that when it introduced the minivan in the early 1980s, which had two functional cup holders sunk into the plastic of the dashboard. They were delighters because drivers no longer had to worry about spilling their beverages as they drove.

Of course, cup holders are now ubiquitous in cars—and an increasing percentage of cars come with GPS navigation as a standard feature. That illustrates an important aspect of the Kano model: Needs migrate over time. Yesterday's delighters become today's performance features and tomorrow's must-haves. Growing customer expectations and competition continuously raise the bar over time. This is another way of describing how, in the importance versus satisfaction framework, the upper value on the right side of the satisfaction scale gets redefined over time, moving yesterday's solutions to the left.

The Kano model also exhibits hierarchy, which I discussed earlier. For example, the fact that your product has a delighter doesn't matter if it's missing a must-have. A navigation system would be pointless in a car with no seat belts. You have to meet basic needs before you can get credit for performance features. And your product must be competitive on performance features before delighters matter.

You can think of this as a three-tier pyramid with must-haves on the bottom, performance features just above that, and delighters at the top.

You can apply the Kano model to gain clarity about the problem space. Think about the customer benefits that are relevant in your product category and classify them into the three categories of must-haves, performance benefits, and delighters. Evaluating competitive products and reading product reviews can help inform you as you create this framework. I will talk more about using the Kano model in conjunction with your competitive landscape when I discuss how to define your product's value proposition in Chapter 5.

PUTTING THE FRAMEWORKS TO USE

This chapter covers a lot of ground, and hopefully solidifies the problem space concept in your mind while illustrating the depth and richness with which you can explain customer benefits. Once you have identified the customer benefits that you could potentially address, you use the importance versus satisfaction framework to determine which ones allow you to create the most customer value. You want to pursue product opportunities in the upper left quadrant of importance versus satisfaction that have as large an opportunity score as possible. For the opportunity you decide to pursue, you will next break down the related benefits and decide which ones you will address with your product. You want to make sure your product delivers enough customer value and is better than other alternatives, which is the essence of product strategy. In the next chapter, I discuss how to define your value proposition using the Kano model, which you'll use to specify your MVP candidate.

Chapter 5

Define Your Value Proposition
(Step 3)

The next step in the Lean Product Process is to define your product value proposition, which is the next layer in the Product-Market Fit Pyramid. At this point, you have identified several important customer needs that you could potentially address. Now you need to decide which ones your product *will* address. You want to do so deliberately and resist the temptation to tackle more needs than you should.

A good product is designed with focus on the set of needs that are important and that make sense to address together. Swiss Army knives are incredibly useful, providing a set of tools to address a wide range of needs all in one convenient package. But at some point, as you add more and more tools, a Swiss Army knife gets wider, heavier, less usable, and less valuable. Focus is critical when defining a new product.

You also don't want to unnecessarily risk wasting resources with an initial product scope that is too large. You do not have perfect information about all those customer needs. There is quite a bit of uncertainty in both your hypotheses and in what you think you know. That's why you want to start off by identifying the *minimum* viable product. Remember, all of your hypotheses about customer needs are hinged on an underlying assumption about your target customer. If you test your MVP and realize that your assumption was wrong, you will have to revisit your hypotheses about the relevant needs to address.

Even if user testing verifies that you are heading in the right direction, you will learn new information that causes you to revise and add to your problem space hypotheses. And this will occur each time you iterate. You'll never have "perfect information." If you are following a good trajectory as you iterate, there will just be "less imperfect" information that you gather with increasing confidence.

STRATEGY MEANS SAYING "NO"

This step in the Lean Product Process is about determining your *product value proposition*, which identifies the specific customer needs your product will address and articulates how it is better and different than the alternatives. When you specify the needs your product *will* address, you are also deciding the other benefits it *won't* address. It can be difficult for some people to say, "No, our product won't solve that problem"—but that is the essence of strategy. One of the best definitions I've heard of strategy is: "deciding what you're *not* going to do." Here's what Steve Jobs had to say about saying "no":

> People think focus means saying yes to the thing you've got to focus on. But that's not what it means at all. It means saying no to the hundred other good ideas that there are. You have to pick carefully. I'm actually as proud of the things we haven't done as the things I have done. Innovation is saying no to 1,000 things.

So you need to start by selecting the customer needs you plan to address. I will show you how to use the Kano model as an organizing framework, with needs classified as must-haves, performance benefits, or delighters. Since you want to make sure your product will be different and better than the alternatives, you should be classifying needs in the context of your relevant competitors. And since your competitors are usually in the same product category that you are, the must-haves will likely be the same and there will probably be significant overlap among the performance benefits. Different products may have different delighters, though.

It's important to list the must-haves, since they are required. However, since all products in the category have to have them, they are not the core part of your value proposition. The core elements are the performance benefits on which you choose to compete and the unique delighters you plan to provide.

VALUE PROPOSITIONS FOR SEARCH ENGINES

I'll illustrate the concept of product value proposition by going back to the early days of Internet search engines. Back then, there were many search engines, and different products focused on different performance benefits. Some focused on having the largest number of pages in their index, which meant that they would return the largest number of results when a customer conducted a search. Some search engines focused on their index's "freshness": how quickly they added new pages and updated existing ones. Others focused on having the highest relevance of results. So there are at least three performance benefits on which early search engines competed: the number, the freshness, and the relevance of results. While early search engines also competed on other benefits, I'll limit the discussion to these three for the sake of simplicity. At this early stage in the search engine market, the relative importance of each benefit wasn't clear, and different companies chose different value propositions by focusing on different performance benefits.

Over time, most search engines were indexing a large number of pages, so the number of results became less important. While users liked knowing that there were many results, they didn't usually take the time to look beyond the first few pages. Similarly, most search engines were eventually able to add new pages relatively quickly so that their results were fresh. Therefore, relevance became the most important benefit and the one that offered the biggest opportunity for differentiation. Google was able to achieve much higher relevance than other search engines due to its unique PageRank algorithm. Because they were best at the benefit that mattered most—and had comparable or better performance on the other dimensions—Google won the search engine wars.

Table 5.1 shows these three different value propositions. The table shows that Google focused on relevance, while search engine A focused on the number of search results, and search engine B focused on freshness.

TABLE 5.1   Value Propositions for Early Search Engines

Performance Benefit	Google	Search Engine A	Search Engine B
Number of search results	Acceptable	**Best**	Acceptable
Freshness of search results	Acceptable	Acceptable	**Best**
Relevance of search results	**Best**	Acceptable	Acceptable

What about delighters? Google Suggest, which automatically suggests search query matches, falls into this category. Instead of having to type their entire query—for example, "how many inches are in a yard"—users can start typing the first few letters or words—"how many..."—and then a list of suggested queries appears. The user can then just click to select the query they have in mind from the list of suggestions, which saves them time—and the longer the phrase, the more time saved. Seeing the top related phrases also helps people who aren't quite certain about their query, which results in reaching more relevant results more quickly.

Google Instant Search is another delighter. This feature brings up search results as the user types, before the user hits the "enter" key (or selects an auto-suggested query). This feature also saves the user time. Google observed that people can read results much more quickly than they type, usually taking 300 milliseconds between keystrokes but only 30 milliseconds to scan results. Google has quantified the benefit of Instant Search at two to five seconds saved per search. Table 5.2 shows a more complete description of Google's value proposition by adding these two delighters to the performance benefits previously discussed. Google Suggest and Google Instant Search are features, not benefits. I listed the feature names in the column for Google, but listed the benefit associated with each delighter in the leftmost benefits column: saving time entering a search query and saving time viewing search results, respectively.

TABLE 5.2   Google's Value Proposition with Delighters

	Google	Search Engine A	Search Engine B
Performance Benefits			
Number of results	Acceptable	**Best**	Acceptable
Freshness of results	Acceptable	Acceptable	**Best**
Relevance of results	**Best**	Acceptable	Acceptable
Delighters			
Save time entering query	**Yes** (Google Suggest)	No	No
Save time viewing results	**Yes** (Google Instant)	No	No

Google isn't the only search engine with delighters. When Bing sought to differentiate itself from other search engines, one innovation they came up with was the picture of the day. Each day, when you go to the Bing search page, the background image is a different, stunning photo. The photos are annotated with trivia or hints about the image, and users can try to figure out what the object or location of the photo is. The nice images don't make searches any faster or improve the relevance of results, but they provide an interesting, pleasant surprise for users each day.

NOT SO CUIL

One last search engine to discuss is Cuil (pronounced "cool"), which was launched in 2008. By this time, the search engine market was already in the upper right quadrant of the importance versus satisfaction framework. Search was very important, but users were pretty satisfied with the existing search engines, with Google having the largest market share (over 60 percent at the time). Given this situation, it would be critical for any new product entering the category to have a clear value proposition articulating how it would be better and different than the current solutions.

It became clear from their marketing efforts that Cuil was focused on having the largest index. At launch, Cuil claimed an index of 120 billion web pages, which they estimated was three times the size of Google's. They presented search results to users differently by displaying them in a magazine-like format with more photos. They also tried to differentiate on privacy by promising not to retain users' search histories.

So how did Cuil do? Not so well. Critics complained about slow response times and the low relevance of results. Search expert Danny Sullivan of Search Engine Watch criticized Cuil for focusing on index size rather than relevance. Two years after launching, Cuil shut down.

The Cuil team's hypotheses about what would create a successfully differentiated search engine didn't pan out. In order to have a shot at beating the incumbent market leader, the value proposition for your new product would have to at least match them on the two important performance benefits of relevance and response time. I'm sure the Cuil team didn't *plan* to have lower relevance or response time; that's just what users encountered when they used the product. Even if Cuil had matched Google on those two performance benefits, they would have still needed a valued differentiator to gain significant market share. It's unclear how valuable their intended differentiators of a larger index and increased privacy really were to customers.

Table 5.3 provides a description of Cuil's intended and actual value proposition compared to Google. Changing customer behavior is always difficult—especially in the upper right quadrant—and you need to create a certain amount of excess value to get customers to switch from a product they routinely use. The notion of needing to have "10×" better performance comes to mind again.

TABLE 5.3   Cuil's Value Proposition versus Google

Performance Benefit	Google	Cuil (intended)	Cuil (actual)
Number of search results	Good	Best	Didn't matter
User privacy	Okay	Best	Didn't matter
How well results are displayed	Good	Best	Didn't matter
Response time	Good	Comparable	Poor
Relevance of search results	Good	Comparable	Poor

BUILDING YOUR PRODUCT VALUE PROPOSITION

Now that the search engine examples have illustrated the concept, let's discuss how you should create your product value proposition. Table 5.4 is a blank template for your value proposition. In the first column, you list the benefits—one per row, grouped by type. You want to include the must-haves, performance benefits, and delighters that are relevant to you and your competitors. You should have a column for each relevant competitor and a column for your product. The blank template lists two competitors. Competitors doesn't just mean direct competitors: in the unlikely case that you don't have any direct competitors, there should still be alternative solutions to your product that customers are currently using to meet their needs (remember how pen and paper was an alternative to TurboTax).

TABLE 5.4   Product Value Proposition Template

	Competitor A	Competitor B	My Product
Must-Haves			
Must-have 1			
Must-have 2			
Must-have 3			
Performance Benefits			
Performance benefit 1			
Performance benefit 2			
Performance benefit 3			
Delighters			
Delighter 1			
Delighter 2			

Once you have established the benefits and competitors, you want to go through each row and score each of the competitors and your own product. If you are assessing an existing product, you can score it; if you are building a new product, you can list the scores you plan to achieve. The entries for must-haves should be "Yes." For performance benefits, you should use whatever scale works best for you: A scale of "High," "Medium," and "Low" usually works well. For performance benefits that are amenable to numerical measurement, you can use the values for higher precision. For example, if you had a restaurant reservations application such as OpenTable, the number of restaurants in your system and the time it takes to make a reservation might be two performance benefits for which you could list numerical values. Delighters are typically unique, so just list each delighter on a separate row and then mark "Yes" where applicable.

See Table 5.5 for an example of a completed value proposition. I've intentionally kept the benefits and competitors generic, so you can more easily envision a similar grid for your product. In this example, there are two existing competitors for the new product you plan to build. All three companies have "yes" for all the must-haves. Competitor A focuses on being the best at performance benefit 1, and Competitor B focuses on being the best at performance benefit 2. You plan to be the best at performance benefit 3. Perhaps you have identified a new customer segment that values performance benefit 3

TABLE 5.5   Example of Completed Product Value Proposition Template

	Competitor A	Competitor B	My Product
Must-Haves			
Must-have 1	Yes	Yes	Yes
Must-have 2	Yes	Yes	Yes
Must-have 3	Yes	Yes	Yes
Performance Benefits			
Performance benefit 1	**High**	Low	Medium
Performance benefit 2	Medium	**High**	Low
Performance benefit 3	Low	Medium	**High**
Delighters			
Delighter 1	**Yes**		
Delighter 2			Yes

more than the others; or perhaps you have a new technology that allows you to achieve higher levels of satisfaction with performance benefit 3. Competitor A has delighter 1, and you have your own idea for a different delighter, delighter 2. Each product's key differentiators are shown in bold.

Completing this grid allows you to clearly articulate what benefits you plan to provide and how you're aiming to be better than your competitors. The column for your product that includes your benefits and intended score for each one is your product value proposition. You have decided on the areas where you plan to play offense and those you are willing to cede as less important. Your key differentiators are the performance benefits where you plan to outperform your competitors as well as your unique delighters. Tying back to last chapter, these differentiators should ideally correspond to underserved benefits that have high importance and low satisfaction, where there are larger opportunities to create customer value.

Few product teams ever complete such an exercise to clarify the value proposition for the product they are planning to build. So merely doing so will put you farther along than most companies. A clear value proposition decreases the likelihood that you are just launching a "me too" product, focuses your resources on what's most important, and increases your chances of success.

SKATING TO WHERE THE PUCK WILL BE

I've described the creation of your value proposition as a static snapshot in time. To be strategic, you want to ensure that you are projecting forward in time, anticipating the important trends in your market and what competitors are likely to do. This is especially important in many high-tech markets, which often have a rapid pace of change. As Wayne Gretzky said, "I skate to where the puck is going to be, not where it's been."

THE FLIP VIDEO CAMERA

A great example related to this is the Flip video camera. Launched by Pure Digital in 2006 as the "Point and Shoot Video Camcorder," many customers found the device superior to traditional camcorders because it was easier to use, more compact, and more affordable. The success of the Flip video camera led Cisco to acquire Pure Digital for $590 million in 2009.

However, two years later, Cisco announced that to align its operations, it would exit aspects of its consumer businesses, including the Flip business. What happened? The Flip video camera achieved product-market fit for several years, but the competitive landscape changed swiftly. In 2009, Apple launched the iPhone 3GS, its first iPhone with built-in video recording. Compared to the Flip, smartphones offered an even more portable solution that avoided the need for a second device. Plus, their wireless connectivity allowed customers to post videos instantly without having to sync to a computer. Cisco corporate strategy aside, it became apparent over time that the smartphone would be the future of easy, portable video recording.

PREDICTING THE FUTURE WITH VALUE PROPOSITIONS

Returning to your value proposition template, to predict the future, you can use separate columns for "now" and "later" for each competitor and your product. "Later" would be whatever length of time is the most relevant for your product strategy purposes. Table 5.6 shows an example of how you could do this.

Table 5.6 has "now" and "in 1 year" columns for the competitor and your product. Competitor A is the best at performance benefit 1

TABLE 5.6   Example of Product Value Proposition with Expected Future States

	Competitor A		My Product	
	Now	In 1 Year	Now	In 1 Year
Must-Haves				
Must-have 1	Y	Y	Y	Y
Must-have 2	Y	Y	Y	Y
Performance Benefits				
Performance benefit 1	High	High	Medium	**High**
Performance benefit 2	Medium	**High**	Low	Low
Performance benefit 3	Low	**Medium**	High	High
Delighters				
Delighter 1	Y	Y		
Delighter 2			Y	Y
Delighter 3		Y		
Delighter 4				Y

right now, while your product is the best at performance benefit 3 right now. You anticipate that Competitor A will invest in improving performance benefit 3, but won't match you. You also anticipate that Competitor A will invest to extend their lead in performance benefit 2. You have decided that performance benefit 2 is less important to your target market. Instead of investing there, you plan to ensure you stay the best at performance benefit 3 and close the gap on performance benefit 1. Turning to delighters, you each currently have your own unique delighter. Looking forward, you expect your competitor to launch delighter 3 and you plan to launch delighter 4.

Analyzing your product strategy in this way ensures that you're not just solving for current market conditions and reduces the risk that the path you're heading down will end up being suboptimal in the future.

Using the tools in this chapter should help you develop a clear understanding of your value proposition. You then need to determine the set of product features you plan to pursue to deliver on your value proposition. The next step in the Lean Product Process is to specify your MVP feature set.

Chapter 6

Specify Your Minimum Viable Product (MVP) Feature Set (Step 4)

Now that you have a clear understanding of your value proposition, the next step in the Lean Product Process is to decide on the feature set for your minimum viable product (MVP) candidate. You are not going to start off by designing a new product that delivers on your full value proposition, since that would take too long and be too risky. For your MVP, you want to identify the minimum functionality required to validate that you are heading in the right direction. I call this an MVP *candidate* instead of an MVP because it is based on your hypotheses. You haven't yet validated with customers that *they agree* that it is, in fact, a viable product.

For each benefit in your product value proposition, you want to brainstorm as a team to come up with as many feature ideas as you can for how your product could deliver that benefit. You have done all this great thinking in the problem space and are now transitioning to solution space. At this point, brainstorming rules should apply. You should be practicing *divergent thinking*, which means trying to generate as many ideas as possible without any judgment or evaluation. There will be plenty of time later for *convergent thinking*, where you evaluate the ideas and decide which ones you think are the most promising. As your team brainstorms, try to build on each other's suggestions and push each other to come up with even more creative and outlandish ideas.

When you are done brainstorming, you want to capture all the ideas that your team generated, then organize them by the benefit that they deliver. Then, for each benefit, you want to review and prioritize the list of feature ideas. You can score each idea on expected customer value to determine a first-pass priority. The goal is to identify the top three to five features for each benefit. There is not much value in looking beyond those top features right now because things will change—a lot—after you show your prototype to customers.

USER STORIES: FEATURES WITH BENEFITS

User stories (used in Agile development) are a great way to write your feature ideas to make sure that the corresponding customer benefit remains clear. A user story is a brief description of the benefit that the particular functionality should provide, including whom the benefit is for (the target customer), and why the customer wants the benefit. Well-written user stories usually follow the template:

As a [type of user],
I want to [do something],
so that I can [desired benefit].

Here's an example of a user story that follows this template:

As a professional photographer,
I want to easily upload pictures from my camera to my website,
so that I can quickly show my clients their pictures.

This template is a good start, but writing good user stories is an acquired skill. Agile thought leader Bill Wake created a set of guidelines for writing good user stories; to make them easier to remember, he uses the acronym INVEST:

- Independent: A good story should be independent of other stories. Stories shouldn't overlap in concept and should be implementable in any order.
- Negotiable: A good story isn't an explicit contract for features. The details for how a story's benefit will be delivered should be open to discussion.
- Valuable: A good story needs to be valuable to the customer.
- Estimable: A good story is one whose scope can be reasonably estimated.
- Small: Good stories tend to be small in scope. Larger stories will have greater uncertainty, so you should break them down.
- Testable: A good story provides enough information to make it clear how to test that the story is "done" (called *acceptance criteria*).

BREAKING FEATURES DOWN

Once you have written high-level user stories for your top features, the next step is to identify ways to break each of them down into smaller pieces of functionality—what I call "chunking." The goal is to find ways to reduce scope and build only the most valuable pieces of each feature. When someone comes up with a feature idea, there are often creative ways to trim off less important pieces. I deliberately use the term "feature chunk" instead of feature to remind readers that you should not be working with items that are large in scope, but rather breaking such items down into smaller, atomic components.

Let's illustrate the idea of breaking a high-level user story down. Say you are working on a photo sharing application and start out with the user story: "As a user, I want to be able to easily share photos with my friends so that they can enjoy them." One way to break this story down is by the various channels a customer can use to share photos: Facebook, Twitter, Pinterest, email, text message, and so forth. Each of those would be a distinct feature chunk or smaller scope user story. You may not need to build out all of these sharing channels for your MVP. Even if you decided that you did, it helps to break the story down to be more specific in your product definition, to enable more accurate scoping from development, and to allow you to explicitly prioritize the order in which you build the chunks. You might also limit scope by enabling the user to share only the photo and nothing else for your MVP. You may have ideas for additional functionality down the road such as adding an optional message to each photo or the ability to tag users in photos. Each of those would be a distinct feature chunk.

SMALLER BATCH SIZES ARE BETTER

The tactic of breaking features down is consistent with the Lean manufacturing best practice of working in small batch sizes. When a product is being manufactured in a factory line, the batch size is the number of products being worked on together at the same time (at each step of the manufacturing process). The parallel for software development is the size of the features or user stories to be coded. Working in smaller batch sizes increases velocity because they enable faster feedback, which reduces risk and waste. If a developer spends a month at her computer developing a feature and then shows it to the product manager and designer, there is a greater chance that there will be a disconnect and that their feedback will require significant changes. If, instead, the developer shows her work to the product manager and designer every day or two, that prevents a large disconnect from occurring. The magnitude of feedback and course corrections will be much smaller and more manageable, resulting in less wasted work and higher productivity.

This advice also applies to product managers and designers showing their work product (e.g., user stories and wireframes) to their teammates, too. The benefit of working in small batch sizes applies to customer feedback as well. The longer you work on a product without getting customer feedback, the more you risk a major disconnect that subsequently requires significant rework.

SCOPING WITH STORY POINTS

Readers who have experience working with Agile development are probably familiar with the idea of breaking features down into smaller chunks. In many forms of Agile, once you've written the user stories, the team discusses each one and the developers estimate the amount of effort required. They often do so by using *story points*, a type of currency for estimating the relative size of different user stories. For example, a very small user story may take 1 point, while a medium scope user story may take 3 points, and a large scope user story may take 8 points. I discuss story points in more detail in Chapter 12.

A good operating principle is that stories that are estimated to require a large number of points—above some maximum threshold value—need to be broken down into a set of smaller stories that are below the threshold value. You can think of a feature chunk as corresponding to a user story that has an acceptably small scope—an estimated number of story points that is below your maximum threshold.

USING RETURN ON INVESTMENT TO PRIORITIZE

This is a good time to introduce the concept of return on investment (ROI). So far, you have only prioritized based on how much customer value you believe each feature will create. You haven't yet taken into account the amount of resources required to build each feature. After you have finished chunking your feature ideas, you should perform a second-pass prioritization that accounts for both the value and the effort.

A simple way to illustrate ROI is to imagine that I invest $100 in a stock. Several months later, it is worth $200 and I sell it. I have a return—or net profit—of $100, since $200 − $100 = $100. My investment was $100. So my ROI is $100 ÷ $100 = 1, or 100%. The formula for ROI is:

$$\text{ROI} = \frac{\text{Final Value} - \text{Investment}}{\text{Investment}} = \frac{\text{Return}}{\text{Investment}}$$

In the context of investing, both of the numbers you plug into the formula are monetary amounts (e.g., dollars). However, that's usually not the case for ROI in the context of product development. When you are building a product or feature, the investment is usually the time that your development resources spend working on it, which you generally measure in units such as developer-weeks (one developer working for one week). It's true that you could probably calculate an equivalent dollar amount, but people use units like developer-weeks because they are simpler and clearer.

Similarly, in the context of developing a new product, "return" is often not a dollar amount. Instead, it is usually some relative measure of the amount of customer value you expect a certain feature to create. As long as you use an appropriate number scale to estimate customer value, the ROI calculations will work out fine. You need to use a "ratio scale," which just means that the scores you use are in proportion to their value. For example, say you use a 0 to 10 scale for customer value and estimate scores for all your feature chunks. Using a ratio scale, if one feature chunk has a score of 10 and a second feature chunk has a score of 5, that should mean that the first feature would create double the amount of customer value as the second.

Visualizing ROI

Figure 6.1—which shows the return, or customer value created, on the vertical axis and the investment, or development effort, on the horizontal axis—illustrates the concept of ROI. Let's start off with

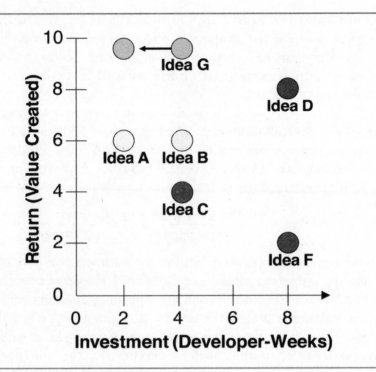

FIGURE 6.1   Return on Investment

feature ideas A and B, both of which are estimated to create 6 units of customer value. However, idea B requires 4 developer-weeks to implement while idea A requires only 2 developer-weeks. The ROI for idea A is 6 ÷ 2 = 3, while the ROI for idea B is 6 ÷ 4 = 1.5. You should prioritize feature A above feature B.

Sometimes two features offer about the same ROI. Look at feature ideas C and D. Idea C offers 4 units of customer value for 4 developer-weeks, for an ROI of 4 ÷ 4 = 1. Idea D offers 8 units of customer value for 8 developer-weeks, for an ROI of 8 ÷ 8 = 1. When you have two feature ideas with the same ROI, it's best to prioritize the smaller scope idea higher because it takes less time to implement. You will deliver the value to customers more quickly—and by having the feature live sooner, you will get valuable customer feedback on it sooner, too.

There are bad ideas out there too—such as idea F, which offers 2 units of customer value for 8 developer weeks, an ROI of 2 ÷ 8 =

0.25. The large effort of a low-ROI idea is often recognized early as the team works on implementing it; however, they usually don't realize the low customer value until after launch. Google Buzz and Google Wave are examples of low-ROI projects that each took a larger number of developer-hours to build but were shut down shortly after launching when customer reaction indicated that they had not created enough value.

Good product teams strive to come up with ideas like idea G in Figure 6.1—the ones that create high customer value for low effort. Great product teams are able to take ideas like that, break them down into chunks, trim off less valuable pieces, and identify creative ways to deliver the customer value with less effort than initially scoped—indicated in the figure by moving idea G to the left.

Some people struggle to create numerical estimates of customer value they feel are accurate. However, that isn't something to worry about too much, since this isn't about achieving decimal point precision. Even the effort estimates aren't likely to be very precise, because you haven't fully designed the features yet. You can't expect developers to give you accurate estimates based on just a high-level description of a feature. The accuracy of the estimates should be proportional to the fidelity of the product definition. The main point of these calculations is less about figuring out actual ROI values and more about how they *compare* to each other. You want to focus on the highest ROI features first and avoid the lower ROI features.

You can sort your list of feature chunks by estimated ROI to create a rank-ordered list—which is a good starting point to help decide which feature chunks should be part of the MVP candidate. However, sometimes you can't just follow the strict rank order to create a "complete" MVP; you might need to skip down to include important features.

The return in the ROI calculation can be a measure of value to your business instead of value to the customer. In those cases, you often have an estimated dollar amount that you can use for the return. This will be an expected gain in revenue or an expected decrease in cost. Let's say, for example, that you have a live product and are trying to improve your conversion rate of free users to paid users. For a given improvement in the conversion rate, you should be able to estimate the expected improvement in revenue. Therefore, you should be able to associate an estimated dollar value with each improvement idea you have. Chapters 13 and 14 discuss how to maximize your ROI as you improve your business and product metrics.

Approximating ROI

I've explained how to think about ROI rigorously, but you can also use this prioritization tool in a less rigorous manner. If you are struggling with creating numerical estimates of customer value or development effort, you can score each feature idea high, medium, or low on customer value and on effort. This will create a three-by-three grid, as shown in Figure 6.2. All of your feature ideas will fall into one of the nine buckets. Even though you won't be calculating ROIs for each feature numerically, you can rank order the nine buckets based on ROI, as shown in the figure. So all the features in square number 1, which has the highest value and the lowest effort, would be higher priority than the features in square number 2, which would be higher priority than the features in square number 3, and so on.

If you find yourself stuck because you're not sure about the estimates for customer value and effort, just use your best guess to place each feature into one of the nine cells. These are just your

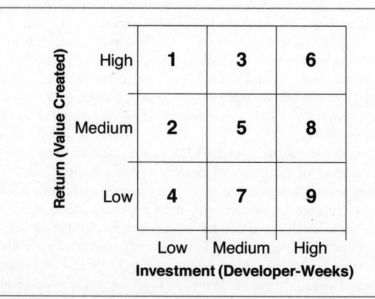

FIGURE 6.2   Approximate ROI

starting hypotheses; you can—and likely will—change them as you learn and iterate.

DECIDING ON YOUR MVP CANDIDATE

Once you are done chunking, scoping, and prioritizing, you can create a simple grid that lists the benefits from your value proposition and that lists, for each benefit, the top feature ideas broken into chunks. See Figure 6.3.

In Figure 6.3 I've listed the top feature chunks for each benefit in priority order, with higher priority on the left. Rather than naming specific benefits or feature chunks, I've intentionally given them generic names so that you can more easily envision replacing them with what would be relevant for your product. "M1A" means feature chunk A for must-have 1. "P2B" means feature chunk B for performance benefit 2, and "D2C" means feature chunk C for delighter benefit 2. In filling out a similar grid for your product, you would instead use the specific labels for your benefits and feature chunks.

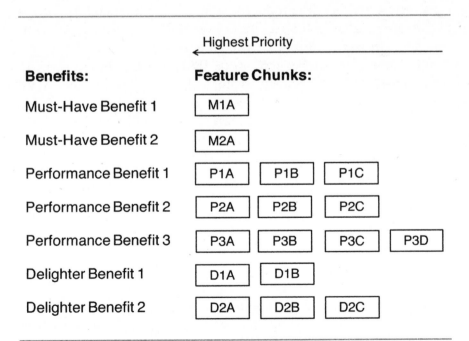

FIGURE 6.3   List of Prioritized Feature Chunks for Each Benefit

Once you have organized your list of feature chunks by benefit and prioritized them, it's time to start making some tough decisions. You must decide on the minimum set of functionality that will resonate with your target customers. You are going to look down the leftmost column of feature chunks and determine which ones you think need to be in your MVP candidate. While doing so, you should refer to your product value proposition. To start with, your MVP candidate needs to have all the must-haves you've identified.

After that, you should focus on the main performance benefit you're planning to use to beat the competition. You should select the set of feature chunks for this benefit that you believe will provide enough for customers to see the difference in your product.

Delighters are part of your differentiation, too. You should include your top delighter in your MVP candidate. That may not be necessary if you have a very large advantage on a performance benefit. The goal is to make sure that your MVP candidate includes *something* that customers find superior to others products and, ideally, unique.

The feature chunks that you believe need to be in your MVP candidate will stay in the leftmost column, which you can label "v1," as you see in Figure 6.4, while the others are pushed out to the right. You can create a preliminary product roadmap by continuing this process and creating columns for each future version with each column containing the feature chunks that you plan to add.

Since you plan to be best at performance benefit 3, you are including the highest priority feature chunk, P3A, in your MVP candidate. You also plan to differentiate with differentiator 2, so you are including feature chunk D2A in your MVP candidate. Your MVP candidate also has the two must-haves.

Looking out to your next version, v1.1, you plan to invest further in performance benefit 3 and delighter 2 with feature chunks P3B and D2B, respectively. In the version after that, v1.2, you plan to start addressing performance benefit 1 with the highest priority feature chunk P1A.

I don't recommend that you plan more than one or two minor versions ahead at the outset—since a lot of things are apt to change when you show your MVP candidate to customers for the first time. You'll learn that some of your hypotheses weren't quite right and will come up with new ones. You may end up changing your mind on which benefit is most important or come up with ideas for new features to

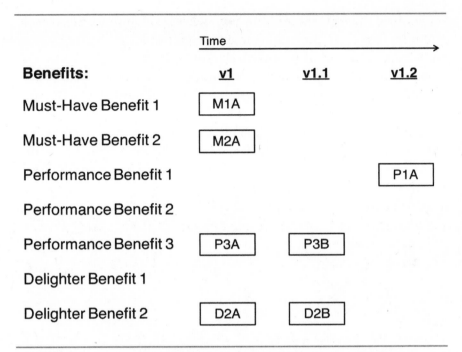

FIGURE 6.4   Deciding Which Feature Chunks Are in Your MVP Candidate

address the same benefits. So if you've made tentative plans beyond your MVP, you must be prepared to throw them out the window and come up with new plans based on what you learn from customers.

The way I've drawn Figure 6.4, there is, at most, only one feature chunk for a given benefit in your MVP candidate. However, it may be the case that you need two or three feature chunks for a given benefit, depending on your situation and how small your chunks are. The idea is still the same: to pick which feature chunks need to be in that leftmost column, which corresponds to your MVP candidate.

Let's take a step back and reflect. At this point in the Lean Product Process, you have done a fair bit of work. You have:

- Formed hypotheses about your target customers
- Formed hypotheses about their underserved needs
- Articulated the value proposition you plan to pursue so that your product is better and different

- Identified the top feature ideas you believe will address those needs and broken them down into smaller chunks
- Prioritized those feature chunks based on ROI
- Selected a set of those feature chunks for your MVP candidate, which you hypothesize customers will find valuable

You have done a lot of rigorous thinking to get this point, but your MVP is still just a candidate, a bundle of interrelated hypotheses. You need to get customer feedback on your MVP candidate to test those hypotheses. But before you can test, you need to create a solution-space representation of your MVP candidate that you can show to customers, which is the next step in the Lean Product Process.

Chapter 7
Create Your MVP Prototype (Step 5)

Once you have specified the feature set for your MVP candidate, you'll want to test it with customers. In order to do that, you need to create a user experience (UX) that you can show to customers, which is the top layer of the Product-Market Fit Pyramid.

The goal is to build a prototype that lets you test your hypotheses. As discussed in Chapter 1, I intentionally use the broad term MVP "prototype" to capture the wide range of items you can test with customers to gain learning. While the first "prototype" you test *could* be your live MVP, you can gain faster learning with fewer resources by testing your hypotheses *before* you build your MVP. Also, as discussed in Chapter 1, even though I'm using the term MVP, the Lean Product Process applies even when you are not building an entire product (e.g., adding a new feature or improving an existing feature). The type of prototype you should create depends on the type of test you want to conduct with customers.

WHAT IS (AND ISN'T) AN MVP?

There has been spirited debate over what qualifies as an MVP. Some people argue vehemently that a landing page is a valid MVP. Others say it isn't, insisting that an MVP must be a real, working product or at least an interactive prototype. The way I resolve this dichotomy is to realize that these are all methods to *test* the hypotheses behind your MVP. By using the term "MVP tests" instead of MVP, the debate goes away. This allows more precise terminology by reserving the use of MVP for actual products.

Many people misinterpret the term MVP by placing too much emphasis on the word *minimum*. They use this as an excuse to build a partial MVP that has too little functionality to be considered viable by a customer. Others use "minimum" to rationalize a shoddy user experience or a buggy product. While it's true that an MVP is

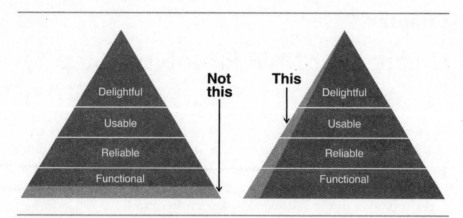

FIGURE 7.1   Building an MVP

deliberately limited in scope relative to your entire value proposition, what you release to customers has to be above a certain bar in order to create value for them.

The diagram in Figure 7.1 illustrates the difference between this incorrect way of interpreting MVP and the correct interpretation. I've adapted this figure from one created by talented UX designer Jussi Pasanen of Volkside, http://volkside.com, who gives his acknowledgements to Aarron Walter, Ben Tollady, and Ben Rowe.

Similar to my hierarchy of web user needs (Figure 4.2), this figure separates the distinct aspects of a product. In this case, a pyramid of four hierarchical layers is used to describe a product's attributes: functional, reliable, usable, and delightful. The pyramid on the left illustrates the misconception that an MVP is just a product with limited functionality, and that reliability, usability, and delight can be ignored. Instead, the pyramid on the right shows that while an MVP has limited functionality, it should be "complete" by addressing those three higher-level attributes.

MVP TESTS

Getting back to MVP tests, there are many different kinds you can use, and you may have heard some of their names: "Wizard of Oz," "smoke test," and "fake door." This chapter will explain the different types of MVP tests and help you decide which one will be most beneficial for your situation. By the way, rather than using the word "test" over and over, I will also use the word "validate." Some people like "validate" because it implies that there is an underlying hypothesis being tested. Other people cringe when they hear the word "validate" because to them it presumes that your test will be successful. I use "validate" synonymously with "test your hypothesis," with no presumption about the results.

While the term MVP test provides a convenient umbrella for all the various tests, there *are* key differences among them. There are two main ways to categorize them.

Product versus Marketing MVP Tests

The first way you can categorize MVP tests is by whether they are aimed at testing your product or your marketing. A landing page test that measures what percentage of prospective customers click the "sign up" button and leave their email addresses is focused on marketing, because there isn't any product functionality the customer can actually use. You're simply describing the functionality to prospective customers to see how compelling they find your description.

In contrast, MVP tests used to validate your product will involve showing prospective customers functionality to solicit their feedback on it. You may be showing them a live beta product or just low fidelity wireframes to assess product-market fit. With either a product or a marketing MVP test, you care about how compelling customers find what you're showing them; but the learning goal of each differs.

Marketing tests can provide valuable learning, but they're not an actual product that creates customer value. At some point, you need to test a prototype of your MVP candidate. If through testing and iteration you reach a point where you feel that you have validated product-market fit with enough confidence, you would then proceed with building an *actual* MVP.

Quantitative versus Qualitative MVP Tests

The second dimension on which MVP tests differ is whether they are qualitative or quantitative. Qualitative means that you are talking with customers directly, usually in small numbers that don't yield statistical significance. Here, you care about the detailed information you learn from each individual test. You may try to discern patterns across the results, but statistical significance isn't a primary concern. If, for example, you conducted one-on-one feedback sessions with 12 prospective customers to solicit their feedback on a mockup of your landing page, then that would be qualitative research.

Quantitative research involves conducting the test at scale with a large number of customers. You don't care as much about any individual result and are instead interested in the aggregate results. If you launched two versions of your landing page and directed thousands of customers to each one to see which one had the higher conversion rate, then that would be a quantitative test.

Quantitative tests are good for learning "what" and "how many": what actions customers took and how many customers took an action (e.g., clicked on the "sign up" button). But quantitative tests will not tell you *why* they chose to do so or why the other customers chose not to do so. In contrast, qualitative tests are good for learning "why": the reasons behind different customers' decisions to take an action or not.

Both kinds of tests are valuable and complement one another. I've seen many teams rely on one type of testing too heavily, usually quantitative. You must be mindful of what is most important to learn for your situation and choose the type of test accordingly. In general, when you are first starting to develop your product or marketing materials, it is most beneficial to start with qualitative tests to gain some initial understanding. If you jump straight into quantitative tests without doing any qualitative tests, they usually don't perform as well—and even if they do, you won't know why. It is common to see product teams alternate between rounds of qualitative testing and quantitative testing as they learn and iterate. Chapter 9 provides additional advice on how to qualitatively test your MVP with customers.

THE MATRIX OF MVP TESTS

I created the two-by-two matrix in Figure 7.2 to list and categorize the different MVP tests based on product versus marketing and qualitative versus quantitative. In each of the four quadrants, I've listed the MVP tests that pertain to that combination of attributes. I'll walk

	Qualitative Tests	Quantitative Tests
Marketing Tests	Marketing materials	Landing page/Smoke test Explainer video Ad campaign Marketing A/B tests Crowdfunding
Product Tests	Wireframes Mockups Interactive prototype Wizard of Oz & Concierge Live product	Fake door/404 page Product analytics & A/B tests

FIGURE 7.2   MVP Tests Categorized by Type

through each of the four quadrants in the figure and describe the MVP tests in each one.

QUALITATIVE MARKETING MVP TESTS

Let's start off with qualitative marketing tests in the upper left quadrant. Clearly, there are many different ways to market your product. Rather than create a long list of tests for each type, I've lumped them all under "marketing materials." These types of tests involve showing customers your marketing materials and soliciting their feedback. Marketing materials include anything you would want to put in front of a customer: a landing page, a video, an advertisement, an email, and so forth. This test is an attempt to understand how compelling they find this marketing material and why. You are not getting feedback on the product itself, but rather how you talk about and explain the product.

These tests can help you understand which benefits resonate with customers and their reactions to different ways of talking about the benefits and describing your product. Conversations like these help you see how compelling they find your product value proposition. You can even show customers your competitor's marketing materials to learn what they've explained well and what they haven't and to test your differentiation.

One good way to test your overall messaging is the five-second test. The idea is to show customers your home page or landing page for just five seconds and then ask them to tell you what they remember and what they liked. Because customers make snap judgements about products all the time, this can be a good way to see how well your messaging conveys what your product does and why someone would want to use it.

QUANTITATIVE MARKETING MVP TESTS

You can use quantitative marketing tests to validate demand for your product. You can also use them to optimize the acquisition of prospects and the conversion of prospects to customers. Because these tests capture user behavior, they can provide significant learning with large sample sizes.

Landing Page/Smoke Test

One of the most popular tests is the landing page or smoke test. In this test, you create a live web page to which you direct traffic. The landing page describes the product you plan to build and asks customers to express some level of interest, which is usually a "sign up" button or a link to a "plans and pricing" page. It's also called a smoke test because there is no real product for customers to use yet. Instead, there is usually a "coming soon" page that thanks the customer for their interest and asks for their email address or other contact information.

The key metric that these tests measure is the conversion rate: the percentage of visitors to your landing page that clicked on the button to convert from a prospect to a customer. For example, if you directed 1,000 prospective customers to a landing page with a "sign up" button, and 250 of them clicked it, then your conversion rate would be 25 percent. The conversion rate will be influenced by which benefits you choose and how well you describe the benefits and your product. Even if you've selected benefits that customers find compelling, good visual design and copywriting are important for landing pages to be successful.

Your development team can create and evaluate landing pages using your existing web technology stack and analytics package. However, handy tools like Optimizely and Unbounce make landing page testing and optimization faster and easier with less development effort.

Landing Page MVP Example: Buffer

Buffer provides a good example of a landing page MVP test. Buffer is a product that helps you post to Twitter more consistently by letting you specify tweets you want to send and schedule them to be posted at preset times. Buffer's CEO and cofounder Joel Gascoigne authored a blog post about how he decided to start out with a landing page MVP test (https://blog.bufferapp.com/idea-to-paying-customers-in-7-weeks-how-we-did-it). Gascoigne writes how he approached Buffer differently from his previous startup: "I started coding Buffer before I'd tested the viability of the business. As soon as I realized that, I stopped, took a deep breath and told myself: do it the right way this time. It was time to test whether people wanted this product."

Buffer's first home page described what the product's value proposition was with a headline and three bullet points. It included a "plans and pricing" button, which was the only thing that visitors could click. Upon doing so, they were taken to a page that said "You caught us before we're ready." Then they could enter their email address to be notified when the product launched.

As Gascoigne explains, "The aim of this two-page MVP was to check whether people would even consider using the app. I simply tweeted the link and asked people what they thought of the idea. After a few people used it to give me their email and I got some useful feedback via email and Twitter, I considered it validated."

Gascoigne felt that he had confirmed that people wanted the product. The next step was to test if people would be willing to pay for it. So he inserted an additional page (before the email form) that described three different product levels: free, $5 per month, and $20 per month. This allowed him to see how many clicks each plan received in addition to how many people submitted their email address. The results were positive. Despite the extra click required, people were still getting to the email form and leaving their email addresses, and some people were clicking on the paid plans.

It's worth noting that, at this point, no one had actually paid any money to use Buffer (because they couldn't yet). But Gascoigne felt that he had enough validation of product-market fit from these two simple tests to confidently move forward with his product idea.

Explainer Video

The explainer video is really just a variant of the landing page test that relies on a video to explain the product. You judge a video's effectiveness by the conversion rate that it drives, for example, on a sign-up page. This type of test is particularly useful for products that are difficult to explain with just words. Cloud storage service Dropbox conducted one of the most well-known explainer video MVP tests. Founder Drew Houston found that people just didn't understand why Dropbox was better when he tried to explain how his company's unique approach to file synchronization made it different from all the other cloud-based file storage products in the market at the time. So he created a video that showed and explained how Dropbox works. The video resonated with customers as solving a real pain point they had managing and sharing their files across multiple devices, driving a large number of sign-ups for Dropbox's private beta waiting list.

Ad Campaign

In order to test a landing page, you need to drive traffic to it somehow—and one way to do so is with advertising campaigns. For example, Google AdWords displays short text ads when customers conduct searches. You can experiment with different search terms and ad copy to try to increase your clickthrough rate, giving you quantitative feedback on what words and phrases customers find most compelling. You can also use display ad campaigns to test different messaging and imagery. Since Facebook ads let you target on demographics, they can offer a good way to test your hypotheses about your target market. Because the ads are usually small, they often don't give you enough room to convey your entire value proposition and are instead limited to a tagline. As a result, this type of test is most useful for optimizing your customer acquisition efforts and not validating product-market fit.

For example, if you were thinking of building a site for people to find jobs, you might run three ad campaigns, each with a different tagline: "We match you with your perfect dream job," "We have the most job listings anywhere," and "We offer the fastest way to scan job listings." You would then compare the clickthrough rates of the three ad campaigns to see which performed best.

Marketing A/B Testing

A/B testing, also called split testing, is a quantitative technique where you test two alternative designs simultaneously to compare how they perform on a key metric, such as conversion rate. You can use A/B testing to try different versions of your marketing materials to see which performs better. For example, you could test two different versions of your landing page—with different messaging, pricing, images, colors, or other design elements—to see which converts better. You can also A/B test most other online marketing materials such as advertising, videos, and emails.

Your tests can have more than two alternatives, for example, an A/B/C test. In a true A/B test, the different versions your are testing run in parallel at the same time, for example, 50 percent of traffic to version A and 50 percent of traffic to version B. It's less desirable to test versions sequentially (100 percent of traffic to version A for a while, followed by 100 percent of traffic to version B for a while). By running alternatives concurrently, you avoid the risk of differences in extraneous factors between the two time periods—such as seasonality or level of promotion—skewing your results.

Often after doing several A/B tests to optimize some aspect of your product, you will have identified the best performing option, which is called the champion. From time to time, you may test new alternatives to see if they can beat the champion. An important aspect of this is statistical significance, which is determined by the difference in performance and the sample size. There are formulas and online tools to help you calculate the statistical confidence level for your specific test.

However, it's important to know that statistical significance is higher for larger differences in performance and for larger sample sizes. If your sample size is too low, you won't achieve statistically significant results. If you have two alternatives with very similar performance, it may take a very large sample size to discern any statistically significant difference.

Popular A/B testing tools include Optimizely, Unbounce, KISS-metrics, Visual Website Optimizer, and Google Content Experiments (part of Google Analytics). These A/B testing tools let you specify several variations and then randomly distribute traffic among the variations. They track the results for the conversion action you care about and show you how each variation is performing, along with the corresponding statistical confidence level.

Multivariate testing is similar to A/B testing, but instead of testing different versions of a page, you test variations of *page elements*. Each page element that you are changing is a variable. Let's say you were working on a landing page and had three different ideas for possible headlines and three different ideas for the main image on the page. A multivariate test would try out all nine possible combinations of headline and image to determine which performs best.

Crowdfunding

Crowdfunding platforms like Kickstarter and Indiegogo can be a great way to test whether or not people are willing to pay for your product and to quantify demand. These platforms let people who want to make and sell a product promote it and accept money from customers who want to buy the product when it comes out. You can set a fundraising threshold for your product and only commit to build it if you reach that limit. This approach where customers pay you *before* you start building your product is consistent with Lean principles, in that it can help you eliminate the uncertainty of whether or not anyone will pay for your product.

The Pebble Watch is a Kickstarter success story. After founder Eric Migicovsky took the startup through the Y Combinator incubator, he was unable to raise enough funding from venture capital firms. He launched a Kickstarter campaign with an initial funding goal of $100,000. Customers could pay $115 for a Pebble Watch when they launched, basically preordering at a discount from the full price of $150. The project met its initial goal in two hours and continued to grow. Pebble ended their Kickstarter fundraising a little over a month later, after over 68,000 people had pledged over $10 million.

Kickstarter has become an exciting new funding channel for startups. Virtual reality headset startup Oculus Rift started off with an initial $250,000 fundraising goal in August 2012. In one month, they raised just under $2.5 million, almost 10 times their target amount. Facebook acquired Oculus Rift less than two years later for $2 billion.

Entrepreneurs who are full-time employees but have a startup idea they want to pursue can use crowdfunding as a way to mitigate risk before taking the plunge. Crowdfunding is an especially good fit for selling consumer products, since it provides a direct-to-consumer e-commerce sales channel. However, because there is no product for people to try out, you have to provide a rich description of both the offering and its benefits. Many campaigns have high-quality videos and extensive FAQs. You should also market to prospective customers in other ways, such as social media, in order to make them aware of your product's campaign.

Crowdfunding sites can be a great way to connect with early adopters for your product. You can readily engage them in discussions about their needs and preferences, and they can be a source of good ideas for improving your product. Successful crowdfunding pages become an active communications hub between the startup and its customers.

QUALITATIVE PRODUCT MVP TESTS

I've covered the marketing MVP tests that can help ensure your messaging is on point with customers and help quantify the expected values of marketing metrics such as conversion rate. Product tests help ensure that customers see value in your actual product. When developing a new product, a redesigned product, or a new feature, qualitative product tests are the most valuable way to assess and improve your product-market fit. There are two fundamentally distinct times when you can conduct qualitative product tests: *before* you've built your product and *after* you've built it. Both are valuable.

You can test your product's design with customers before you build your product. Typical product design deliverables include wireframes, mockups, and interactive prototypes—all of which are representations of what your product will be like without being the actual product itself. You'll want to validate your design before you start coding your product to reduce waste. It's usually much faster and less costly to make changes to your designs than your code. I'll discuss this further, but design artifacts can vary in *fidelity*—that is, how closely they represent the real product.

After you build your product, you can test it with users—which has the advantage that the fidelity of what you're testing is 100 percent. As a result, you may learn things that you weren't able to observe in testing your design artifacts. For example, you may get feedback on a mockup of your web page about how well the information is laid out, how clear the copy is, and how compelling the visual design is. However, you wouldn't catch things like the fact that the web page is very slow to load or that it doesn't work properly in a certain browser. There are no inherent negatives to live product testing; however, if you *wait* until your product is live to test it with customers, you are unnecessarily taking a big risk. You want to reduce this risk by showing customers design deliverables earlier in the process to ensure that customers will value the product that your developers are going to spend their valuable time building.

You can show customers a variety of design artifacts to solicit feedback. Figure 7.3 classifies these artifacts by their level of fidelity on

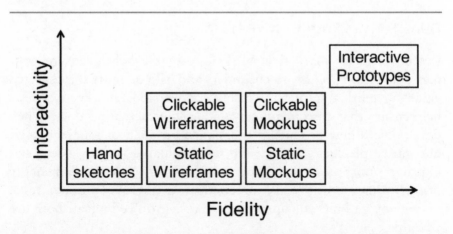

FIGURE 7.3　Design Artifacts by Fidelity and Interactivity

the horizontal axis and their level of interactivity on the vertical axis. Again *fidelity* refers to how closely the artifact looks like the final product, whereas interactivity means the degree to which the customer can interact with the artifact relative to a live, working product.

See Figure 7.4 for an illustration of low versus high fidelity. Both of the design deliverables shown in the figure are for the same product, the iOS app Pointedly (https://itunes.apple.com/us/app/pointedly-simple-score-keeper/id933257819). Built by talented UX designer Ben Norris, the app makes it easy to keep score when you're playing games (like Scrabble), instead of needing pen and paper. On the left side of the figure is a low-fidelity wireframe. It doesn't use any colors

**FIGURE 7.4   Low Fidelity Wireframe versus High
                Fidelity Mockup**

(it's grayscale) and only shows the screen elements and their locations without any visual design details. The high-fidelity mockup on the right is meant to look much more like the actual product (although the color image appears in grayscale in the printed version of this book). The app's user interface elements have been given a visual design using specific colors, fonts, and graphics.

Hand Sketches

In the bottom left of Figure 7.3 is the hand sketch, which has the lowest fidelity and the lowest interactivity. Hand sketches are a great way to start visualizing your ideas, especially to share and discuss them with your teammates and other internal stakeholders. Sketching on a whiteboard or paper allows you to iterate your design quickly. I'm a big fan of whiteboarding, especially in the early stage of design. In fact, the whiteboard could very well be the ultimate Lean tool because it enables teams to iterate their ideas so rapidly. As useful as hand sketches are for internal use, they are too low fidelity to show to customers for feedback (which is why they do not appear in the MVP test matrix).

Wireframes

The design artifact with the next level up in fidelity is the wireframe, which is a low to medium fidelity representation of a product that gives a sense of the product's components and how they are arranged. Wireframes are not "pixel perfect"; rather, they show relative size and position. They are usually devoid of any visual design details such as colors, images, and fonts. Instead, they are often grayscale and use placeholders for images to avoid distracting reviewers with visual design elements. Some wireframes may also use a placeholder for text—such as "lorem ipsum"—in place of the final copy, although that is becoming less commonplace. I recommend using real copy from the start, even if it is just a preliminary draft, to identify potential layout issues early.

Wireframes can be drawn by hand, but are usually digital artifacts created using a software application—either a general-purpose design application or a special-purpose wireframing application. Illustrator and Sketch are graphic design applications used mainly by designers. OmniGraffle and Visio are more general-purpose tools. Some non-designers create wireframes in PowerPoint or Keynote. I recommend using more capable tools specifically designed for wireframing, such as Balsamiq, Axure, and UXPin for web products.

Because mobile products—whether native applications or mobile websites—tend to have different user experience elements than traditional web applications, tools that specialize in mobile wireframing have emerged. I recommend the mobile wireframing tools Flinto and Marvel for designers. POP and Dapp are easy to use mobile wireframing tools for nondesigners.

There are new, more powerful wireframing tools coming out all the time. If it's been a while since you've tried out the latest ones, I'd encourage you to do so. I've seen too many designers and product managers miss out on the next big thing because they keep clinging to an older tool with which they're comfortable and proficient. Productivity is obviously important, and switching tools does require a time investment. But adopting a new tool can be worthwhile because of the new capabilities it adds and the higher level of productivity it enables once you master it.

Some signs that you should probably evaluate a new wireframing tool include:

- You are drawing basic page elements from scratch using shapes and lines instead of leveraging a library of predefined widgets
- The wireframes you're creating aren't clickable or tappable
- It's hard to share your wireframes with other people
- You're creating wireframes for mobile screens with a tool that is not optimized for mobile
- It takes you longer than you'd like to create wireframes
- You're not creating wireframes at all

Today's tools make it so easy and affordable to wireframe that there's really no excuse for anyone involved with developing a product not to. If you have one or more interaction designers on your team, they may be the ones doing most of the wireframing. But it is still a valuable skill to be able to quickly bang out a visualization of an idea you have to share with others. And if you don't have a dedicated wireframer on your team, you may have to step up.

A common feature of modern wireframing tools is a widget library containing most common user interface elements that you would want to use. For example, if you wanted to wireframe an iOS app, you shouldn't draw the standard iOS controls by hand or use generic controls. Your tool should have a set of the common iOS user interface elements available in its library.

Since the wireframe shows a representation of the user interface, product teams often find it useful to add explanatory notes. Such annotations could convey important details, such as the list of options that should be displayed in a dropdown menu, the maximum number of characters a user should be allowed to type into a particular form field, or the wording for a particular error message. Such annotated wireframes can be powerful design tools, containing much of the product specification required for development. Obviously, the version of the wireframes shown to the user should not display these annotations.

Until several years ago, wireframes were usually static—that is, not clickable or tappable. But modern wireframing tools have made it very easy to create clickable wireframes that let you connect a set of wireframes for different pages into a logical navigation flow that the user can experience. You usually only make selected user interface controls clickable—the ones that are pertinent to the design and what you want to learn from the specific test. Such a user scenario is called the "happy path"—the one that you intend the user to follow through the user experience you have designed.

Clickable and tappable wireframes have essentially replaced static wireframes as the norm. A static wireframe test requires the user to tell you, "I'd click this button," after which you would show the next static wireframe. Clickable wireframes create a more immersive experience for the user—one where they can independently explore and navigate your product. Plus, because clickable wireframes are usually tested on the device on which the product will be used (e.g., computer, tablet, or phone), the experience feels more realistic.

Mockups

As shown in Figure 7.3, the design artifact with the next level up in fidelity is the mockup, which looks much more like the final product than wireframes. Mockups convey visual design details such as colors, fonts, and images. Some are intended to be "pixel perfect" while others may only represent the approximate size and position of design elements. Mockups are also sometimes referred to as "comps," and are usually created with a graphic design application such as Illustrator, Photoshop, or Sketch.

As with wireframes, mockups can be static or clickable. The output of a graphical design application is usually a static image file like a JPG, GIF, or PNG, which is not inherently clickable. To create a set of clickable mockups, those images are combined using another application that lets you specify "hot spots," which are click or tap targets that navigate from one mockup to another.

The prototyping web application InVision does this well. This tool lets you upload your images and link them together via clickable hot spots. Balsamiq also lets you do this. As with clickable wireframes, clickable mockups create a multiple page or screen user flow that the customer can experience. But instead of seeing low to medium fidelity wireframes, the customer sees high fidelity mockups. Again, the happy path through the user experience is usually enabled while other navigation flows are not. Because clickable mockups can look and feel so close to the real application, they can yield very valuable feedback from users. Some teams that are adept at creating clickable mockups start their user testing of design artifacts there. Those teams often create wireframes before the mockups, but don't solicit user feedback on the wireframes.

Interactive Prototype

The next step up in fidelity and interactivity from clickable mockups is an interactive prototype. The word prototype by itself can be used to describe any clickable design artifact; it simply denotes that it is either not a fully functional product or only a facsimile of a product. Interactive prototypes provide a level of interaction that goes beyond that of just clickable mockups. For example, an interactive prototype might include many types of functioning user interface controls, such as drop-down menus, hover effects, input forms, and audio or video players.

Interactive prototypes can be created with a variety of developer tools. Web prototypes are usually built with HTML, CSS, and

JavaScript. Popular front-end frameworks such as jQuery and Bootstrap are often used for more rapid development. Prototypes can also be built using Ruby on Rails or other rapid development frameworks if you want to have some lightweight server-side functionality, too. Powerful tools such as Axure—which lets you export your prototype to HTML, CSS, and JavaScript—enable you to create interactive prototypes without any coding. Mobile prototypes can be built in HTML or in native code, for example, iOS or Android.

Wizard of Oz and Concierge MVPs

None of the qualitative product tests discussed so far have been a live, working product or service. The Wizard of Oz MVP and concierge MVP allow you to actually test your live product or service; but instead of the final version, you are using manual workarounds. I call MVPs like this "manual hack" MVPs, since they are inefficient and not meant for the long run. The idea behind a concierge MVP is to be very involved with a small number of early customers to really understand your target market, their needs and preferences, and how to tailor your product to best meet these. Doing so helps you validate what your product or service should do before you actually build it. Concierge MVPs work best with services, especially those with processes that require a fair amount of interaction with and input from the customer.

Concierge MVP Example: Airbnb

For example, the lodging rental site Airbnb used a concierge MVP to grow their service. In a talk at South By Southwest (SXSW), Director of Product Joe Zadeh described how the Airbnb team hypothesized that property listings with professional photos would get more business. So they manually recruited hosts to offer them professional photography, and recruited photographers to match up with the hosts. After scheduling the photo shoot and taking the pictures, the photographers would upload their pictures to Dropbox, and Airbnb employees would upload them to the associated property listing. Airbnb would then pay the photographers. The Airbnb team saw that their hypothesis was true: listings with professional photographs had two to three times more bookings than the market average.

After proving their hypothesis, Airbnb replaced most of their manual process steps with automated steps. So, instead of being done by a human, the Airbnb system invites hosts to take advantage of professional photography, assigns photographers to hosts, and updates each listing with the photos. Airbnb mitigated risk and potential waste by validating their hypothesis before investing the resources required to build an automated solution.

The Wizard of Oz MVP is similar to the concierge MVP in that you perform certain steps manually in the short term. However, the difference is that it's not obvious to the customer that you are performing these steps manually; like in the movie *The Wizard of Oz*, they are hidden behind a curtain. The Wizard of Oz MVP appears to users as the real live product. The goal is to validate the manual steps that are required before making the investment to build out an automated solution.

Live Product

You can also test live product with customers. Ideally, before building your MVP, you will have validated its design by testing increasingly higher fidelity artifacts with customers. When you iterate to a point where you feel that you have validated product-market fit with enough confidence, you would proceed with building a real MVP. Chapter 12 discusses how to build your product using Agile development.

Even if you've tested design artifacts along the way, it's a good idea to test your actual MVP once it's built. Changes often occur between the design and development phases. Because live product is the highest fidelity possible, you may learn new things from customers that you didn't uncover during lower fidelity tests; for example, how a web product looks and behaves on different screen sizes and browsers.

You can test your live product in a moderated or unmoderated fashion. In moderated testing, you are present with the customer as they use your product, whereas the customer is alone with unmoderated testing (and the test is recorded so you can watch it later).

Moderated tests can be conducted either in-person or remotely using screen sharing software such as Skype, WebEx, or join.me. I discuss this further in Chapter 9.

QUANTITATIVE PRODUCT MVP TESTS

Once you have a live product with a meaningful amount of usage, you can conduct quantitative product tests. Unlike qualitative product tests where you are asking smaller numbers of customers for their opinions, quantitative product tests measure the customers who are actually using your product (usually with large sample sizes).

Fake Door/404 Page

The fake door or 404 page test is a good way to validate demand for a new feature that you are considering building. The idea is to include a link or button for the new feature and see what percentage of customers click on it. This lets you gauge whether customers actually want the feature before you spend the resources to build it. Since you haven't built the feature yet, the customers usually see a page thanking them for their interest and explaining that the feature is not built yet when they click on the link or button. You can also add a form asking the customer to share why they would find this feature valuable.

The extreme case of this type of test is to not even bother building the destination page, since you can technically track the clicks without it. In that case, clicking on the link or button goes to the website's generic 404 page (404 is the HTTP error code for "page not found").

The gaming company Zynga, which has a strong reputation of quantitative product testing, uses fake buttons often. In a talk he gave at the Stanford Technology Ventures Program, Zynga cofounder Mark Pincus described how his team would test new game ideas by coming up with a five-word pitch for each one. They would then publish the pitch as a promotional link in their live games for a short period of time to see how much interest it generated from customers.

Of course, you want to be mindful of how long and how often you run fake door tests to avoid making your customers unhappy. Rather than leaving fake door tests live for an extended period of time, it's best to run them only for the amount of time required to achieve the sample size you need and then take them down.

Product Analytics and A/B Tests

Product analytics aren't a test per se, but they can give you insights into how your customers are actually using your product. For example, you can see which features they use the most and where they spend most of their time. When you roll out product changes, you can look for changes in key product metrics to test your hypotheses. Product analytics also form the foundation for A/B testing, because they are used to calculate the results of the tests. Leading product analytics solutions include Google Analytics, KISSmetrics, Mixpanel, and Flurry.

Product A/B tests or split tests are used to compare the performance of two alternative user experiences (A and B) in your product. For example, say you developed a new registration flow for your web application that you think will have a higher completion rate than your current registration flow. Rather than just replacing the old flow with the new flow, you could A/B test the flows: randomly direct 50 percent of traffic each to the old flow (A) and the new flow (B) and compare the completion rates. There are several popular product A/B testing tools available such as Optimizely, KISSmetrics, Visual Website Optimizer, and Google Content Experiments (part of Google Analytics).

Most companies use third-party tools for marketing A/B testing. However, when it comes to product A/B testing, many eventually choose to build their own testing infrastructure to achieve more flexibility through tighter integration with their code. One of the main reasons for this is because most A/B testing tools use a JavaScript solution, which works fine for testing front-end (client-side) product variations. However, these tools don't offer as much help when complex back-end (server-side) variations need to be tested. That being said, leading A/B testing tools such as KISSmetrics offer ways to integrate with your internal server-side A/B platform.

You don't have to split the traffic evenly between your A and your B variations. As long as the variation with fewer users has enough data points to calculate statistical significance, it will work out fine. Many companies are constantly experimenting, subjecting small subsets of their users to dozens or hundreds of alternative features or designs. You may notice a new button, feature, or design every once in a while on Google, Amazon, or other large websites. If you compare what you're seeing to another user and it's different, one of you is most likely an A/B test subject.

Analytics and A/B testing are powerful empirical tools that help you understand your customers' behavior and optimize your product. Competency with these tools enables rapid iteration and separates great product teams from others. Given the importance of analytics and A/B testing, Chapters 13 and 14 discuss these topics in more detail.

This chapter has covered a variety of MVP tests and clarified the difference between qualitative versus quantitative, and product versus marketing tests. Once you've selected the MVP test that you want to conduct, you must design the page, screen, or other user experience artifact to test. Good user experience design is important and helps all the MVP tests discussed in this chapter be more successful. So before jumping into how to test your MVP, I want to discuss the principles of great UX design, so that you can apply them as you design the artifacts for your MVP tests.

Chapter 8

Apply the Principles of Great UX Design

At this point in the Lean Product Process, you are clear on the feature set you believe should be in your MVP. User experience (UX)—the top layer in the Product-Market Fit Pyramid—brings your product's features and benefits to life for the customer. Even if you have made good decisions on the other four layers, you will not achieve product-market fit without a good UX.

Unlike the other chapters in Part II of the book, this chapter does not represent a separate step in the Lean Product Process. Instead, the advice in this chapter applies to Step 5, "create your MVP prototype," covered in Chapter 7. This entire chapter is devoted to UX design because it is so critical to achieving product-market fit. You should use the guidance in this chapter when you are designing your MVP prototype.

This chapter won't transform you into a world-class designer, but it will give you an overview of UX design and an understanding of key concepts. This information is especially beneficial for product managers, developers, and others who work closely with designers. This knowledge should equip you to have richer discussions with designers, to contribute more to the design process, and to ultimately create better products.

WHAT MAKES A GREAT UX?

We have all experienced products with either a fantastic or a poor user experience. The latter feel unintuitive and hard to use. You can't find what you're looking for, and you're not clear what to do next. You may navigate to a dead end or receive a cryptic error message. It may be hard to read the text, or the design may not be aesthetically pleasing. All of those problems are symptoms of bad UX design.

In contrast, a product with a great UX feels easy to use. It's effortless to find what you're looking for and to figure out what to do next. You don't even notice the user interface and are able to focus on accomplishing the task at hand. The product may even be fun to use and convey emotional benefits such as confidence in your abilities or peace of mind. A great design may lead you to what psychologists call a state of "flow," where you are completely immersed in using the product. In this state, everything else falls away, and you experience full involvement and enjoyment of the task at hand. An incredible UX can be a strong product differentiator.

So what leads to an exceptional UX? No matter how easy to use or beautiful a product is, it can't deliver a great user experience if the customer doesn't value the benefits the product provides. In the Product-Market Fit Pyramid, the customer benefits that a product aims to deliver live in the value proposition layer, which is two levels below the UX layer. These benefits are addressed in the solution space by the feature set the product team has chosen. So, one way to evaluate UX is to consider how much it helps or hinders the functionality in conveying the desired customer benefits. Poor UX gets in the way, preventing the user from realizing the benefits. Great UX makes it easy for the user to realize the benefits that the product's functionality offers. In addition to addressing benefits that customers find valuable, a great UX also achieves a high degree of *usability* and *delight*.

Usability

The first key attribute of a great UX is usability, which indicates how easy it is for customers to use the product. Usability focuses on the users' goals and the tasks they need to perform to achieve those goals. What percentage of users are able to successfully complete each task? What percentage are able to do so, but encounter problems along the way? You obtain answers to these questions through *usability testing*, where you ask users to complete key tasks and observe what they do.

Beyond the successful completion of tasks, usability also includes efficiency. If customers are able to figure out how to use a feature, but it requires too many steps or takes too long, that results in poor usability. Efficiency is easy to assess by measuring effort. You can simply count the number of clicks, taps, keystrokes, or other user actions required to complete a task in a certain UX. Likewise, you can measure how much time it takes users to complete each task. You should compare these efficiency metrics as you evaluate different designs or try to improve a given design.

In addition to actual physical effort such as clicks and keystrokes, perceived effort is also important. You should be mindful of the cognitive load that your UX places on the user. You can mentally overwhelm users by showing them too much information or giving them too many choices. You can also tax their knowledge or memory. A great UX avoids requiring users to exert much physical or mental effort.

The likelihood of a user successfully completing a task is directly related to the amount of effort it takes. After observing usability tests and analyzing usage metrics for many products, I came to a general realization I call "Olsen's Law of Usability":

> The more user effort required to take an action, the lower
> the percentage of users who will take that action.
> The less user effort required, the higher the percentage of
> users who will take that action.

I have seen this law ring true time and again when evaluating user experiences. It is valuable to keep this principle in mind not only for achieving better usability, but also to improve the conversion rate for user actions that are important to the success of your business. Examples of such actions include submitting a registration form or completing a payment flow.

In addition to the objective behavioral measures I mentioned, your users' perception of your product's ease of use is important. For example, you can ask users, "How easy or difficult is the product to use?" and allow ratings on a seven-point bipolar scale:

1. Very difficult to use
2. Difficult to use
3. Somewhat difficult to use
4. Neither easy nor difficult to use

5. Somewhat easy to use
6. Easy to use
7. Very easy to use

At the end of a usability test, you can also ask customers other questions such as, "How well did the product meet your needs?" or, "How satisfied are you with the product?" They will not base their responses on what your intended value proposition or feature set is—which they likely don't even know about. Instead, their answers will depend on their actual experience using your product. You won't get any credit for having a valuable feature if users can't find it or can't figure out how to use it.

You determine a product's usability with respect to a particular user profile. Your target customers will have a certain level of knowledge or skill. Different target customers can vary in how tech savvy they are and how much relevant domain knowledge they have. Usability expectations would be quite different for a product intended for highly trained power users as opposed to one for a mainstream consumer market. Your personas, discussed in Chapter 3 and later in this chapter, should help inform this.

Ease of learning is also an important usability attribute. How much time and effort does it take a user to progress from having no knowledge of how your product works, to working knowledge, to mastery? This is especially important for new users. They will decide very quickly whether your product is right for them or not, and ease of learning is critical in that assessment. Many products that deliver a great user experience address the need for "user onboarding" with helpful tutorials and guides for first-time users. These guides often disappear later or can be dismissed by the user when no longer needed.

Delight

The second key attribute of a great UX is delight. Strong usability helps avoid a poor UX, but it is not enough to deliver a great UX. Usability answers the question, "Can customers use your product?" *Delight* answers the question, "Do customers *enjoy* using your product?" Delight, which goes beyond simply avoiding user frustration, means evoking positive emotions. Products that delight users are enjoyable and fun to use.

One aspect of delight is *aesthetics*—ensuring that the product looks appealing. Customers see your product before they start using it, and visual appeal helps create a positive first impression. A pleasant design can convey a sense of high quality, make a product seem more credible, and make users feel at ease. The positive emotions that aesthetics help evoke can lead to higher customer enjoyment when they use your product.

Simplicity helps some user experiences deliver delight. Less is often more in UX design—eliminating visual clutter reduces cognitive load and helps a user focus on what's important. Think of the minimalistic design of the Google home page with its search box and not much else.

User experiences that seem to read the user's mind can help create delight. By selecting smart default choices on the user's behalf or proactively addressing top-of-mind questions, a product can make users feel like it understands them and is empathetic. Google Suggest, described in Chapter 5, is a good example of such a feature.

Products can convey personality to evoke emotion from users. This is typically done through the tone of the language used. Humor is another good way to create delight, both with text and with funny images.

Delight often involves a dynamic response by the product based on user action. A great example is the "rubber band" effect that occurs in iOS when a user attempts to scroll past the end of a displayed document or webpage. It's such an amusing effect that many people—whether consciously or not—can't help but fidget with it. Animations and sound effects can also contribute to delight. I know that many Quicken users love hearing the cash register "ka-ching" sound after they enter a transaction. The Apple Mac startup chime is another sound that evokes a positive emotion for many users.

Surprise is an important component of delight. Your product can amuse users by doing unexpected things. In Twitter's early days, the social media platform experienced service outages. When that happened, instead of seeing a typical, unremarkable error page, users were treated to Twitter's infamous "fail whale" graphic.

I recall a pleasant UX surprise I encountered while using email marketing service provider MailChimp. After you finish composing a marketing email you plan to send, MailChimp lets you preview how the email will look at different screen widths. As you vary the preview width, the user interface shows the MailChimp mascot pointing to the number of pixels on a ruler with his outstretched arm. The instructions warn that the width of your email should not exceed a certain number of pixels. When you increase the width past a certain point, the expression on the chimp's face changes from happy to pained, and text warnings such as, "Too big!" and, "Stop it!" appear. If you keep increasing the width past the recommended maximum, the chimp's arm actually detaches, showing a "POP!" graphic. I found this delightful UX so clever, funny, and surprising that I still vividly remember it years later.

THE UX DESIGN ICEBERG

So how do you create a user experience that customers find usable and delightful? Designing a great UX requires skill in several different areas, collectively known as UX design. My framework for UX design is the iceberg shown in Figure 8.1. Like an actual iceberg, only a small

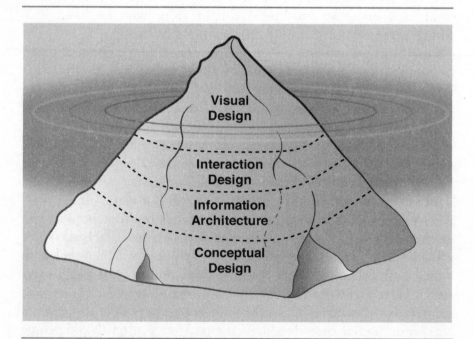

FIGURE 8.1   The UX Design Iceberg

portion of UX design is visible and immediately apparent—but there is much more beneath the surface. Starting at the bottom, the four layers of the iceberg are conceptual design, information architecture, interaction design, and visual design. I will describe each layer in detail, but here's a quick overview: The conceptual design, the iceberg's bottom layer, is the underlying concept that forms the essence of the user experience. The next layer is information architecture, which determines how you structure your product's information and functionality. The next layer is interaction design, which defines how the user and your product interact with one another. The top layer that sticks above the water—the portion of the iceberg that users see—is visual design: how your product looks. We are visual creatures; visual processing is the main way our brains ingest information. But just looking good on the surface is not enough to create a great user experience. Excellent UX design requires attention and skill at all four layers of the iceberg, as well as a good design workflow that progresses from the bottom layer to the top.

CONCEPTUAL DESIGN

The iceberg's bottom layer, conceptual design, has to do with the core concept you are using to design your product. Ideally, your conceptual model should resonate with how your target customers think. A product based on a good conceptual design feels intuitive and easy to use.

This layer of the UX iceberg can often contribute greatly to product innovation. You can envision the UX iceberg as sitting at the top of the Product-Market Fit Pyramid where the UX layer sits. Doing so highlights the fact that the conceptual design layer is just above the feature set layer. Conceptual design is what breathes life into the features and gives them form. By that, I don't mean the details of how the features look and feel, but rather the essence of how they function to create value for the user.

Examples are helpful to explain the idea of a conceptual design. Recall from Chapter 1 how the Quicken team achieved significantly greater ease of use than 46 competing products. The product's success was largely due to its conceptual design of using the checkbook as a metaphor, which customers found very intuitive.

Uber's Conceptual Design

Let's discuss the example of Uber, the popular service that lets you easily book car rides. What conceptual design did the company use for its mobile application? The Uber app uses a map-centric design. While map-centric designs are relatively common, the innovation of Uber's conceptual design was to show users the location of nearby cars in real time: those available for hire before you book, as well as the car that you end up booking. It's worth pointing out that implementing this design required technical innovation in order to track the position of Uber drivers in real time. Uber knew that taxi customers are frustrated when they are victims of late pick-ups or no-shows. As part of its value proposition, the company decided that it was critical to give users transparency into when their car would arrive. Uber's innovative design shows you the estimated wait time, along with the car's location as the driver comes to pick you up. The conceptual design that Uber chose for its UX makes the app's value proposition immediately obvious to the first-time user and instantly conveys how the service is fundamentally different than trying to hail or schedule a taxi.

User Research

Coming up with a good conceptual design is easier when you have a deep understanding of your target customers and their needs. An important but often overlooked part of UX is the "U": the user. Recall that the Product-Market Fit Pyramid starts with the target customer; this is the person for whom you are designing the experience.

You gain the understanding of your customer through user research, which is a specialized field within UX design. User researchers utilize a range of techniques to learn about customers, such as discovery interviews, usability tests, and surveys. Chapter 4 shared advice on customer discovery interviews. Chapter 9 describes how to conduct customer interviews to solicit valuable feedback on your designs. Chapter 13 provides a framework for UX research methods and describes the other techniques (besides interviews). User research informs all levels of the UX iceberg. When customers provide feedback on your UX, it's helpful to parse their feedback and map it to the relevant layer of the UX design iceberg.

It's critical when you conduct user research to ensure that the UX researcher isn't the only person who gains most of the learning. Product team members should observe as much user research as they can. Experiencing user research firsthand is much more impactful than just reading a research report. It's like the difference between watching a sports event live from a front row seat versus reading an article about it the next day. Team debriefs, where individuals share and discuss their observations, help maximize learning and should be held promptly after the research occurs. Documenting the summary of results and key takeaways is also important to solidify the learning and capture it for others. One common and useful deliverable from user research is the *persona*.

Personas

You need to understand your users in order to design a great user experience for them. The UX design tool used for this is the persona, which I first discussed in Chapter 3 in the context of defining your target customer (refer to Figure 3.1 to review). As a quick recap, a persona is an archetype of actual users. Good personas convey your target user's goals along with any relevant psychographic, behavioral, and demographic attributes. Personas help inform your decisions as you design a product that delivers the customer benefits in your value proposition.

In addition to the user's goals, several other aspects of the persona are relevant in the context of UX design. The first is how tech savvy the user is. Users who are less comfortable with technology will need very simple interfaces that focus on the most important tasks along with clear instructions and a good help system. However, a technically advanced user would care less about those things and instead prefer more powerful tools that offer greater flexibility and productivity. There is often a tension in UX design when you need to address both types of users in a single product.

Another aspect of personas that can help inform good UX design is the context in which customers will be using the product. If the user is rushed for time, then you need to make key information and frequently used functionality readily available without much effort. If, instead, the product context is more of a "lean back" experience, the user interface controls should probably be less visible and fade into the background so that the content can be front and center. If the product is used in a loud environment with lots of ambient noise, then you probably shouldn't rely on voice commands.

Teams use personas in the UX design process to remind themselves for whom they are designing the product. That's why *naming* your persona is so critical. As the team wrestles with a decision over different design alternatives, they can ask themselves: "Which would best meet Nancy's needs?" Many teams even create cardboard cutout photos of their personas that they place in the team's workspace to help ensure they keep their user in mind as they work on the design.

Once you have a conceptual design that you believe your persona will find intuitive and valuable, the next step is to define the high-level components of your product and how they should be organized.

INFORMATION ARCHITECTURE

The second layer from the bottom in the UX design iceberg is information architecture, or IA for short. IA is the design discipline responsible for defining how the information and functionality of a software product should be structured. Products typically consist of multiple pages or screens, and there are numerous ways to organize them. The customer accesses the various parts of the product by using the product's navigation system. When looking for a certain page, the customer relies on the navigation labels to infer how the product is organized and guess where the desired page is located. *Card sorting* is a research technique used to learn how customers think about the different parts of the product and how they are related in order to identify their preferred organization scheme. Good IA organizes a product in a manner that users find intuitive, with labels that are easy to understand, resulting in good usability and findability.

Findability refers to how easy it is for users to find what they're looking for in the product. To measure this attribute, you could ask a group of test users to try to find a certain page or screen in your product and see what percentage are successful. You can also assess findability by looking at navigation patterns from an analytics tool. Are your users taking the shortest path to get to each page? Or are they getting lost and taking longer paths or hitting the browser's back button?

Note that IA deals with the product's feature set at a high level: what the features are, how they should be organized, and how they should be labeled. At this point, you are not yet thinking about user flows, page layout, or look and feel. Information architecture is a foundational layer that contributes to a great UX by making the product's structure feel intuitive to users. The main IA deliverable used to do that is the sitemap.

Sitemaps

A sitemap is used to define a product's structure. Even though the term "sitemap" comes from "site" (as in "website"), it's the name of the design deliverable used to specify structure for any software product, including mobile apps. A sitemap shows all of the pages or screens, how they are organized into sections, and the high-level navigation patterns provided. A sitemap also specifies page titles and the words used to label sections of the product. You should test your sitemap with users to ensure that your labels convey the intended meaning and that, when asked to find pages or screens pertaining to different features, they are able to easily do so with your proposed structure. Figure 8.2 is an example sitemap for a web application that enables video advertising campaigns.

Each box in this sitemap represents a page. Lines connect the boxes to show navigation paths between pages. In a few cases, the navigation is one-way, indicated with an arrow (refer to the legend on the left side). The global navigation items—pages to which the user can navigate from any page—are clearly identified. The global navigation shows the major sections of the product, which correspond to the main links you would see at the top of a website. The sitemap indicates which page users navigate to when they click on each of those top-level links. For each section of the website, its subpages are shown in a clear hierarchical format. The sitemap also shows which pages behave differently from normal—by either opening in a popup or opening in a new browser tab.

Once you have created a sitemap that defines your product pages and how they are organized, the next step is to identify how the user experience flows across those pages—that is, how the user will interact with the product.

122

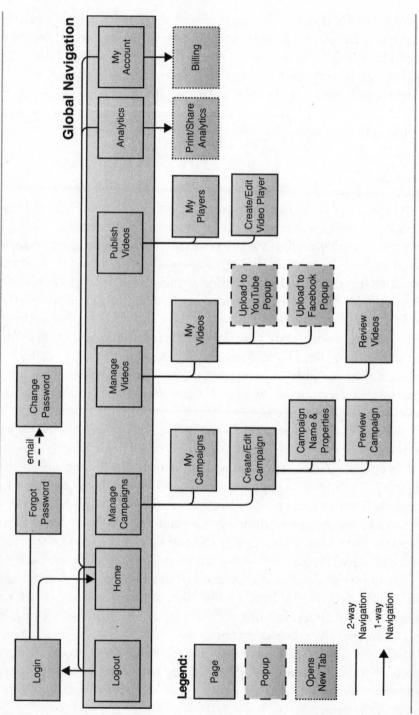

FIGURE 8.2 Sitemap Example

INTERACTION DESIGN

The next layer up in the iceberg is interaction design, which determines how your product and the user interact with one another. Interaction design specifies user flows: That is, what actions can the user take at each step, and how will the product respond? It also governs how users enter information, such as in a form. Any user interface control or link with which the user can interact (click, hover, drag, type, tap, swipe, etc.) falls under the umbrella of interaction design.

For example, let's say that your product has a registration form. Decisions about what information you ask your user to provide, how you design the fields in the form, and what you consider valid versus invalid input are all part of interaction design. So is deciding what happens after the user clicks the "register" button. Any user task that consists of multiple pages or steps requires interaction design. Navigation—when the user goes from one page or screen to another—is a common user interaction, which is also affected by your IA.

If your product offers the user any "operating modes" aside from normal operation—such as an edit mode or preview mode—those are part of your interaction design, too. Similarly, if your design involves different states that impact what the user can and can't do, they are also part of your interaction design. For example, a product for sale on an e-commerce site can have various states: in stock or out of stock, in your shopping cart, or ordered. There is an allowed flow through those states that your interaction design will enforce: The product must be in stock to add to your cart and must be in your cart to be ordered. A good design would make these states clear to the user throughout the flow. States that are important for interaction design can also often be closely tied to your conceptual design (the bottom layer of the iceberg). In the example above, the conceptual design is based on a virtual shopping cart, meant to be analogous to a real-world shopping cart. The Uber app also has a fundamental connection between its conceptual design and the state of the user's trip. Before you book a car, the app shows you all nearby cars; but once you book a car, it only shows you that car.

Another important part of interaction design is the feedback the product gives the user: how the system responds when the user takes a certain action. Error messages fall into this category. For example, if you fill out a registration form on a website and enter an invalid email address (e.g., due to a typo), the website should show you an error message asking you to please check to ensure the email address is valid. Error messages should be well written and clearly explain to the user why the error occurred and what they can do to fix it.

Response time is another aspect of product feedback. If users click a button and there is no resulting indication that something is happening, they will assume their click didn't register or that your product isn't working. Slow performance creates poor interaction design. Users need confirmation that the system is receiving their actions. Even if the system's final response to the action cannot be accomplished quickly, users should receive some feedback to acknowledge their click or tap if they will experience a perceptible delay. Animated spinners are a common solution for this, but you could also display a message explaining what the product is doing (e.g., "searching thousands of flights to find the best matches for your request").

If the product is going to take a while to complete the requested task, it is important to give users a sense of progress and how much time remains. The progress bar is a good tool for doing that, like the ones you see when you are downloading or uploading large files. For long user flows—such as a multipage wizard—giving the user a high-level sense of the steps involved and a progress indicator showing "you are here" as he or she completes the steps is helpful.

TurboTax's Interaction Design

Let's discuss a product that has taken a complex process with many steps and made it easy for users to accomplish through great interaction design. There are few things as complex as preparing one's income taxes. There can be countless questions across many forms that the user must answer to prepare their annual tax return. Yet the product team at TurboTax has managed to create a user experience that guides the novice through that process step by step, which is no small feat.

The product offers two modes, the first of which is "EasyStep." The conceptual design of EasyStep is a structured interview that guides the user through the process by asking them to answer one or two questions at a time. The product dynamically determines what question to show the user next based on the user's previous answers. This design enables the user to focus on one thing at a time while hiding all the other questions and the complex dependencies between questions.

The main user interaction is answering the question at hand— presented in a wizard interface—and then clicking the "continue" button. The product meticulously guides users step by step through the long process until their tax return is completed. Through good interaction design, TurboTax makes this formidable task easy for users. EasyStep's interaction design also allows knowledgeable power users to skip steps, jump around in the interview, and fill out information as they please.

EasyStep is the product's main, default mode. The second mode is "forms" mode, where you see the actual tax forms and worksheets with their values populated (from the EasyStep interview) and can edit them directly if desired. TurboTax users can finish their taxes without ever going to the forms mode, and they can easily toggle between the two modes. Many users never even see the forms that are behind the scenes, which are mainly used by power users. By utilizing these two distinct modes, TurboTax's interactive design effectively addresses the needs of both novice and expert users with the same product.

Flowcharts

So how do you take a complex process or task—like preparing a tax return—and make it simple? Flowcharts are the primary design artifact for doing that. They specify the possible flows for key tasks in your user experience. They show the actions that can be taken and the decisions that can be made by both the user and your product. Actions are represented with rectangular blocks, and decisions points are represented with diamond-shaped blocks (also called conditionals). The blocks are connected with arrows to show the allowed flows.

Figure 8.3 shows an example flowchart for the CarMax mobile application designed by talented UX designer Christine Liu http://christineliu.info. The app's goal is to help the user find a car they like and then connect them with a CarMax dealership. The app uses

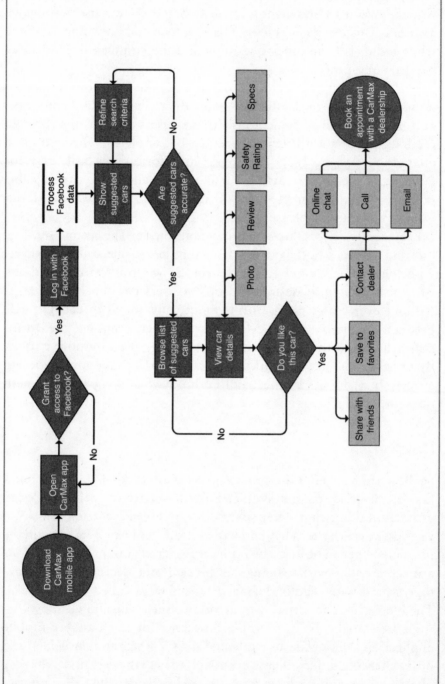

FIGURE 8.3 Flowchart Example

customers' Facebook data to suggest cars they might like. Users can browse suggested cars and can view detailed information on each car until they find one they like. At that point, they can contact a CarMax dealer via email, chat, or phone to book an appointment to see the car. The flowchart starts with the user downloading and opening the app, then shows the paths the user can take through the various screens to the end of the user experience. Notice that the flowchart defines the UX at a high level without addressing the design details of any screen (e.g., layout or visual design).

Aside from their role in UX design, flowcharts can help ensure that everyone on the product team understands the end-to-end user experience the product should deliver. This can be especially valuable for the team members who will be implementing and testing the product.

For simple flows, many teams skip the formal creation of flowcharts and jump straight to clickable wireframes. Because they are more visual and interactive than flowcharts, clickable wireframes are often more effective at communicating the desired interaction design. They do a good job of illustrating the flow and interactions for the "happy path"—that is, when users do what you expect them to do. You can supplement a wireframe with annotations to address error states and call out other important notes. However, if there are many different branches in the user flow and many possible states that need to be specified, then a flowchart helps capture and communicate that complexity.

Wireframes

You typically create wireframes, first discussed in Chapter 7, after you are clear on the desired user flows for your product. Wireframes represent an important threshold in the Lean Product Process. Up to this point, you have spent a lot of time thinking about customers, their needs, your value proposition, the feature set, the IA, and the user flows. Now, for the first time, you are actually specifying what customers will see when they use your product—what each page or screen will show.

At this point in the UX design process, you are not worried about pixel-level precision or visual design aspects such as color. You are trying to determine the layout of each page or screen: which components should be there and how they should be arranged. You are asking questions like, "Should this page have one or two columns?" and, "For this page, should I put the image on the left and the form on the right or vice versa?" Historically, wireframes were static, focusing only on layout. Clickable and tappable wireframes that bring the user flows to life are increasingly common. Modern design applications make it easy to create such wireframes relatively quickly.

You won't be able to finish designing the wireframes for any non-trivial product in one sitting; it requires iteration, and there is no "right answer." You know what your problem space objectives are, and you are trying to identify different solution space alternatives to meet those objectives. Rather than fixating on the first design direction you come up with, it is beneficial to deliberately apply divergent thinking. Such an approach encourages you to come up with as many different possible design directions as you can. It's like brainstorming: You are focused on *generating,* not evaluating ideas at this point. There will be plenty of time down the road to shoot down the bad ideas. At a later point in the design process, you will evaluate the top design approaches and use convergent thinking to narrow your focus. However, if you narrow down too early, you run the risk of exploring only a small portion of the solution space and ending up at a local maximum when there is actually a better solution yet to be discovered.

Instead of designing the wireframe for each page or screen from scratch, good designers look across a product and identify groups of pages or screens that should be similar. Each group will share a distinct template that defines its layout. For example, you may create a template that all two-column pages share. Using a standard set of page or screen templates across your entire product helps ensure a consistent design. You should also standardize components that appear on multiple pages.

Once you have created your initial set of wireframes, you now have—for the first time—a solution space artifact that you can and should test with customers. Chapters 9 and 10 describe how to solicit user feedback on your wireframes and use it to iteratively improve your designs. It's okay to start out with static wireframes if that's your preference, but you should create and test wireframes that are clickable or tappable. These enable you to test your user flows in addition to your layout, and give customers an interactive experience that feels more realistic. Once your target customers validate that your wireframes are easy to use and deliver on your value proposition, it's time to move to the next layer of the UX iceberg: visual design.

VISUAL DESIGN

Visual design is the tip of the iceberg—the part that is most immediately obvious to anyone looking at your product. It is also called graphic design, look and feel, or chrome. And as with the chrome on a car, it doesn't determine what the product does or how you use it, but it does impact how it looks. Aside from creating an aesthetically pleasing product, good visual design helps reinforce the visual hierarchy (discussed later in this chapter) and contributes to ease of use. It can also convey your brand personality, create user delight, and differentiate your product from others. Three major components of visual design are color, typography, and graphics.

Color

Color is an important aspect of a product's visual design. You can create design artifacts for all the other layers of the iceberg in black and white and they will work just fine. But when you create high-fidelity mockups to specify the visual design, you need to decide on colors.

Color contributes to aesthetics and is used to make certain elements on the page stand out more than others. You can also use color to convey certain attributes or emotions. Warm colors such as red, orange, and yellow are typically more energizing and passionate, whereas the more subdued cool colors such as green, blue, and purple are more calming and reserved. Many applications and websites use a blue color scheme because it conveys trustworthiness and calm. Green is associated with nature, growth, and money. Purple suggests luxury and creativity. Red is associated with aggression, passion, power, and danger. Orange is energetic and vibrant. Yellow conveys happiness and sunshine. Brown is associated with warmth and the earth. Black can suggest sophistication, elegance, and mystery. White is associated with purity, cleanliness, and simplicity. These are common generalizations, and the meaning of colors can vary around the world. So if your target customers are of a particular culture, you should be mindful in your design about how they perceive color.

Instead of using colors willy-nilly, a good visual design has a deliberate *color palette*—the set of colors used in the product. The idea is to pick a combination of colors that look good together and to use only those colors in your design. Using color with consistency helps create a cohesive visual design. A color palette will usually have one or two main colors and one or two background colors. It can also have one or two accent colors, which are used to complement the main color. The full palette will also include additional colors created from the main color—usually lighter or less saturated versions of the same hue.

Your use of color can help or hinder readability and usability. To ensure readability of text, there must be a strong contrast between the colors used for text and for the background. Black text on a white background is high contrast, but light blue text on a light gray background is low contrast and barely visible. For better usability, the use of color for key controls such as buttons and primary navigation should make them stand out clearly. An orange button on a black background will pop, but a blue button on a slightly darker blue background will not.

Typography

Typography—defining the arrangement and appearance of text—is another important element of visual design. In the earlier days of the web, browsers only supported a small number of typefaces, such as Arial, Georgia, and Verdana. But the widespread adoption of CSS3 web fonts has provided a multitude of choices.

Different typefaces convey different attributes: formal versus informal, classic versus modern, light versus dramatic. You should select fonts that reinforce the tone you want to set with your product. A key distinction among typefaces is serif versus sans serif. Serifs are the small decorative flourishes that extend from the edges of letters; sans serif fonts do not have these. Traditional design advice has been that serif fonts work better for print materials, which have a very high resolution (dots per inch), whereas sans serif fonts work better for the web, which has lower resolution. However, you see an increased use of serif fonts online with the proliferation of web fonts. At small sizes, serif fonts can be hard to read on a screen; however, they are often used in headings and other large text elements. Even more so than with color, you want to limit the number of different fonts you use in your product. A common approach is to select two fonts: one for body text and one for large text, such as headings. It's common to see websites and mobile applications use a sans serif font for body text and a complementary serif font for headings.

Font size is an important part of your typography. Your body text, which usually has the smallest size, should of course be large enough to be readable. Titles and headings will have a larger size. As with color and typefaces, you want to avoid using too many different text sizes and be consistent throughout your product. Fonts can also have different weights and styles such as bold, italic, or underlined.

Typography usually plays an important role in establishing your design's visual hierarchy (discussed later). You should deliberately design the color and relative size, weight, and position of the text elements on your pages to create the desired visual hierarchy.

Graphics

Images, both photographs and illustrations, are often used in visual design. For certain product categories, such as ecommerce, using images well is critical. Take Airbnb: In order for customers to feel comfortable renting a place to stay, they need to see pictures of it. Chapter 7 discussed how Airbnb more than doubled their conversion rate by using higher-quality photos. Images are often used on landing and other marketing pages. The use of *hero images* is common—where a large, prominent photo shows your product, a typical customer, or some other artistic or inspirational object or scene. For example, Netflix often uses large photos of customers watching and enjoying a show.

Illustrations are often used to explain how your product works. You can also use other graphical elements such as lines, shapes, textures, gradients, and shadows in your visual design. These smaller touches can help you achieve the look and feel you want for your product by adding structure, depth, and pizzazz.

Icons are small symbols used to represent objects or concepts. They are most commonly used for buttons or other user interface controls, especially when space is at a premium. In many applications, icons are the main way to use the product. Browsers use icons for their back, forward, and refresh buttons. Adobe Photoshop utilizes a toolbar packed with icons as the main way for customers to access its functionality. Similarly, Microsoft Office products use a "ribbon" full of icons. Aside from user interface controls, icons are also used on marketing pages to support and complement the text. Iconography is a specialty within visual design; iconographers have to tweak individual pixels by hand to create their tiny masterpieces. The importance of good icon design has grown with the increased usage of mobile devices. Their small screen size puts space at a premium; so many controls in mobile applications are icons.

Customers need to be able to look at an icon and understand what it means. However, it can be challenging to convey an icon's intended meaning because it is so small and is just a symbol without any text. If a standardized symbol already exists for an icon in your design, I strongly recommend you use it instead of trying to invent a new symbol. Let's say you're creating an app that plays audio and are designing icons for the play and pause buttons. It would be silly to create your own symbols when everyone is familiar with the triangle pointing to the right that means "play" and the two vertical lines that mean "pause."

Most applications use a set of multiple icons, in which case it is important to have design consistency across the icons. Each icon needs to have a unique symbol, of course, but the overall shape, color, and style should be consistent with the set. Consistency in your product's visual design is important to create a good UX. Two useful tools for achieving consistent visual design are *style guides* and *layout grids*.

Style Guides

A style guide is a visual design deliverable that is used to achieve a consistent look and feel. They are especially important for products with many pages or screens. A style guide specifies the visual design details—such as color, size measurements, fonts, and graphics—for commonly used elements. A style guide helps maintain consistency, especially if multiple designers are working on the product, and also reduces work for your UI developer.

Layout Grids

The layout grid is a design tool that helps you ensure consistent alignment of the design elements on each page or screen. Grids have long been used in print design, and their use in web and mobile design helps deliver a better UX. A grid consists of a specific number of columns of the same size separated by a "gutter" or margin.

You select the size of your grid to match your situation. The sample grid in Figure 8.4 consists of 12 columns, each 94 pixels wide, separated by 18-pixel wide gutters. The total width of 1,326 pixels is optimized for screens that are 1,366 pixels wide, so that users don't have to scroll horizontally. This width allows up to 40 pixels for a vertical scrollbar and any other visual elements from the browser or operating system.

The idea is to align all page or screen elements to the grid as you lay them out. Examples of a page or screen element would be a block of text, an image, or a button. Elements can span more than one column. The key is that the left and right horizontal edges of elements should

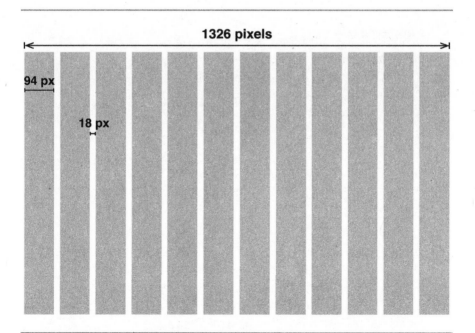

FIGURE 8.4   Layout Grid Example

begin and end on the grid. The grid I've shown has 12 columns, which is evenly divisible by 2, 3, 4, and 6, and allows a wide range of possible element widths. See Figure 8.5 for an example of a wireframe that utilizes a grid to arrange page elements.

The grid shown in these two figures only divides the space horizontally (into columns). Grids used in print design often specify vertical divisions (rows) as well. Grid lines for vertical positioning have been less useful on the web due to the large variation in screen heights. In addition, it can be hard to control the exact vertical position of elements because browsers dynamically render content based on the width of the screen. As a result, digital grids tend to focus only on the horizontal divisions. With the advent of responsive design, discussed later, designers now have a greater ability to control the vertical position of elements in their web designs.

Recall that at the wireframe stage, your layout usually describes only the approximate position and relative size of elements. By enabling precise, pixel-perfect layouts, grids help you make the transition from lower fidelity wireframes to high fidelity mockups.

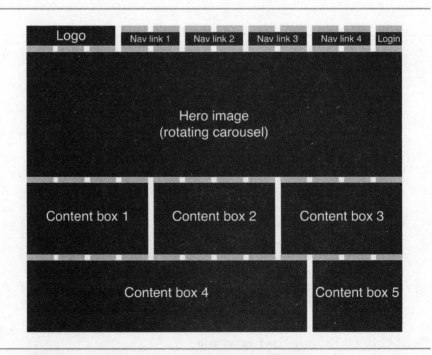

FIGURE 8.5   Wireframe Using a Layout Grid

Mockups

Mockups, discussed in Chapter 7, are higher-fidelity design deliverables that capture your visual design. They build on your wireframes, using color, typography and graphics to create the look and feel of your product. Mockups are typically created by a visual designer in a tool such as Adobe Illustrator or Sketch and then exported as an image file (PNG, GIF, or JPG). You can solicit feedback from users on static mockups such as these, but it is more valuable to show users a set of clickable or tappable mockups. These give users a better sense of your product and how it works. Tools such as InVision let you take a set of static mockups and string them together into a user flow. These tools let you identify a clickable area on a mockup (e.g., a button or a link) and specify to which other mockup it should navigate. Chapters 9 and 10 describe how to solicit user feedback on your mockups and use it to iteratively improve your designs. Once you have a set of clickable or tappable mockups that your target customers agree is easy to use and delivers your value proposition, then you have finished your UX design. The next step would be to implement your UX by building your product. Chapter 12 discusses how to do that using Agile development.

I've explained the UX design iceberg and how to bring your feature ideas to life by progressing through its four layers. I've also described the key design deliverables along the way, including the ones you should test with customers to assess your UX and product-market fit. In this next section, I share several important design principles that will help you create a great UX.

DESIGN PRINCIPLES

Design is a magical part of the Lean Product Process. It's where intangible ideas about benefits and features get transformed into an actual user experience. In many ways, design is more art than science, but there are several design principles that can help you create a better user experience.

Gestalt Principles

The Gestalt principles are a set of useful theories that describe how humans visually perceive objects. The word gestalt means "an organized whole that is perceived as more than the sum of its parts." That's what our visual processing system attempts to do with what we see. There are several Gestalt principles, but I will focus on the principles of proximity and similarity.

According to the Gestalt principle of proximity, the brain perceives objects that are closer together as more related than objects that are farther apart. Therefore, you should put related objects close to one another in your designs. You should apply this principle when you are determining the layout in your wireframes. This applies to both arranging content as well as user interface controls. For example, you can see in Figure 8.5 that all of the primary navigation links are together. If your user interface gives the user three choices on how to proceed, then the three buttons or links should be shown together. You should avoid putting unrelated items close to each other or else the user may infer they are related. For example, placing a cancel button for one feature too close to another feature on the same page may lead to user confusion about which feature the cancel button affects.

The Gestalt principle of similarity maintains that the brain perceives objects that share similar characteristics as more related than objects that don't share those characteristics. Therefore, in your designs, objects that are similar or related should look similar by having the same shape, size, or color. You should avoid making unrelated objects look alike. You should apply the principle of similarity when you are determining your visual design. For example, you could require that all your hyperlinks be blue and underlined or that all your action buttons have the same rounded rectangle shape. Because they describe how our visual perception works, the Gestalt principles lead to the next design principle: visual hierarchy.

Visual Hierarchy

Visual hierarchy is an important design principle that determines which elements of your design the user considers most important. This importance drives the user's attention, influencing the order in which they look at the various elements.

The size and color of elements are two of the main attributes that create a visual hierarchy. The brain assumes that larger objects are more important and smaller objects are less important. It also assumes that elements with high contrast—for example, a color that makes them stand out or "pop"—are more important. Images that stand out can have the same effect. Our eyes are naturally drawn to pictures of people, especially faces.

The location of elements also affects visual hierarchy, because users start reading at the top of the page. In English and other left-to-right languages, users start reading on the left side of the page. Therefore, all other things being equal, people will look at elements near the top left corner of the screen first.

A nice hack to quickly determine the visual hierarchy of a page or screen is to squint your eyes. You will not be able to read the text or see details, but you will notice the location, size, and color of major design elements. You can also take a screenshot and blur it (using a graphic design application) to create the same effect. When you try this test on a product with strong visual hierarchy, you will be able to identify the most important design elements.

Designers should use the principles of how human visual processing works to reinforce the desired hierarchy of information. To create a visual hierarchy, you should first identify the relative importance of the different components that should be on the page. Then design the location, size, and color of your components to reinforce that prioritization. The design of a page with good visual hierarchy will attract the user's eyes to the most important element. The design then guides the user's eyes from one element to the next in priority order, usually moving along intuitive top-to-bottom and left-to-right paths. This helps the user find what they are looking for and successfully complete tasks. It also leads to higher conversion rates for key user actions. A good visual hierarchy is a critical component of a good UX.

Principles of Composition

In addition to the Gestalt principles and visual hierarchy, you should also consider these principles of composition when creating and evaluating your designs:

- **Unity:** Does the page or screen feel like a unified whole or a bunch of disparate elements?
- **Contrast:** Is there enough variation in color, size, arrangement, and so forth to create visual interest?

- **Balance:** Have you equally distributed the visual weight (position, size, color, etc.) of elements in your design?
- **Use of space:** How cluttered or sparse does your design feel? Ensuring your design has enough white space—the space you don't use on the page or screen—is important to avoid designs that feel crowded to the user.

Responsive Design

When you specify the arrangement of design elements on a page or screen, you have to make assumptions (either explicit or implicit) about the size of your "canvas." In print design, you know the exact width and height of the paper on which your design is going to be printed. Unfortunately, the digital world is not so simple. Your customers will be using your product on devices with a variety of screen sizes, so the size of your canvas is not so straightforward.

Clearly, smartphones have much smaller screens than laptops and desktop monitors. The original iPhone was 360 by 480 pixels, for example. There is now a wider range of smartphone sizes than ever. Tablets emerged to populate the gap in screen size between smartphones and computer monitors. Phablets have filled the gap between smartphones and tablets. At the high end of the screen resolution spectrum, desktop monitors with large resolutions have become popular. The range of different screen resolutions has grown even further with the advent of wearable devices, such as Apple Watch, and their tiny screens.

How should your product team deal with this large and highly fragmented variation in screen resolutions? You can use *responsive design* for web-based products. Rather than trying to accommodate all users with a single design, responsive design allows users on different size screens to see different versions of your user interface. The design responds to the user's screen size, usually the width. You start by determining the screen width "breakpoints" you want to use and then apply the desired differences in styling to each width. It's common to have a large width version for computer screens and a small width version for phone screens. Many products also use an intermediate width breakpoint for tablets.

With responsive design, as the screen width shrinks from wide to narrow, some page elements start "wrapping"—that is, getting pushed to the next line. Some elements become smaller in size or just disappear at smaller screen widths. Responsive design enables these types of dynamic UX changes without requiring a lot of additional coding effort or complexity.

Designing for Multiple Screen Sizes

The need to accommodate multiple screen sizes is a reality of modern-day software design. For web-based products, responsive design is a great tool for doing so elegantly and without too much additional effort. Native mobile applications share the same problem, and mobile software development kits (SDKs) include tools that enable an app to have different layouts optimized for different screen sizes.

But should you begin your UX design process with the larger or smaller screen size? If you've initially designed your product for a larger screen size, modifying it for a smaller screen size can be challenging. The same amount of content just won't fit, so it can be hard to choose what to remove. You will probably have to change your navigation. You will need to rethink and replace content that is just too wide for the smaller screen. Often such teams end up creating a second, separate product with a different code base—a situation that isn't ideal. For one thing, the need to make changes and additions in two separate pieces of code leads to inefficiency and an increased chance of errors. And because the mobile and non-mobile products were not designed together, they often look and feel very different from one another—which results in an inconsistent user experience that can confuse customers.

It is harder to design for a smaller screen due to the space constraints, which require more tradeoffs. As a result, many teams embrace a "mobile first" approach—designing for the smallest screen first since this forces them to prioritize what is most important. After the mobile design is far enough along, they design the larger sizes, which can often easily accommodate additional content and functionality. Note: The intent is not for the two designs to be designed sequentially or separately. They should be done in parallel; it's just that the mobile design leads the process. Often, rather than just being a smaller version of the full-size product, the mobile version of the product will play a complementary role in relation to the web version. It may have unique functionality that the web product doesn't have (e.g., taking advantage of geolocation or other sensors). Or it may offer a more focused subset of the full functionality of the web product. Designing the two in parallel helps ensure that they work together to deliver a user experience that achieves product-market fit.

COPY IS ALSO PART OF UX DESIGN

Before concluding this chapter, let's touch on an often-overlooked component of the user experience: copy. This is the text that your customers see, whether it's on your marketing pages or in your product. The quality of the copy on marketing pages can result in major differences in your conversion rate. But the copy you use in your product—labels, instructions, descriptions, and error messages—can really affect usability. Users often have very little text to guide them, so labels on buttons and links need to be clear and easy to understand. It is a major usability problem if a user wants to perform an important action but isn't sure which button to use. Descriptions of features and instructions should be written in simple text using words that users understand—*not* internal or industry jargon. Error messages should be helpful and explanatory instead of cryptic. The good news is that it is relatively easy to identify and fix problematic copy; you just need to conduct usability tests of your product. In your tests, if users encounter difficulty with a particular word or phrase, you should ask them what they would call it, since they often have great suggestions.

THE A-TEAM

As you can see from the topics covered in this chapter, UX design is a discipline that spans several different skills. Many companies have a "design gap"—a situation where all of the skills required to create a great UX design just aren't present. Many teams don't have a designer. Even if you have a designer, that person probably isn't strong in all the UX design skills. It is possible for a single designer to be strong in several of the different UX design skills, but it is more common for a designer to be stronger in either visual design (how the product looks) or interaction design (how the product works). To create a great UX, your team needs to be talented in both of these areas. You also need a front-end developer who can skillfully implement the design, as well as a strong product manager. Aside from each person individually possessing the requisite skills, it's crucial for these team members to work together effectively in order to deliver a great UX. I like to call a team who has this set of four essential skills—product management, interaction design, visual design, and front-end development—the "A-Team" (like the popular 1980s television show). Other roles or skills are obviously important to deliver a great product: back-end developers, quality assurance (QA), DevOps, and so forth. But when it comes to creating a great UX, having an A-Team is critical.

UX IS IN THE EYE OF THE BEHOLDER

At the end of the day, your customer is the ultimate judge of how good your user experience is, which impacts your product-market fit. Recall from the technology adoption life cycle in Chapter 3 that innovators may be willing to tolerate a substandard UX for a breakthrough product that provides cutting edge benefits. But as you try to advance through the technology adoption lifecycle to penetrate additional segments, they will not be as tolerant, and UX becomes more important to product-market fit. Even though great design takes a lot of skill and work, there's really no excuse for having a bad user experience. As I've discussed, you should be showing your designs to customers to identify and resolve any issues. In fact, that's what the next chapter is about: how to test your MVP prototype with customers.

Chapter 9

Test Your MVP with Customers (Step 6)

Once you have applied the principles of great UX design to create the prototype of your MVP candidate, the next step in the Lean Product Process is to test it with users. This is where the rubber meets the road. You'll recall that Chapter 7 discussed two fundamentally different types of test you can run: quantitative and qualitative. That is, you'll either pay attention to the details of what you're hearing from a small number of customers (qualitative) or to the aggregated results for a large number of customers (quantitative).

Quantitative tests, such as A/B tests and landing page tests, are relatively straightforward to conduct and analyze. Since they don't involve talking to users, they're just about the data. You track the conversion rate (or other metric) for your MVP test and see how it compares to the target value that represents a successful outcome (or to the value for other alternatives). You need to be mindful of your sample size, which will affect the level of confidence of your results.

This chapter focuses on how to conduct *qualitative* user testing of your MVP. User feedback is incredibly valuable because it identifies what you don't know. When you are so close to your product, it is difficult—often impossible—to perceive it as a new customer does. You have become more familiar with your product than any new user could ever be. As a result, you have "product blindness": blind spots for the issues that a new user will readily encounter within minutes of using your product.

User testing is the antidote for product blindness. User testing validates or invalidates your hypotheses, whether you made them explicitly or they are implicit assumptions. Because of product blindness, the first time you test with users often leads to the most surprising learning. I recall when I conducted the first user feedback sessions for cloud collaboration startup Box—it was quite an eye-opening experience for the team. They learned so many new things that they instantly saw the value of user testing and wanted to do more.

Qualitative user tests require that you show customers your product or design deliverables—wireframes, mockups, or prototypes—to solicit their feedback. It takes skill to design and run these tests successfully. I'll be sharing lots of advice—both what to do and what not to do—to help you get the most value out of your qualitative user testing.

HOW MANY CUSTOMERS SHOULD I TEST WITH?

I recommend conducting user tests with one customer at a time for the best results. You *can* speak with more than one customer at a time, but you usually get suboptimal results due to group dynamics. You especially see this negative affect in focus groups, which involve talking to anywhere from 6 to 12 people at once. Some participants may not speak their mind openly for fear of being judged or criticized. One or two outspoken people often dominate the discussion, drowning out other voices. Participants also often experience groupthink, where all or most of the group artificially converges on the same opinions, which leads to inaccurate data.

By speaking with one customer at a time, you don't experience any of those negative group dynamics, and you're able to have a richer, more in-depth conversation. The customer is much more likely to speak up and share his or her true feelings, especially if the moderator is the only other person present. In my experience, the more observers you have, the more worried about being judged some customers can be. Many moderators like to have a note-taker present so they can focus on conducting the user test, which is fine. I personally prefer taking my own notes—that way, I'm certain that my insights get captured, and it's truly a one-on-one interview. If you want observers to be able to watch testing sessions live, then using a webcam that projects the video feed to a monitor in another room is a good alternative. If the user test is remote, then the observers can join the screen sharing session.

I *have* conducted user testing with two and three customers at a time. It worked out fine because I was getting feedback on printed mockups; we were all seated at a table and could see and point to the papers on the table. It probably wouldn't have worked so well if each customer was looking at the designs on a laptop. I took this approach instead of one-on-one sessions because my client wanted to obtain the results of the research very quickly, and this allowed me to speak to more customers per day. Sometimes research subjects don't make their appointment; no-shows are just a reality of user research. So another benefit of having two or three people scheduled for each session was that I wasn't left twiddling my thumbs if one person was a no-show.

Product teams often ask, "How many customers should I test with?" If you talk to too few, you run the risk of not catching all the issues you need to address. And you might discover opinions that aren't really representative but not realize that's the case. On the other side of the spectrum, talking to too many people takes additional time and resources. You can go past the point of diminishing returns where you just keep hearing the same feedback and aren't learning anything new. I've found that testing in waves of five to eight customers at a time strikes a good balance. That number of tests is enough to uncover major issues and identify patterns across users. After each wave, you will be revising your product or design artifact based on what you learned and then testing it with a new wave of customers until you've validated that you've achieved product market fit.

You should plan for the fact that some customers will not show up for their user test. The typical no-show rate is usually around 10 percent. From a practical standpoint, I would just schedule one more test than my desired sample size. If I knew I wanted to speak to seven people, I would schedule eight to hedge for a no-show.

IN-PERSON, REMOTE, AND UNMODERATED USER TESTING

You can conduct user testing research either in-person or remotely. In-person is straightforward: the moderator and the customer are in the same room. Remote testing is possible using screen sharing or video recording technology. With remote testing, you can have either moderated or unmoderated tests. Moderated means that the researcher is present and conducting the test with the customer. Unmoderated implies that no moderator is present; instead, customers are provided with the artifact or product to test and guidance on what to do. These sessions are recorded for the product team to watch later. Most tools capture the customer's screen (i.e., so you can see where they were clicking in your product), and many also record audio so you can hear the user's thoughts. Some tools also capture video of the customer's face (i.e., using a webcam).

Of the three qualitative testing methods—in-person, moderated remote, and unmoderated remote—I would recommend in-person if possible. You can gather much richer data sitting next to a user versus sharing a screen. You can see the user's screen and face when you're in his or her presence, and can pick up little things like sighs, facial expressions, and other subtle cues. You can see where the user's eyes are looking. You are also likely to build a better rapport in-person, which usually leads to better data because the customer feels more comfortable talking to you.

Of course, sometimes it can be difficult to find target customers nearby. If this is the case, then remote moderated testing is a good way to reach them where they are. While not quite as good as in-person testing, you can still get valuable information. To see the customer's screen, you will use a screen sharing application such as GoToMeeting, WebEx, Skype, Screenleap, or join.me. As with any situation like this, you should be prepared to encounter technical difficulties. When you're ready to start a remote session, it's common to find that customers have not installed the software required to share their screen or need help getting it running properly. Additionally, the screen-sharing program can get in the way of the test, for example, by causing user confusion or shrinking the size of the design artifact you're showing. There is often some lag between the customer's actions and when you see them on your screen, and firewalls can cause problems as well. However, when you don't run into technical difficulties, remote-moderated testing can yield a lot of valuable information from users.

The third type of testing is unmoderated remote testing, which you accomplish using a service such as UserTesting or Validately. Such services provide access to your design artifacts, facilitate users through the session, and capture what they do. Many of these services also offer a panel of users to test your product. One advantage of this approach is that you can get results more quickly. You usually don't have to spend any time on recruiting or scheduling users, and multiple users can perform the user testing at the same time versus being constrained by moderator availability. However, you are not present to guide the user through the experience. The user follows written instructions, so you have to put more thought into structuring the flow of the test and the directions you give the user. It's best to pilot the test with one or two people before recruiting many users. Additionally, the fact that you are not present means that you cannot ask questions as they arise, such as, "Why did you click that button?" You must provide all the questions you'd like the user to answer in advance—so you need to give more thought and attention to detail to how you word the questions compared to moderated testing.

Most unmoderated remote testing tools focus on recording what users are doing on their screens, capturing their mouse movements and clicks. While seeing the user's screen is helpful, hearing audio from the user adds even more value. Some tools even include video of the user's face. Other tools don't record the user or the screen and just capture clicks and calculate clickthrough percentages. That type of quantitative information will be useful once you have launched at scale, and you can get it from your analytics package. But when you are trying to test product-market fit with unmoderated tests, it's preferable to have both screen recordings and user audio, which most of the leading tools provide.

One advantage of unmoderated testing over moderated testing is that there is no risk of the moderator influencing the results. In reality, customers are going to be evaluating, signing up for, and using your product on their own, without anyone by their side. This makes unmoderated testing more prototypical of the user's real world situation. Most customers who sit with a moderator pay more attention and try harder than they would if they were on their own.

So how should you select which method to use? When you are early in defining and validating your MVP, moderated testing is the way to go to ensure you can ask questions and get rich customer feedback. As I've emphasized, in-person is ideal—unless it's a challenge to find target users and remote testing is more feasible. When you are farther down the road and feeling more confident about your MVP, unmoderated testing can be a useful tool to compliment moderated testing since it takes less time and is less expensive. That's why unmoderated is also a good option if you just don't have the resources to conduct moderated testing.

HOW TO RECRUIT CUSTOMERS IN YOUR TARGET MARKET

Of course, you want to make sure that the customers with whom you are testing are in your target market. Otherwise, their feedback could send you iterating in the wrong direction. You can ensure a good fit by using a screener—a set of questions, like a survey, that you ask prospective participants. For example, if you were targeting younger males, you would ask questions about age and gender. You create multiple-choice answers for each question and decide which answers qualify versus disqualify respondents from your target market. Chapter 3 discussed the different types of customer attributes you can use to specify your target customer.

In addition to demographic attributes, behavioral attributes are typically very useful. If, for example, you were targeting hardcore videogamers, you would probably ask, "Do you play videogames?", and filter out people who replied "no." You might then ask people who replied "yes," "In a typical week, how many hours per week do you play videogames?" The respondents would select from a list of possible responses such as "less than 5 hours per week," "5 to 10 hours per week," "10 to 20 hours per week," "20 to 30 hours per week," and "over 30 hours per week." You could decide that gamers need to play 20 or more hours per week to be in your target market, and therefore only accept people who selected the last two choices.

Psychographic attributes—users' opinions and feelings—can also be useful for screening. Sticking with the same target customer, one possible psychographic question could be, "Do you consider yourself a hardcore gamer?" You could also ask, "How much do you enjoy playing videogames?" and provide a scale for responses.

You should refer to the personas you created for your target market as you develop your screener questions. As with everything else, the screener questions serve as hypotheses for you to test and iterate. If you notice while running your initial user tests that your first set of screener questions didn't get you the right kind of customer, then you should change them for the next round of tests.

You'll often discover additional criteria to add to your screener after your first tests. For example, let's say we had a portfolio management application targeted at investors. Our first screener might ask questions about trading frequency and portfolio value. We discover after our first set of user tests that there are two distinct types of investors: those that like to make their own investing decisions, and those that prefer to delegate decisions to a professional advisor. Our value proposition resonates with the first group but is not appealing at all to the second group. For subsequent user tests, we would add a question to our screener to target the do-it-yourself investors and filter out the delegators. We should update our persona accordingly, too.

Once your screener reflects the customers from whom you'd like to get feedback, the next step is to recruit them. This can be the most challenging step for many people who are excited about Lean user testing. If you are trying to improve an existing product, you can often talk with your existing customers. If not, you have to figure out how to find your target customers. You might be lucky enough to have a list of prospective customers you can contact. Otherwise, you'll have to hunt for them.

One approach is to try to recruit local participants by posting online to Craigslist, TaskRabbit, and similar websites. A best practice is to include in your posting a link to an online survey hosted at SurveyMonkey, Google Forms, or another survey site with your screener questions. The volume of responses you receive can vary quite a bit depending on where you post, what you say, and the size of the incentive you offer.

If you experience a low response rate in your recruiting efforts, using remote testing lets you expand beyond your local market to any-one online. Some companies use Amazon's Mechanical Turk (MTurk) as an affordable recruiting source for remote testing, and several ser-vices have been built on top of MTurk to make this easier to do. Many remote testing services, such as UserTesting, have a panel of customers available for testing. The amount of control these services give you over screener questions can differ. Some limit you to prespec-ified attributes such as gender, age, employment status, and so forth, while others let you ask your own questions. When selecting a remote testing service, ensure that you have the required level of control over screener questions. Getting feedback from customers that aren't in your target market is a waste of time and money that can lead you in the wrong direction.

It can be harder to reach your target customers if they are not consumers—for example, if you're aiming for marketing executives or doctors. One creative way is to target conferences, meetups, or other events where they congregate and conduct some guerrilla on-the-ground testing. One of my clients had an idea for a product related to purchasing carbon offsets. He was originally planning to build a web application, which would have taken a lot of time and money. I explained why I thought a Kickstarter MVP would make more sense, since it would allow him to validate his value proposition before spending any money on coding—and he agreed. He targeted a local conference on alternative energy and brought his iPad along. As he spoke with attendees, he figured out which ones were in his target market and showed them his Kickstarter page. He received tons of valuable feedback in a short amount of time.

Events like that can be a good way to get concentrated feedback. Unfortunately, relevant events probably aren't taking place often enough near you to support rapid testing and iteration. A remote testing service with a panel can be a good option for recruiting users frequently with relatively short notice.

Customer research companies are another option for conducting in-person tests. Many research companies have a local panel of participants from which they can recruit. Such companies often offer an end-to-end service that includes testing facilities and a moderator, but you can usually just pay them to recruit for you. The price per recruit can vary but is often between $75 and $150. If your target customers are relatively scarce and place a high value on their time—say heart surgeons or CEOs—it can cost a lot more or simply not be feasible to recruit them. In my experience, research companies are a great way to recruit local participants for in-person testing. The main disadvantage is the cost. But you frequently get more than your money's worth back in valuable feedback, especially if you've done a good job on your screener and conduct a good test.

How to Avoid the Scheduling Trap

I see a lot of companies who want to conduct user tests struggle with the logistics of scheduling the sessions. Product teams spend much of their time heads-down, working on defining their value prop, writing user stories, and designing wireframes. When they're ready to test their wireframes with users, they pop their heads up and scramble to recruit users quickly so they don't lose time. It's very hard to recruit users at the drop of a hat like that. At that point, most teams haven't thought about their screener or test script. If the team doesn't have any resources to help with recruiting users, it often falls on the product manager or designer—both of whom already have a full plate. It can take a week or two (or longer) until the first user test is scheduled. By that time, the team has probably received a lot of pressure to move forward and succumbed, proceeding with high fidelity design or even coding. By the time they're able to digest the feedback from the wave of user tests, it's too late for it to impact the product. They complete an iteration or two of development and then this frustrating cycle repeats itself, leading many teams to reduce their frequency of user testing or stop altogether. What's a Lean product team to do?

The best way out of this trap is to just blindly schedule users on a routine basis. For example, you might schedule three users to come in every Tuesday afternoon or five users every other Wednesday. I use the term "blindly" because when you schedule the users, you probably won't know exactly what you'll be testing with them. Instead of waiting until your product or artifact is ready to schedule users, teams can just count on users being available at the designated recurring time. This breaks the dependency between having your test ready to go and scheduling users, and enables a much higher frequency of user testing with a lot less work. I also recommend that teams get a resource to help recruit and schedule users for tests. Junior employees or interns can be good options, as well as part-time contractors. They mainly just need a well-written screener to do the job.

Starbucks User Testing

If you're up for guerrilla tactics, another option is what I call Starbucks user testing, where you spend time at a cafe and test with people you recruit on the spot. The main benefits of this method are its low cost and immediacy. The main drawback is that you're not able to closely control the type of customers with whom you speak. If you have a mainstream consumer product like Google or Facebook, it can be feasible to find people who are in your target market. However, this approach probably won't work if you have a very specific target customer. You can try to visually screen people and make inferences from their appearance (e.g., gender, age, how they're dressed, etc.).

Be prepared for a fair amount of rejection; many people don't like being approached by strangers or are too busy. Personally, I've found the shopping mall to be a good alternative to the cafe, since people there seem to be less busy and more open. Your opening line is critical to your success rate. Make it a point to quickly inform people about what you're asking of them and what you're offering in exchange for their time. For example, you could say, "Hi, sir, do you have 10 minutes to share your feedback on a new website in exchange for a $25 Starbucks card?"

Compensating Customers

Speaking of cost, how much should you compensate testers for their time? The typical range is $75 to $125 per hour, but it depends on your target customer and how much their time is worth. Talking with a heart surgeon probably would cost much more than that—while talking to a high school student would be much less. Many resourceful startups are able to recruit testers without compensation by finding people who have sufficient interest in their product category. I've used admission to an exclusive private beta as a carrot, as have other companies. If your company has nice swag (e.g., a T-shirt, hoodie, or track jacket), that can work, too.

There are several options for payment. Gift cards are convenient for both parties since they are easy to buy and easy to use. A general-purpose gift card such as Visa or MasterCard has more appeal than a specialty gift card. If you're doing Starbucks user testing, a Starbucks card works well. Cash works but can be a pain to obtain from a company account. Some companies prefer to issue checks for accounting purposes. Cashier's checks are a good option because the respondent doesn't have to worry whether they will bounce or not. If you are testing with current customers, then an alternative to giving them money is giving them credit toward your service or future purchases.

USER TESTING AT INTUIT

I was first introduced to user testing at Intuit, a pioneer in the field. After the launch of each new version of Quicken, product managers would conduct "follow me homes." They would wait in the store aisle where Quicken was being sold. When they saw a customer who was going to purchase Quicken, they would ask if they could follow the person home, where they would observe the customer install and use the product. The ability to watch customers use our product in their real world setting gave us lots of valuable insights. You may have heard of "contextual inquiry" or "ethnographic research"; these are UX research methods that also focus on observing customers in their real-life setting.

It's not always feasible or economical to go to where your users are; sometimes it makes more sense to have them come to you. Intuit also created a state-of-the-art usability lab with several rooms for conducting tests. We would invite customers to the lab to test software as we developed it. The moderator would be the only person in the room with the customer, but a one-way mirror enabled additional people to watch the test live. The lab's cameras captured the computer screen as well as the customer's face and relayed the video to monitors in the back room.

RAMEN USER TESTING

Intuit's usability lab was very impressive and fun to use as a product manager. But the reality is that you don't need such an elaborate setup to conduct user testing. Since I left Intuit, I've worked at many startups, which usually have to be scrappier with their limited resources. I've helped them conduct what I call Ramen user testing, a technique that eliminates everything but the essential parts of user testing. Instead of using a dedicated facility, you just use a conference room at your office. Instead of hiring a dedicated moderator, someone on the team (usually the product manager or designer) runs the session. If you've never run a user test, I recommend you give it a try. I've found that many people who are initially intimidated by the notion of running a user test just need a little encouragement. It isn't rocket science—like most things in life, it just takes practice to get better at it. But because it can be challenging to try to moderate and take notes at the same time, I recommend having a dedicated note-taker.

Have customers bring their laptop or device for the test if possible, since this tends to work out much better than making the customers use a device with which they're not familiar. I've seen differences in operating system (Windows or Mac), keyboard, mouse, or browser throw users for a loop and interfere with a test. It's good to observe customers using your product on the actual devices they use at home or work. You often learn something new that didn't come up in your team's internal discussions and tests.

Once in the room, I like to seat the customer at the table with their laptop or mobile device and have the moderator and note-taker sit next to the customer, one on either side. This allows you to face the same direction as the customer and see the screen. Plus, sitting next to them allows you to notice facial expressions and other subtle cues.

I encourage others on the team to watch the user tests, too. It is very powerful when multiple people observe the same customer feedback at the same time. The problem and solution spaces can be a bit murky as you are seeking product-market fit, which can cause team members to have different hypotheses and opinions. Watching user tests together helps team members achieve a shared understanding. That being said, you don't want to overwhelm the customer with lots of people in the room. A maximum of three people in a conference room with the customer is enough. It's also important for anyone but the moderator to remain quiet and not disrupt the test. If more people want to watch, then you can set up a webcam that transmits to a screen in a separate viewing room. I've also used a setup in a larger room where I attached a projector to the customer's laptop for others to watch. I arranged the projector and observer chairs behind the customer's field of view but close enough for the observers to hear the customer.

Some people on your team might be tempted to record in-person user tests instead of watching them live with the idea of watching them later. I've been involved with a large number of tests, and I've never seen anyone actually go back and watch the recordings. Chances are that if someone on your team isn't motivated enough to attend the test, they aren't going to be motivated enough to watch the recording. Plus, many customers don't like the idea of being recorded. Now, if your team really sees value in it and is really going to watch the recordings, then go for it—as long as the customer doesn't object. Otherwise, skip the recordings and focus on watching the live sessions.

HOW TO STRUCTURE THE USER TEST

So you've successfully recruited a handful of target customers and have the first one in the room with the moderator. Now, how do you run the test? First off, it's helpful to prepare a test script that lists what you plan to show and ask the user. This helps you plan ahead to make sure that you cover what you want, that the flow of the test makes sense, and that you manage your time effectively. The test script should identify exactly which design artifacts or parts of the product you plan to show the user, what tasks you plan to ask the user to attempt to accomplish, and what questions you plan to ask the user, all in the desired order.

It can help to conduct a pilot test with a team member first to work out any kinks and become comfortable with the flow, especially if you're nervous about running the test. It can also be helpful to print out the test script (or a shorter outline of it) to have by your side and refer to as you run your tests.

User tests typically run about an hour plus or minus 15 minutes, maybe longer if the user is excited about your product and giving you lots of feedback. I recommend spending the first 10 to 15 minutes of the session warming the user up and conducting discovery about his or her needs and current solution. Then I like to spend about 40 to 45 minutes getting feedback from the user on the product or design artifacts. I close with 5 to 10 minutes of wrap-up, where I answer any questions from the user and ask any closing questions that I have.

It's important to start the user test off on the right foot. It's a good idea to try to spend a minute or two chit-chatting to get to know the person a bit. Building a rapport and making them feel comfortable usually results in the user being more honest with you and giving you more feedback during the test. It's also important to set some expectations. Most people are nice and don't want to say critical things, especially right to your face. They know you are probably on the team that designed or built the product, and they don't want to hurt your feelings. Compensating them for their time can cause a positive bias, too. To help counter all these natural tendencies, it's important to explicitly tell users up front that you want their honest feedback, even if it's negative. Let them know that they won't hurt anyone's feelings. I like to point out that their critical feedback will help make the product better—which is the whole reason for conducting the user test.

During the test, it's important that the user verbalize his or her thoughts so you can hear them. Some people have a natural tendency to do this while others are naturally more quiet and reserved. To help ensure you receive enough feedback, it's a good idea to explicitly encourage the user to share thoughts out loud as they occur (i.e., stream of consciousness) throughout the user test. This is called the *think aloud protocol*. If you find a user who is still quiet after you've given them this guidance, you can try to remind them again.

These tips for the beginning of the user test will help improve your odds of receiving valuable feedback from users, but there's no guarantee. No matter what, some people will not say anything critical about your product, and others just won't say that much. You might find that around 10 percent of users who show up are "duds." If you're not getting good feedback from a significant percentage of your user tests, then you should reevaluate your screener, test script, or moderator—since this is a sign that one or more of these could probably use some improvement.

HOW TO ASK GOOD QUESTIONS

Discovery questions are great for exploring the problem space and your value proposition with customers. You can start by asking them about their current behavior and feelings about the key benefit you plan to provide. For example, if you were Uber, you could start by asking people how frequently they take taxis, what types of trips they take with taxis, and how they find a taxi when they need one. You could also ask them to walk you through the end-to-end details of a recent taxi experience. Then you could ask them what they like and don't like about their experiences with taxis and their overall level of satisfaction. Notice that you haven't even mentioned Uber at this point in the interview. You're just trying to understand the customers' needs, their current solution, what they like and don't like about it, and how satisfied they are. You're trying to discover qualitative information you can use to validate your hypotheses about your target customer and your value proposition. Discovery questions also help warm the user up to the context of your product before you show it to them.

After discovery, you transition to the product feedback portion of the user test. The moderator's job is to solicit the user's feedback on the product in an effective manner without perturbing the results. The top way that moderators perturb the results is by asking leading questions, such as "That form was easy to fill out, wasn't it?" or "So, do you think you would want to click the 'buy' button?" Moderators who ask rhetorical and leading questions like this care more about confirming that the product is good than they do about getting actual, authentic feedback. The point of user testing is not to make ourselves feel good; the point is to get objective feedback from real customers. It's up to the moderator to ensure objectivity. It's understandable that it can be hard to disassociate yourself and remain impartial when you're testing a product you've worked so hard on—but that's what you must strive to do. The best moderators engage the user with the product with as little intervention as possible. They refrain from any commentary, and mainly observe and ask questions.

If a user takes an action on a prototype but doesn't verbalize that they did or why they did, a good moderator might say, "I see you just clicked on that button. Could you tell me why?" You'll notice that instead of just asking the user "why," the moderator started by stating what he observed. Such "echoing back" is a powerful technique to ensure you understand the user and to probe deeper. For example, if the user answered, "I clicked on the button because I was looking for [_____]," the moderator might ask, "Why were you looking for [_____]?" This is reminiscent of the "five whys" technique. Asking a customer "why" too many times can make them feel defensive, so it's a good idea to mix it up with other phrases such as "Could you please tell me more about that?," "Could you please help me understand [_____]?," or "What thoughts were going through your head when you did [_____]?"

It's common for users to ask the moderator questions during the test. For example, a user might ask a moderator, "So, should I click here to log in?" Rather than replying yes or no, a good moderator might ask, "What would you expect to happen if you clicked there?," or might say, "Do whatever you would do if you were by yourself."

Good moderators often use the judo move of answering a question with a question.

ASK OPEN VERSUS CLOSED QUESTIONS

There is a big difference between open and closed questions. Open questions give the customer plenty of latitude in answering. They usually begin with "why," "how," and "what." In contrast, closed questions limit the customer's possible responses (e.g., to yes or no). For example, asking the closed question "Do you select which flight to book based on price?" is not as good as asking "How do you select which flight to book?" Closed questions often start with "do," "did," "is," "are," or "would." Asking open versus closed questions is less a matter of moderator bias and has more to do with the moderator's skill level. In normal conversation, when you're not moderating a user test, closed questions are perfectly fine. But as moderator, you have to be mindful of this. Writing your intended questions in advance in the test script can help. But you also have to be able to focus on asking open-ended questions on the fly as well (e.g., in response to something the user did or said). A helpful technique is to get in the habit of saying your next question in your mind before you verbalize it. That way, if it is a closed question, you can change it to an open-ended question before you pose it to the customer.

Another error to avoid is embedding a preferred or possible answer in your question. This turns what starts off as an open-ended question into a closed question. For example, I could ask a user, "How would you like the application to sort your transactions? By date?" Sometimes, inexperienced moderators can't help but eagerly provide what they think is a likely response. Even if the suggestion wasn't the top reply the user would have told you, he or she may now say yes because you just suggested it. Sometimes this occurs because the moderator doesn't feel comfortable and is attempting to make things "easier" for the user. Long pauses are going to happen; users need time to process what you are showing them and formulate their thoughts. While such periods of silence would feel awkward in a normal conversation, they're totally fine during a user test. You should avoid suggesting an answer and just stop talking after you ask a question to keep it open-ended and give users latitude in how they can answer.

They will often surprise you with things you didn't already know. It's fine (and can be fun) to try to predict how the customer will reply; but keep your predictions in your head and don't verbalize them.

Again, you want to intervene in the test as little as possible. You will have to start by showing the user the particular part of your product or artifact on which you'd like feedback; but once you do this, you should recede into the background. They may look at the first page and then ask you, "So, what should I do?" I like to reply, "Pretend I'm not here. Just do whatever you would do if a friend told you to check out this product and you were by yourself on your computer at home." If the person isn't verbalizing his or her thoughts, you should ask for feedback—for example, "What are your impressions of this page?"

I like to let the user interact with the parts of the product that he or she discovers naturally on his own (again, without moderator intervention). But if you want feedback on a certain part of the product that the user hasn't discovered, then you can ask him or her to navigate there. After doing that, I would again recede into the background.

As the user interacts with the product and makes comments, you should ask probing questions as necessary. For example, if the user comments after filling out a form, "That was complicated," you should follow up by asking, "Could you please tell me why you felt that was complicated?" or saying, "Tell me more about that."

I FEEL YOUR PAIN

If users have difficulty understanding or using your product, it's important not to help them, as painful as that may feel. Your goal is to keep the test as real as possible; you're not going to be able to hold every customer's hand after your product launches, so it's important for the product to stand on its own. You should simply act as though you were a fly on the wall and not break character during the feedback portion. If users complain or ask questions, you should refrain from explaining confusing text or UI to them, telling them what to click on, or grabbing their mouse and doing it for them (yes, I've seen moderators do that). You can let users know that you will address their questions at the end of the test. If the quality or

UX of your product or artifact is so poor that it prevents users from effectively interacting with it on their own, then you should stop doing user tests and solve those problems.

Though it's not very common, I have seen moderators respond to user criticism by getting defensive and trying to argue with the user's opinion—or blaming the user for a test that didn't go well. Such behavior is unproductive and unprofessional. If the user couldn't understand your product, it's clearly your company's fault—not the user's.

WRAPPING UP THE USER TEST

The wrap-up section starts after the feedback portion is over. This is a good time to ask users to reflect on everything they've seen and provide overall impressions and feedback. You may want to ask the user to provide some ratings. For example, you could ask, "On a scale of 0 to 10, with 10 being best, how valuable did you find the product?," or "Based on what you saw today, how likely would you be to use the product?" You could also ask, "How easy to use was the product?" You can ask verbally or you can give the customer a short form to fill out, which may lead to less biased results. I call this "semi-quant" because although you're asking for numerical ratings, the data will be limited to a small sample size. As you iterate and improve your MVP candidate, you should see ratings improve from one wave to the next.

The wrap-up section is also the time to answer any questions that came up during the test or that the customer has at the end. If the user had trouble using the product due to known bugs or issues, you can explain that. This is also when you should give users any compensation for their time and thank them. I usually ask users to sign a form acknowledging receipt of payment. On that form, I will often include prompts for the users to write their email and phone number if they want. I also like to include two yes-no questions: "Would you be willing to participate in future research?" and "Would you like to be notified when this product is available?" These are both meant to be a more honest measure of interest. If a user has nothing but positive feedback during the test and gives your product high ratings but doesn't circle "yes" for those two questions, they were just being nice.

I ran one test where I didn't give users any form at the end. After giving them their checks and thanking them, a high percentage asked me when the product was launching, gave me their contact information, and asked me to please notify them when it launched so that they could buy it. The product had tested well, but this additional evidence of product-market fit was a welcome surprise.

HOW TO CAPTURE AND SYNTHESIZE USER FEEDBACK

As the user goes through the test, you're trying to uncover data that supports or refutes the hypotheses you have made to get to your MVP candidate: your target customers, their underserved needs, the differentiators in your value proposition, and so forth. There are three distinct elements of your product that users will give you feedback on: functionality, UX, and messaging. Feedback on functionality has to do with whether your MVP addresses the right benefits or not. Users may complain that a key feature is missing or tell you that a feature you've included is not important to them. It's important to tie such feedback back to benefits and your value proposition. You may have the right feature set that's addressing the right benefits, but have a poor UX that prevents users from taking full advantage of your feature set. Finally, you may have the right features and UX, but the way you talk about your features, benefits, and differentiators—your messaging—may not resonate with customers. When you receive critical or positive feedback from customers, it can be very helpful to map it to those three high-level categories of functionality, UX, and messaging. Documenting feedback this way after a test allows you to develop a clearer picture of what is and isn't working well.

Let's discuss an illustrative example where we capture user feedback. Table 9.1 shows a summary of feedback from a wave of five user tests. You can see that I've captured the results for each user in a column. I've organized the feedback into separate sections for feature set, UX, and messaging. I've also captured quantitative ratings for value and ease of use that I asked for at the end of each test. Both positive and critical feedback is included, one item per row. I indicate which users gave each item of feedback with a "Y" for yes. This makes it easy to eyeball patterns across users. In the right column, I've calculated overall results for all five users (percentages and median

TABLE 9.1 Tracking Key Results from User Tests

	Vanessa O.	Sofia D.	Xavier G.	John G.	Rich S.	Overall
Feature Set						
+ Thought feature X was valuable and unique	Y	Y		Y	Y	80%
− Complained that feature Y was missing	Y	Y	Y		Y	80%
UX Design						
− Didn't see "sign up" link		Y		Y	Y	60%
− Had difficulty with registration	Y		Y	Y		60%
+ Thought the design looked professional		Y		Y		40%
Messaging						
+ Liked the hero figure on our home page	Y	Y	Y	Y		60%
− Didn't understand our tagline		Y			Y	40%
How valuable? (1–10)	7	7	6	8	7	7 (median)
How easy to use? (1–10)	5	7	5	4	7	5 (median)

ratings). In the interest of simplicity, I'm not including in this table any feedback that fewer than 40 percent of users mentioned.

You can see that in Wave 1, we received positive feedback from customers on feature X, our professional-looking design, and the hero image on our home page. Wave 1 also revealed four issues:

1. 80 percent of users complained that feature Y was missing.
2. 60 percent of users didn't see the "sign up" link.
3. 60 percent of users had difficulty with the registration flow.
4. 40 percent of users didn't understand our tagline.

After we act on this feedback to improve our product and conduct a second wave of user testing, we would expect and hope to see progress toward greater product-market fit in three ways. First, we should hear more positive feedback items from a higher percentage of users, especially those related to our value proposition. Secondly, we should no longer hear the negative feedback that we heard in earlier waves. Remember, the users in your new wave never saw the earlier version of your product. So no new user is going to tell you, "Nice job fixing issue [_____]." Instead, you measure such progress by silence—the absence of hearing complaints you heard in prior waves. The third measure of progress is in your key ratings. You should see user ratings for value and ease of use (and any other key metrics) rise between waves.

USABILITY VERSUS PRODUCT-MARKET FIT

It's crucial as you conduct your user tests to differentiate between feedback on usability versus product-market fit. Feedback on usability has to do with how *easy* it is for customers to understand and use your product, whereas feedback on product-market fit has to do with how *valuable* they find your product. You'll notice at the bottom of Table 9.1 that I included a rating question devoted to each of those two attributes.

You may get a lot of feedback from customers early in the design of your MVP that your UX needs improvement. In that situation, poor usability often prevents users from seeing the full value your product provides. You may discover that you have bugs that get in the way, too. Messaging that doesn't resonate with customers can also be a stumbling block.

As you eliminate those dissatisfiers, the value of your product can better shine through, and you can get a more accurate read of product-market fit. After making many improvements, you may get to the point where users get through your tests easily, without running into any usability issues. However, you should not infer from those results that you have product-market fit. You need to explicitly assess product-market fit by asking how much they value your product.

I experienced this firsthand working on a product that provided users with real-time news tailored to their interests. In the first wave of tests on our rough live product MVP, users provided feedback on lots of usability issues. We also discovered a few bugs and some unclear messaging in the tests, too. After we fixed those issues, we heard a smaller number of issues in the second wave, which we also fixed. In the third wave, the user tests starting going much better. Most users sailed through the test with no problems, which made me excited about our progress.

I started asking users at the end of each test how likely they would be to use our product. Even though the tests went well, around 20 percent of users said they wouldn't use it. This result surprised me, mainly because the tests had gone well and hadn't garnered much negative feedback. Also, most of the customers with whom we tested expressed a certain amount of interest in a personalized news product, so I felt that they fit our target customer profile well enough. I then asked the 20 percent why they wouldn't use our product, and I learned that a segment of users have a strong preference for getting their news a certain way. This was a great, unexpected insight, which led me to start asking people how they preferred to get their news during the discovery questions at the beginning of my interviews. I discovered that there were three very different ways that people preferred to get their news—and our product approach had been designed to most resonate with *one* of those ways. Learning this helped us make more sense of the market. Online news is a mainstream consumer product with a large audience, so it seems natural that the market would contain different segments with distinct preferences. The team agreed that a design that tried to address all three different ways would be schizophrenic and not make any of the three types of users happy. So we used what we learned to refine our target customer definition.

This example shows how usability issues can prevent you from assessing product-market fit and how great usability does not mean you have strong product-market fit. It also shows how user testing can help you validate and refine your hypotheses (in this case, who your target customer is).

User testing is a powerful tool in the Lean toolkit. Done well, you can get very valuable feedback on your hypotheses at multiple levels of the Product-Market Fit Pyramid: underserved needs, value proposition, MVP feature set, and UX. However, it's important to note that user testing is inherently based on the assumption that you are talking with the right type of customer. It's very important that you ensure that the customers with whom you are talking are in your target market. You can do a great job defining your value proposition and MVP feature set, design an amazing set of clickable wireframes, and run your tests perfectly. However, if you are talking to the wrong type of customer, you will not get the data you need. In fact, you may get *bad* data that is very different from what your target customers would have told you. Iterating your MVP based on data from the wrong type of customer can send you in the wrong direction—heading off a cliff instead of toward the Promised Land of product-market fit.

If your user tests are showing that you don't have product-market fit once you get past any major usability issues, you might need to revisit your hypotheses about your value proposition, MVP, or UX design. But it could be the case that you need to revisit your hypotheses about your target customer, so keep an open mind to that possibility.

In the next chapter, I discuss how to use the data you capture from user testing to improve your MVP candidate and how to use rapid iteration to achieve product-market fit.

Chapter 10

Iterate and Pivot to Improve Product-Market Fit

I explained in the previous chapter how to conduct a wave of user tests to assess your MVP's product-market fit. This chapter is about what to do after you complete each round of testing. Lean is about learning and iterating quickly. This means that you want to use what you have learned after you receive a round of feedback to modify your hypotheses and your MVP so that you can test them with customers again. You want to iterate quickly from one round of user testing to the next with the goal of improving product-market fit each time. This chapter will walk you through how to do that.

THE BUILD-MEASURE-LEARN LOOP

Eric Ries discusses the above concept of iterative learning in his book *The Lean Startup* (The Lean Startup is a registered trademark of Eric Ries). His "build-measure-learn" loop has helped many people understand the importance of iteration and validated learning. But based on my observations of how some people talk about and try to apply the loop, there are some nuances worth discussing.

It's important to clarify that "build" doesn't mean that you have to actually build a product. Creating a set of clickable wireframes that you test with users is perfectly acceptable. "Build" simply means having something that you can test with customers, which could be a live product or design artifacts, such as wireframes or mockups. "Design something to test" is a broader, more accurate description, so I prefer the label "design" for this step. The goal is to identify and create what will let you test your hypotheses while consuming the least resources.

"Measure" implies numerical data—but keep in mind that "measure" doesn't have to be as quantitative as it sounds. Many people have a bias for trying to prove things with quantitative data. I agree that's nice when you can do it, but A/B testing is not the only way to test hypotheses or gain learning. All information you gain by observing customers falls under "measure." Even though they aren't statistically significant, the results of qualitative testing fit into "measure," too. The key point is that you are testing your hypotheses with customers. Therefore, "test" would be a broader and more accurate label for this step.

The "learn" step is interesting. There are actually two things going on in this step. First, you are learning new things from the results of each test. Second, you use what you learn to modify the hypotheses that led to the test you just ran. It makes things clearer to split "learn" into two distinct steps: "learn" and "hypothesize." In fact, if you think about it, this whole process doesn't start with "build"—it starts with some initial hypotheses. How else would you have a basis for deciding what to build?

THE HYPOTHESIZE-DESIGN-TEST-LEARN LOOP

For the above reasons, I use a modified version of the build-measure-learn loop that I call the hypothesize-design-test-learn loop—shown in Figure 10.1.

As you go through this loop, you transition from problem space to solution space and back again. You start with the "hypothesize" step, where you formulate your problem space hypotheses. In the "design" step, you identify the best way to test your hypotheses. Creating a design artifact or product based on your hypotheses takes us from the problem space to the solution space. In the "test" step, you expose your product or artifact to customers and make observations, which lead to validated learning (the "learn" step). You complete the loop by using this validated learning to revise and improve your hypotheses. These revised hypotheses will inform your next iteration through the loop. To summarize: you test and improve your problem space thinking by showing customers a product or design artifact in the solution space and soliciting their feedback on it.

The more quickly you can learn, the more quickly you can deliver additional customer value and improve your product-market fit. But learning is just one of the steps in the process. In order to gain additional learning, you have to go around the entire loop again.

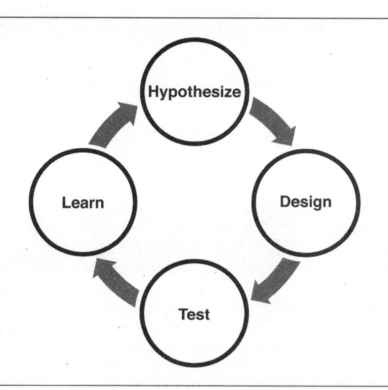

FIGURE 10.1   The Hypothesize-Design-Test-Learn Loop

If you think of the loop as the Monopoly game board, "learn" is the "Go" square that you pass each time around. In the game, you earn $200 for passing "Go"; in the Lean Product Process, you earn validated learning. The "learn" and "hypothesize" steps tend to be fairly quick, so your speed through the loop is usually governed by how quickly you can design and test.

As you validate and invalidate your hypotheses and form new ones, you should refer to the Product-Market Fit Pyramid, shown again in Figure 10.2. For each hypothesis, you should identify to which layer of the pyramid it corresponds. Each layer builds on top of the layer of hypotheses below it. It's easier to make changes near the top of the pyramid, but changing hypotheses near the bottom can have significant ramifications for higher layers. For example, having to change a page's UX design to make it more usable is relatively minor. Let's say instead that your value proposition presumed that a certain customer benefit wasn't important, but you learn from users that it actually is. You will now need to modify your value proposition, which will

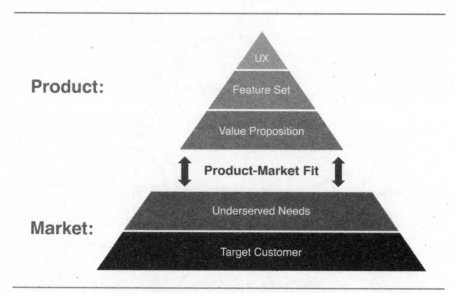

FIGURE 10.2   The Product-Market Fit Pyramid

impact your MVP feature set, and your UX design. This is why you want to focus on addressing the issues at the lowest level first as you process what you learn in your user testing. Once you validate that you have eliminated those issues, you can then focus on addressing issues at the next higher level.

ITERATIVE USER TESTING

As I discussed in Chapter 9, each user test is going to give you valuable information about your MVP. It is helpful to debrief each test with the product team soon afterward to share observations and synthesize the learning. I recommend using a table like Table 9.1 to capture key observations from each wave of user testing.

At the end of each testing wave, you want to look across all the users to see how many gave the same feedback, either positive or negative, which you can express as a percentage. Those percentages should help you prioritize the changes you make to your MVP. If all or most of the users in the wave raised an issue, then addressing it should be higher priority. If only one or two users mentioned an item, it can be lower priority. You should identify which items you plan to address before the next testing round.

Wave 1

Let's continue with the example that was introduced in Chapter 9. First, we're going to summarize the test results from those five users in Wave 1 into a single column. See the Wave 1 column in Table 10.1. You'll notice that I removed the positive feedback, in order to keep the example simple. We discovered four issues in Wave 1:

1. 80 percent of users complained that feature Y was missing.
2. 60 percent of users didn't see the "sign up" link.
3. 60 percent of users had difficulty with the registration flow.
4. 40 percent of users didn't understand our tagline.

Let's go through each of the issues from Wave 1. The fact that feature Y is missing is an MVP feature-set issue. In this case, it turns out that we had considered feature Y, thought it was valuable, and

TABLE 10.1   Tracking Results across Multiple Waves of User Testing

	Wave 1	Wave 2	Wave 3	Wave 4
Feature Set				
− Complained that feature Y was missing	80%	0%	0%	0%
− Said features X and Y should work together	N/A	80%	0%	0%
UX Design				
− Didn't see "sign up" link	60%	0%	0%	0%
− Had difficulty with registration flow	60%	40%	0%	0%
+ Thought that feature Y was hard to use	N/A	80%	40%	0%
Messaging				
− Didn't understand our tagline	40%	0%	0%	0%
How valuable? (1–10, median)	7	8	9	9
How easy to use? (1–10, median)	5	6	7	9

planned to build it later, but didn't think it was critical to include in our MVP. Now that we have learned from customers that they need it, we decide to add it to our MVP. Our designer comes up with a design for feature Y and we add it to our design artifacts.

The fact that users cannot see the "sign up" link is a visual design issue. To address this, our visual designer puts the link in a more prominent position, makes it bigger, and renders it as a button using a color that pops on the screen. She updates our design artifacts accordingly.

Difficulty with the registration flow is an interaction design issue. Our interaction designer addresses the problems that users experienced by coming up with a revised registration flow and updating our design artifacts.

The fact that a large percentage of customers didn't understand our tagline is a messaging issue. It turns out that the specific wording we used didn't convey the meaning we had intended. As a result, the tagline didn't effectively communicate what we view as our differentiating customer benefit. We brainstorm alternative taglines, identify our new favorite, and update our design artifacts accordingly.

Wave 2

Now that we have addressed the four issues we saw in Wave 1, we are ready to test again with a new wave of users. We test our new wireframes with five more users and see the results shown in the Wave 2 column of Table 10.1. After adding feature Y, we see that none of the new users complained about it missing, so that represents progress. We also see that all five users in Wave 2 saw the "sign up" link now, which is a big improvement.

However, 40 percent of users are still complaining that the registration flow was difficult, even though we redesigned it. This happens. The first time you revise your product based on customer feedback, you don't always get it perfect. In the Wave 2 tests, we saw that users no longer encountered some of the specific UX problems that were experienced in Wave 1. But our fix for one of the previous UX issues didn't work as well as we thought it would. Plus, we saw minor issues with some of the new design elements. Given these results, we decide to have a cross-functional team meeting to share the issues we are still seeing with the registration flow, brainstorm possible solutions, and identify the best ones. We come up with a new version of the flow that we think should be much easier and incorporate it into a new version of our design artifacts.

We also see that our new tagline didn't have the issues that we saw in Wave 1, so we are excited by that result. It's great to see an issue go from a high percentage in one wave to zero percent in the next wave after making a fix based on what we learned. That usually means you have adequately addressed that issue and can focus on others.

After you eliminate an issue, you may discover new issues with your updated MVP. Case in point, our Wave 2 customers were happy that our MVP had feature Y, but 80 percent of them felt that this feature was hard to use. We discuss the detailed usability problems we saw users experience, come up with an improved design for feature Y, and update our design artifacts accordingly.

We were also surprised to learn from 80 percent of customers that they want feature Y to work with feature X—since we had added feature Y as a new, standalone feature. In hindsight, what we learned from users about how the two features should work together makes a lot of sense and makes both features more useful. We revise the designs of the two features and update our design artifacts.

We should see the magnitude and number of issues decrease as we iterate. In this case when going from Wave 1 to Wave 2 we successfully addressed three issues (feature Y, "sign up" link, and tagline). We tried but were unsuccessful in solving the registration flow issue. And we discovered two new issues: Feature Y is hard to use, and it should work with feature X.

We should also see our overall ratings improve as we iterate. In this case, we can see that our value rating increased from 7 to 8—most likely due to the addition of feature Y. And our ease-of-use rating increased from 5 to 6, likely as a result of the improved "sign up" link and our partial improvement to the registration flow.

Wave 3

Given what we learned from Wave 2 and our updated design artifacts, we're ready for Wave 3. We conduct tests with another five customers and get the results shown in the Wave 3 column in Table 10.1.

We didn't get any complaints about features X and Y not working together, so we accomplished our mission on that front. We see that after our second attempt to redesign the registration flow, all five users got through it without complaining about it being difficult—which shows we made significant progress. Even though we redesigned feature Y, 40 percent of users still thought it was hard to use. That's down from 80 percent, which is good; but we still have some work to do since it is such an important feature.

As a result of our product improvements, our value rating increased to 9, and our ease of use rating improved to 7. We've made good progress since our initial MVP. We're no longer getting major feedback on missing functionality. Our messaging seems solid. We're mainly getting feedback on the need to improve our UX design, which is common early in the life of a product. I've kept my example simple by using only a small number of major feedback items. When we test with users, we will also receive a large number of minor feedback items. We can and should incorporate improvements to address those as well. We should see our product-market fit improving as we iterate through the hypothesize-design-test-learn loop.

Wave 4

We decide at this point to further improve the design of feature Y to make it easier to use and conduct a fourth wave of testing. We see in the Wave 4 column of Table 10.1 that no one complained about feature Y being hard to use in that wave. And we didn't discover any new major issues. Our value rating stayed at 9 and our ease-of-use rating improved to 9.

At this point, we should feel good enough about our MVP design to proceed to the next step in our product process. If the artifacts we tested with users were high fidelity (e.g., clickable mockups on InVision), we would proceed to building our MVP. If the artifacts we tested were low fidelity (e.g., clickable wireframes), we could proceed to clickable mockups. In certain cases, we might choose to skip high fidelity design and go straight to coding if we felt really confident about our design and didn't think there would be much risk from skipping user testing after visual design. This could be the case if we were adding new functionality to an existing product and already had a visual style guide that we could easily apply.

There is no hard-and-fast rule to determine when you've validated your MVP "enough." There certainly is a risk of continuing to test past the point where it is of much value. You want to avoid analysis paralysis. Conversely, you can launch before you've validated enough, which can result in the need for painful rework on the design and coding fronts. So you want to try to strike the right balance. At some point, though, your baby bird needs to leave the nest; that is, you need to stop testing design artifacts and build your MVP. This is an exciting transition. It puts you that much closer to delivering real customer value with a live product, and also enables the next level of testing your product with customers.

Testing with design artifacts is valuable to validate your assumptions and ensure that you're achieving product-market fit. Testing with a live product is even better. When you test artifacts, customers are telling you what they would do if the product were live. But what customers say they will do and what they actually do can be quite different—and actual customer behavior trumps customer opinions any day. In addition, your live product is the highest fidelity possible. Lower fidelity artifacts may lack some of the details that your final product contains. Or deviations from the design artifacts may have been introduced in the process of building your product.

Once you build your live product, it's best to conduct another wave of tests to see where you stand. Hopefully you measure the same or a higher level of product-market fit from your last wave of tests with design artifacts. If not, you should iterate through the hypothesize-design-test-learn loop with your live product until you do. Many companies use a private beta for this phase, so that only a limited number of customers can see the product until it is ready for prime time.

PERSEVERE OR PIVOT?

I've painted a pretty rosy picture. Sure, it takes several waves of iteration and hard work, but you'll get to product-market fit eventually, right? Unfortunately, many teams don't have that experience. When they test with users, they don't get glowing feedback. They try to iterate, but don't make progress with customers. They feel like they've hit a brick wall.

Several things can go wrong along the path I've described. One or more of your hypotheses may be incorrect. Or even if your hypotheses are correct, your execution in designing, building, or marketing your product may fall short. If you find that you are not making progress as you try to iterate, I recommend you pause and take a step back. Brainstorm with your team about what all the possible problems could be. Map each problem back to the corresponding layer of the Product-Market Fit Pyramid in Figure 10.2. You may find that you are iterating at a higher level than where the true problem lies. For example, if your hypothesis about your target customer is wrong, iterating your UX design won't make much difference. You want to start at the bottom of the pyramid and work your way up until you identify which of your hypotheses are incorrect.

When you change one of your main hypotheses, it's called a *pivot*. A pivot is larger in magnitude than the change you normally see as you iterate along the path you have chosen; it means a significant change in direction. For example, switching to a completely different target customer would be a pivot. Deciding to change the differentiators in your value proposition would be a pivot. Making tweaks to your UX design is not a pivot.

There are many examples of successful pivots. Photo-sharing site Flickr began as "Game Neverending," a web-based massively multiplayer online role-playing game focused on social interaction. After the company added a tool that made it easy to share photos on web pages, they saw how much customers loved using it. The company pivoted and launched photo application Flickr in February 2004, which experienced incredible growth and was acquired by Yahoo! in March 2005.

Photo-sharing app Instagram began as "Burbn," an HTML 5 social app that combined elements from check-in app Foursquare and the game Mafia Wars. After reimplementing Burbn as a native iPhone app, the cofounders felt it was cluttered with too many features. They decided to build a new app from scratch, cutting everything except for the photo, comment, and like capabilities. They launched Instagram in October 2010, which experienced tremendous growth and was acquired by Facebook for approximately $1 billion in April 2012.

One of the hardest parts of the Lean Product Process can be deciding whether to persevere with the opportunity you are pursuing, pivot to a new opportunity, or stop altogether. Let's get that last one out of the way first. You don't have all the time in the world to achieve product-market fit—resource constraints usually limit how much time you have. In a startup setting, you have to rely on external funding from investors before you are profitable. If you don't achieve product-market fit or make significant progress toward that goal, it can be challenging to raise the next round of investment. Even new product efforts within a successful company have fixed budgets as well as timeframe expectations for making progress.

I've seen some startups that always seem to be pivoting. You shouldn't change direction every time you hit a rough patch, nor should you drop what you're doing to chase each cool new idea you come up with, also known as shiny object syndrome. I like to joke that if you've pivoted three times, you're heading in the opposite direction from where you started. At the other extreme are people who stubbornly keep banging their head against the wall and don't take a step back to reevaluate.

So how do you decide whether to persevere or pivot if you still have cash in the bank and time on the clock? You should consider pivoting if you just don't seem to be achieving gains in product-market fit after several rounds of trying to iterate. If, despite your best efforts, your target customers are only lukewarm on your MVP, you should consider a pivot. Said another way, if you haven't yet identified a customer archetype that is very excited about your MVP, then you should consider pivoting.

Sometimes the best way to pivot becomes relatively clear from your tests. For example, you might find that a less central part of your value proposition is what most resonates with customers. In this case, you should trim the rest and focus your efforts on that part. Or you may discover your target market consists of distinct submarkets and learn that one of those submarkets really loves some aspect of your value proposition.

Figure 10.3 uses a mountain climbing analogy to explain product-market fit and pivoting. You start out at the bottom of the first mountain, which represents the market opportunity you are pursuing based on your target market and value proposition hypotheses. The higher

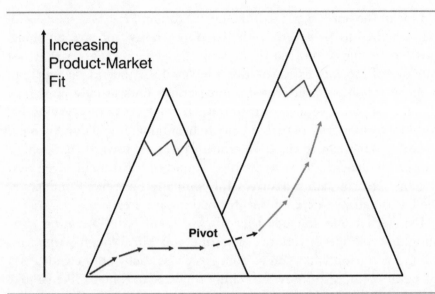

Increasing Product-Market Fit

Pivot

FIGURE 10.3   Pivoting to Achieve Higher Product-Market Fit

you climb, the stronger your product-market fit. After your first wave of testing, you learn a lot and improve your product. You see in your second wave that you have improved product-market fit; but you get much smaller gains in your next wave. Your product is better than when you started, but you haven't managed to reach a high enough level of product-market fit. You try different things in your next two waves but can't seem to make any progress.

In the process of user testing, you discover an adjacent market opportunity represented by the second mountain. This second mountain is taller than the first because the amount of market value that can potentially be created is greater. You decide to revise your hypotheses and pivot to pursue this new market opportunity. You iterate through the hypothesize-design-test-learn loop and find that you are able to improve your product-market fit, reaching much higher heights.

This analogy serves as a reminder to pay attention to how high up the mountain you are climbing (your level of product-market fit) as you iterate. Try to measure your rate of ascent (improvement in product-market fit) after each wave of user testing. If it feels like you are not making much progress, try to find other paths up the mountain (revisit and revise your hypotheses). If, after doing that, you're still not making decent progress, stop to reconsider the mountain you're on (your hypotheses about your target customer and value proposition) and look around for other mountains that might be easier to climb (other market opportunities). Pick your new mountain (pivot) and try to climb up that one (iterate to greater product-market fit).

Before concluding Part II of this book, I want to walk you through the details of a real-world example where I applied the Lean Product Process, which I share in the next chapter. In that example, I pivoted from one mountain to another after the first wave of user testing. I will walk you through my decision to pivot and show how pivoting resulted in much higher product-market fit.

Chapter 11

An End-to-End Lean Product Case Study

Now that I've described each of the six steps of the Lean Product Process in detail, I want to walk through a real-world case study to further solidify the concepts I've covered. I've shared this example in talks and workshops that I've given, and many participants have told me how helpful it is to see the application of the Lean Product Process with an end-to-end example.

MARKETINGREPORT.COM

One of my clients asked me to help define and evaluate a new product called MarketingReport.com. This client's company had a successful consumer web service and was contemplating a new web service to pursue a potential market opportunity. I worked closely with two company executives and a UX designer on this project.

The new service idea centered on a widespread customer problem associated with direct mail—namely, that many people who receive direct mail do not find it valuable and consider it a nuisance. The executives had some insight into the direct mail industry and knew that the mailings were targeted based on marketing databases that profiled customers. For example, you might receive an unsolicited coupon for cat litter from a certain pet store chain because a marketing database somewhere indicates that you have (or are likely to have) a cat in your household.

The idea was to solve this problem by providing a product that gave customers transparency into the profile that marketers had built of them and empower them to make that profile more accurate. So, if I don't own a cat but own a dog, I could correct the marketing databases so that I receive coupons for dog food instead of cat litter. The executives saw parallels with the credit industry.

Every day, thousands of credit-related decisions are made based on people's credit scores. Before the advent of credit reporting services, consumers didn't have much visibility into why they had the score they did; their credit worthiness was based on "behind the scenes" data about their credit history. They might therefore get declined for a loan and not know exactly why. Inaccurate data about their past payments—such as a loan payment reported as unpaid that actually wasn't—could negatively impact them. By providing transparency, credit-reporting services enable customers to see the data behind their credit rating and correct any inaccuracies. MarketingReport.com would do for personal marketing data what credit reports had done for personal credit data.

The initial idea was to provide the service for free and to monetize the marketing data that the service generated. By giving customers access to the data, and the ability to correct inaccuracies and provide additional information, we planned to build a collection of rich and accurate profiles. Therefore, it was critical to define a service with which customers would *want* to engage.

STEP 1: DETERMINE YOUR TARGET CUSTOMERS

You'll recall that Step 1 of the Lean Product Process is to identify your target customer. We agreed at this early point that this would be a mainstream consumer offering. Steps 1 (target customers) and 2 (customer needs) are closely related, so we didn't narrow our target market hypothesis any further than mainstream consumers at this point. We knew we would refine our target customer hypothesis as we gained additional clarity about the customer benefits we could deliver.

STEP 2: IDENTIFY UNDERSERVED NEEDS

We then started working on Step 2: identifying underserved customer needs. Both executives agreed that the service's core benefit was empowering customers to find out what "they" (the direct marketing databases) know about the customer. However, there were a lot of different ideas for what the service would do beyond that core benefit. So we brainstormed a long list of different potential customer benefits that our service could deliver, which included these five ideas:

1. Discover money-saving offers of interest to me
2. Reduce the amount of irrelevant junk mail I receive
3. Gain insights into my spending behavior
4. Meet and interact with other people with similar shopping preferences
5. Earn money by giving permission to sell my marketing-related data

To identify which customer benefits we wanted to pursue, we came up with a set of evaluation criteria, some of which were positive and others negative. We evaluated each benefit on the following criteria:

- Strength of user demand (+)
- Value of marketing data obtained (+)
- Degree of competition (−)
- Effort to build the v1 product (−)
- Effort to scale the concept (−)
- Fit with the company's brand (+)
- Amount of reliance on partners that would be required (−)

We scored each customer benefit on these criteria based on our estimates, which allowed us to weed out less appealing ideas. Customer benefits 1 through 4 from the above list were considered worth further consideration.

STEP 3: DEFINE YOUR VALUE PROPOSITION

At this point, I wanted to nail down which benefits were in scope versus out of scope for our envisioned product so we could solidify our value proposition. So I led the executives in an exercise to map out the problem space for our product, shown in Figure 11.1.

You can see that I grouped related benefits together. We had our core benefit of finding out what "they" know about me (in the middle). A second cluster of benefits (at the top) included reducing junk mail and saving trees (being friendly to the environment). A third cluster of benefits (at the bottom) included saving money on

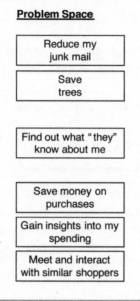

FIGURE 11.1   Initial Value Proposition for MarketingReport.com

purchases, gaining insights into my spending, and interacting with similar shoppers.

I felt that the three clusters on this problem space map were too much to bite off in a single product. Plus, it wouldn't feel coherent if we tried to build one service that addressed all these benefits; the top cluster and bottom cluster were very different. Additionally, while one executive liked the top cluster of benefits more, the other preferred the bottom cluster. I thought they were all good ideas, so I recommended that we pursue two distinct product concepts, each with its own value proposition. The first concept, dubbed "Marketing Shield," would consist of the top two clusters. The second concept, dubbed "Marketing Saver," would consist of the bottom two clusters. By using this approach, each concept included the core benefit of "find out what 'they' know about me" but wasn't too broad in scope. The executives agreed.

In Chapter 5, I recommend that you articulate your product value proposition using the Kano model to classify each benefit as a must-have, performance benefit, or delighter, while taking your competition into account. We viewed the core benefit of "find out what 'they' know about you" as a delighter because this type of service didn't exist. We knew that there were other products in the market that gave customers money-saving offers; so we viewed that as a performance benefit. Similarly, although social networking products existed, they weren't necessarily focused on shopping; so we viewed that as a performance benefit as well. We weren't aware of other products that let you compare yourself financially to others, so we viewed that as a delighter. On the Shield front, we viewed reducing junk mail as a delighter. There were plenty of other ways to be environmentally friendly, so we viewed "save trees" as a performance benefit.

STEP 4: SPECIFY YOUR MVP FEATURE SET

Now that we had the value proposition for each of our two concepts, we started talking about the solution space and brainstormed features that would deliver those benefits. See Figure 11.2 for the features that we settled on for each product concept.

The main feature for the core benefit of "find out what 'they' know about me" was a marketing report containing a collection of marketing-related information about the user built over time. The report originates from data about a customer's purchases and their responses to surveys, mailings, and phone calls. The idea was to provide customers with transparency into the data that the marketing databases contained about them.

Two key components we envisioned for the marketing report were the marketing profile and the marketing score. The profile was based on a set of consumer segmentation clusters used by direct marketing firms. Each cluster has a catchy, descriptive name—like "young digerati," "soccer and SUVs," or "rural retirees"—and is based on key demographic data such as age, marital status, home ownership, children, and zip code. Marketers use these profiles to target relevant offers to people.

We were inventing the idea of a marketing score from scratch. It was intended to be analogous to a credit score—a single number that represents your overall credit worthiness. In the same way, the marketing score was a single number that represented your overall

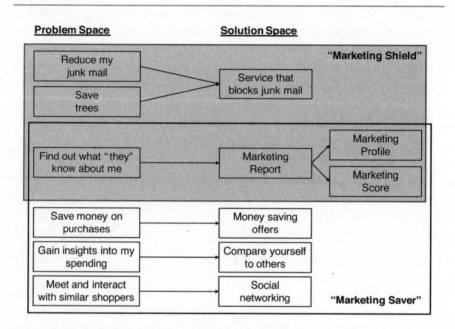

FIGURE 11.2 Features for Marketing Shield and Marketing Saver

attractiveness to marketers. A higher credit score garners you a better interest rate; a higher marketing score would garner more and better money-saving offers. We identified several factors that would go into determining a customer's marketing score.

Turning to the bottom cluster, the main benefit was money-saving offers. The idea was that the customer could identify what types of products and services interested them and would then receive relevant money-saving offers. We would basically be playing matchmaker between consumers and companies who wanted to promote their products. The feature would consist of a user interface where the customer could specify their preferences, a marketplace of vendors, matchmaking logic, and delivery of the offers via the website and email.

The second feature in the bottom cluster was comparing yourself to others. The idea was that customers could compare their spending patterns with similar customers to see if they are spending more or less on certain areas such as dining, clothing, entertainment, and so forth. Gaining this insight would allow them to modify their spending behavior as they saw fit.

The third feature in the bottom cluster was the ability to interact with similar shoppers. The idea was that customers might discover new products or learn about great deals from similar shoppers. Social networking was relatively hot at the time and we wanted to experiment with some social functionality related to online shopping.

The feature in the top cluster was a service that would block junk mail. This addressed both the "suppress junk mail" and "save trees" benefits. The idea was that we would start out with a "Wizard of Oz" MVP by manually filling out and submitting "do not mail" requests on behalf of customers. We would eventually transition to a more automated solution if warranted.

STEP 5: CREATE YOUR MVP PROTOTYPE

With our feature set defined, it was time to move on to Step 5 to bring these features to life with some design artifacts. We knew that we wanted to test design artifacts with customers in person before we did any coding, so we decided to go with medium fidelity mockups. The mockups had enough visual design—coloring, fonts, graphics, and styling—to effectively represent the product to users, but we didn't worry about making them pixel perfect.

We started by thinking through and defining the product's structure (information architecture) and the flow of the customer experience (interaction design). The customer would start by receiving an email describing the service. The email's call to action was "see your marketing report" with a link to a landing page, which further described the service and had a key conversion button labeled "see report." Each customer was assigned a unique code that was included in the email. After clicking the "see report" button, the customers were taken to the "verify information" page. This page contained a form listing their name, address, marital status, household income range, and other key demographic information. This page showed customers the information contained in marketing databases and allowed them to correct any inaccurate information. After clicking the "continue" button on this page, they were taken to the Marketing Report page.

The Marketing Report page was the main page of the product after going through the onboarding flow. It was a dashboard of modules that enabled us to use the same general design for the two product concepts by just swapping out different modules for the "Marketing Shield" versus the "Marketing Saver." For both product concepts, the Marketing Report dashboard included modules for the Marketing Profile and the Marketing Score, since these were the core feature ideas. The remaining modules would vary by concept. The Marketing Shield version had a "block junk mail" module. The Marketing Saver version had modules that covered money-saving offers, comparing yourself to others, and social networking.

The Marketing Report page was the hub from which customers would navigate. They could click on each module to drill down to a more specific page dedicated to that topic. For example, the page dedicated to money-saving offers allowed the customer to select which types of products and services were of interest to them, such as vacations, electronics, and so forth. The page dedicated to "block junk mail" displayed a list of different categories of direct mail and allowed users to select which ones they no longer wanted to receive. That page also included an upsell offer to "Marketing Shield Premium," a paid service that would further reduce the amount of junk mail you received and provide greater privacy for your marketing profile data. With the exception of this upgraded offering, the "Marketing Saver" and "Marketing Shield" services were intended to be free to customers.

STEP 6: TEST YOUR MVP WITH CUSTOMERS

With our mockups done, it was time to proceed to Step 6: testing with customers. At this point, we needed to revisit and refine our target customer definition before we started recruiting. Since we had two distinct MVPs, each with its own value proposition, we had to define the target customer for each. The target customers for the Marketing Shield remained mainstream consumers, but we refined our definition to be people who highly valued their privacy. The target customers for the Marketing Saver also remained mainstream consumers, but we refined our definition to be people who place a lot of value on saving money on their purchases and getting good deals.

Recruiting Customers in our Target Market

We decided to use in-person moderated testing, and I moderated the sessions. In the interest of collecting data more quickly, I spoke with two or three customers at a time instead of one-on-one. I selected a local research firm to recruit customers for us, and they used a screener that I created to qualify customers. Let's walk through the screener questions I used and the rationale behind them.

First off, I wanted the research subjects to be employed full-time (at least 30 hours per week) to ensure that they were in our target market. Many unemployed or retired people participate in market research because they have ample free time, but they wouldn't necessarily be representative of our target market. I required at least a high school diploma and recruited a balance of education levels, consistent with our mainstream audience. I also recruited for a mix of household incomes with a minimum of $40,000. They also had to have a computer in their household and use the Internet a minimum number of hours per week (since our service was going to be delivered via the web). We also wanted to make sure they had recently purchased a product on the Internet (so that they would be comfortable paying online for our service). I viewed all those requirements as ensuring the person was a mainstream, working adult in the target market for web-based services.

Next, I had to decide how to ensure the person was in the target market for the particular concept (Saver or Shield). I decided to use past behavior as an indicator for fit with our two target markets. Since the distinct benefit of Marketing Saver was saving money, for that group I asked about several different money-saving behaviors:

- Have you used three or more coupons in the past three months?
- Are you a Costco member?
- Have you made a purchase on eBay in the past six months?
- When making purchases, do you usually or always spend time researching to make sure you've found the lowest price?

The respondent earned one Saver point for each "yes" response. We considered anyone with two or more Saver points to be in the Saver target market.

Similarly, since Marketing Shield was about privacy and security, I asked that group about several behaviors related to those topics:

- Have you ever asked to be put on the "do not call" list?
- Do you have caller ID blocking?
- Do you own a paper shredder at home?
- Have you paid for antivirus software in the past six months?

Respondents earned one Shield point for each "yes" response—and we considered anyone with two or more Shield points to be in the Shield target market.

We did not select respondents that failed to qualify for either of the two segments. A small number of respondents qualified for both segments, since the criteria were not mutually exclusive (i.e., it is possible to care about saving money *and* about privacy).

Once respondents qualified for the research, we also asked them for their address, age, marital status, number of children, home ownership, household income, education level, occupation, and ethnicity. We used this information to create a personalized version of the "verify information" page mockup for each customer. We also used this information to tailor each customer's Marketing Profile to the matching segmentation cluster. This personalization of the mockups allowed us to develop a much more realistic experience for customers in our tests than we'd be able to do using a generic page and asking them to use their imagination. In fact, most customers expressed surprise when they first saw this page: They asked, "How did you get all this information?" We successfully provoked the realization in customers that "they" (the marketing databases) *really do* know a lot about you, which was the core value proposition for Marketing Report.com.

We worked out the days and times when we would hold research sessions. Since we were talking to people who worked full-time, we selected times later in the day after working hours (6 and 8 P.M.) to better accommodate their schedules. One common mistake companies make is to force research sessions during *their* working hours for *their* convenience. If it's not a problem for your target customers to meet at that time, that's fine. But meeting during the workday is inconvenient for most working adults. As a result, you can skew the type of customers who show up to your research to the point of not being truly representative of your target customers.

To make scheduling more efficient, we asked respondents when we screened them to let us know all of the session times that they would be able to attend. Once we had all this info for all the respondents, scheduling them later to fill all our time slots was easy. The research firm successfully recruited customers for all our slots.

User Testing Script

While the recruiting was taking place, I created the script I planned to use in moderating the user testing. Each session was 90 minutes long. Here is the high-level outline of my user testing script showing the time allocation:

1. Introductions and warm-up (5 minutes)
2. General discovery questions (15 minutes)
   a. Direct marketing mail
   b. The data about you that companies have
   c. Comparing yourself to others financially
3. Concept-specific questions (45 minutes total)
   a. Discovery questions related to concept's main theme (10 minutes)
   b. Feedback on concept mockups (35 minutes)
4. Review: What did you most like/dislike about what you saw? (5 minutes)
5. Brainstorm: What would make the product more useful/valuable? (10 minutes)
6. Feedback on possible product names (10 minutes)
7. Thanks and goodbye

To test out my script and our mockups, I ran a pilot user test first with someone from the company before the first session with real customers. Based on the pilot test, we made some tweaks to my questions and to the mockups. Then we were ready to go!

On each of three evenings, I moderated two sessions with three customers scheduled for each. Half the sessions were for Marketing Saver and half were for Marketing Shield, so nine customers were scheduled for each concept. We ended up having two no-shows, so we spoke with eight customers for each concept. As I mentioned, we personalized the data in the mockups for each customer. Because this was before the days of clickable mockups, I printed out each mockup—one per page. I put them in a stack in front of each customer in the order that they would be seen. I followed my script, and as the customers navigated through the mockups, I flipped the pages.

What We Learned from Customers

The sessions went well. The customers were engaged and articulate. We received a lot of great feedback—in fact, so much that I typed eight pages of notes to capture everything we learned. The bottom line is that neither concept was appealing enough to customers. However, there were a few rays of sunshine that managed to poke through the clouds.

The core part of the value proposition in both concepts—"find out what 'they' know about me"—only had limited appeal. Customers found the Marketing Report and Marketing Profile somewhat interesting, but not compelling. Most of them found the Marketing Score confusing and it had low appeal.

The features for comparing oneself to others and social networking in the Saver concept had low appeal with customers. However, customers did like money-saving offers (one of our rays of sunshine). This was the most appealing part of the Saver concept. The idea of reducing junk mail had strong appeal in the Shield concept, as did the idea of saving trees as a secondary benefit. I should clarify that "strong appeal" was still far from a slam dunk. Customers had plenty of questions and concerns about what we showed them. However, I was confident we could use what we learned to avoid those concerns and make the next revision even stronger. I could tell there was enough latent interest in those benefits.

After the research, I took the map of our problem and solution spaces—originally shown in Figure 11.2—and colored each box green, yellow, or red for strong, some, or low appeal. When I looked at the results, I saw two separate islands of green: the Saver target customers liked money-saving offers and the Shield target customers liked blocking junk mail. The two options for moving forward were clear: we just had to pick which direction we wanted to pivot.

ITERATE AND PIVOT TO IMPROVE PRODUCT-MARKET FIT

While these two distinct concepts had strong potential appeal, the appeal for Shield was stronger. Because a lot of websites already provided money-saving offers (such as coupons.com) for Savers, it wasn't clear to customers how our offering was differentiated. Also, customers were less willing to pay for this service and said that they would only be willing to pay a price that was less than the actual savings it achieved for them. In addition, it would take a lot of effort to sign deals with the companies that would make the offers, and this service wasn't a great fit with the company's brand.

In contrast, we detected a stronger potential product-market fit for Shield. Customers seemed more willing to pay for a service that reduced their junk mail. We had introduced the concept of paying for the service with the "Marketing Shield Premium" upgrade option. Some customers told us that if the service really worked as expected during an initial free trial period, they would be willing to pay afterwards. When asked how much they would be willing to pay for a service like this, some people indicated that it would be a small amount—but we didn't get a strong response. This service was also a better fit with the company's brand.

The Pivot

Based on what we learned, we decided to abandon our previous core value proposition of "finding out what 'they' know about me" and pivot to a service that only dealt with blocking junk mail. We tentatively named it JunkmailFreeze. At this point, we identified three options for how to proceed. The first was to create a new set of mockups, test it with customers, and then build the product. The second option was to code a higher fidelity prototype in HTML and CSS to test with customers and then build the product. The third option was to design and build the product without bothering to test with customers again beforehand.

We decided go with the first option. JunkmailFreeze was quite a pivot away from our core concept, and we had learned a lot about how to improve the junk mail blocking service. Plus, it wouldn't take much time to generate a new set of mockups and recruit another batch of customers. We decided to speak with fewer customers this time in the interest of saving some time and money.

Iterating Based on What We Learned

We tossed out our old mockups and started fresh to design a new product focused on reducing junk mail, with a secondary benefit of saving trees. We came up with a pretty straightforward user experience for our new MVP prototype. It started with an email from a friend recommending JunkmailFreeze with a link to the home page that explained the benefits and had a big "get started" conversion button. It also had a "learn more" link. Clicking the "get started" button led to a simple sign-up page where the user entered their name, address, email address, and password. After clicking the "register" button on that page, the user was taken to the "my account" page where they could specify which types of junk mail they no longer wished to receive. The other pages up to that point explained the benefits of using JunkmailFreeze; but this was the key page where the user interacted with the product to achieve those benefits.

Before we had conducted our first round of user testing, our view of the relevant benefit was simply to reduce the amount of junk mail a customer received. We learned so much more about the problem space after talking with users. We learned that there were certain types of junk mail that almost all customers hated the most: preapproved credit card offers and cash advance checks. Most customers do not have a secure (locked) mailbox. So they were worried that someone could steal a preapproved credit card offer from their mailbox and open a credit card in their name, or steal a cash advance check and use it. We used that knowledge to craft relevant messages in our new designs.

In general, finance-related junk mail was the top area of concern—including the types just mentioned, as well as loans and insurance. Customers had concerns about these types of junk mail increasing the risk of identity theft. It seemed that every customer we spoke with knew someone who had been a victim of identify theft. So we added the benefit of reducing the risk of identity theft to our messaging.

We learned that many privacy-conscious customers spend a lot of time shredding their junk mail. Several told us that when they get home from work, they take their mail out of their mailbox and stand next to their paper shredder as they read through it, shredding as they go. This nightly routine takes five minutes for some people, which adds up over time. We realized that there was also a "save time" benefit associated with reducing junk mail and added that to our messaging.

We also learned that customers considered catalogs to be a pain because they are so big and bulky. People discard many unwanted catalogs and consider it a hassle and quite a waste of paper. However, we also learned that people still wanted to receive certain catalogs, and that different people had different preferences for the types of catalogs they wanted to receive.

We also learned that many customers consider local advertising a nuisance. One form was the pack of local coupons, which many people tossed out without opening. Another form was circulars and flyers from local business such as supermarkets. People also complained about being sent free local newspapers to which they hadn't subscribed.

This is a great example of how talking to customers helps you gain such a deeper understanding of the problem space. We learned so much that our new "My Account" page let the user block up to 31 different types of junk mail across seven categories. After users selected which types of junk mail they wanted to block, they clicked the "continue" button to complete their registration.

The "registration complete" page told users what to expect next: that in the next couple of months, they should see a dramatic reduction in the amount of junk mail they receive in the categories that they selected. For our first round of testing, we learned that customers expected that the service would take a while to "kick in." We also knew that operationally it would take a while for the service to go into effect for each customer.

The page also explained that users could return to Junkmail-Freeze at any time to change the types of junk mail they wish to freeze. We had learned from our first round of research that it was important to customers that they be able to change their settings. Several expressed concern that by blocking their junk mail, they may inadvertently not receive some type of mailing that they would want to receive. Because the messaging on this page matched customer expectations, most nodded or said, "That sounds good," when they read it.

We provided a "learn more" path for customers who weren't ready to sign up right away. We explained on the "learn more" page how JunkmailFreeze contacts direct mailing companies on your behalf to get off their mailing lists. We explained that you would still be able to receive direct mail items that were important to you. Because identity theft was such a large concern related to junk mail, we also provided a page that explained how the two were connected. It included a photo of a row of vulnerable mailboxes and explained how you could reduce your risk of identity theft by using our service.

Because customers had a lot of questions about who was providing this service during the first round of user testing, we also added an "About us" page. They wanted to know about the company and its background.

Wave 2

Now that our JunkmailFreeze mockups were done, we recruited another group of customers using the same Shield screener, since it had worked so well. For this second wave, we scheduled three groups of two customers each. I updated the research script to focus on junk mail. The sessions were 90 minutes long starting at 6 and 8 P.M. (same as last time). Because we had done a fair amount of discovery in the first wave and wanted to focus on getting the product details right in this wave, we spent more time on the mockups (45 minutes instead of 35). I moderated the user testing, and our recruits were again engaged and articulate.

Climbing the Product-Market Fit Mountain

The second wave of user testing was one of the coolest things I've seen—and the results were very different from the first. None of the customers had any major concerns or questions with the product. Instead, there was a lot of head nodding as they went through the mockups, and unsolicited comments like "Oh, this is great." They did have minor comments, questions, and suggestions. But because we had learned what the major issues were in the first round and had adequately addressed them in our second wave mockups, everyone really liked our product.

That being said, the mockups we showed weren't "done." We gained an even deeper understanding about what customers wanted in a junk mail blocking service. For example, we learned that category-level controls for blocking weren't adequate for junk mail related to credit cards and catalogs. For those items, customers wanted to the ability to specify their preferences at the individual company level (e.g., Chase or Wells Fargo for credit cards, Nordstrom or L.L. Bean for catalogs). We also received feedback on our messaging and UX that would further improve the product.

This time when we asked customers how much they would be willing to pay for a service like this, we saw a stronger willingness to pay and a willingness to pay a higher amount compared to the first wave. You always have to be a bit skeptical when you discuss pricing with customers. Again, what they say they would do and what they would actually do can be different. You don't really know what they will be willing to pay until you have a real product and they have to vote with their wallet. But there was clearly much stronger interest in our Wave 2 product. I felt confident that we had achieved an adequate level of product-market fit with our mockups to move forward.

There was one more reason I felt confident. After each test was over, I thanked the customers and gave them their compensation checks. After receiving his or her check, every customer asked me if this service was live now and if they could sign up for it. When I explained that it hadn't been built yet, they all asked if I would please take their email address and notify them when it was available. None of the customers in the first wave had exhibited any behavior like this. Because this was genuine, positive customer interest outside the scope of our user test, I took it as further proof of product-market fit.

REFLECTIONS

Before this particular project, I had conducted various types of customer research to solicit user feedback on a product or product concept, and I had been on teams that practiced user-centered design.

But this project was the first time that I created and tested a product idea in such a Lean way. Focusing on mockups and not coding anything allowed us to iterate rapidly. By being rigorous about our target customer with our screener we were able to recruit customers that gave us great feedback. The whole project took less than two months and used resources very efficiently. I was excited that in so little time—and with just one round of iteration—our small team was able to improve our product idea so much and achieve a high level of product-market fit.

I also like to share this example with others because we didn't really do anything special or unique. We just followed the Lean Product Process. There's no reason anyone else couldn't replicate the results we achieved. By following the process I describe in this book, any team should be able to achieve similar results with their product idea. Of course, the details of how it works out in your case will vary. It may take you more waves. You may not have to pivot, or you may have to pivot more than once. And there's no guarantee you will achieve product-market fit for every product idea you pursue. But you should be able to test your hypotheses and assess your level of product-market fit with confidence.

As previously discussed, you can conduct user testing with design artifacts or a live, working product. To minimize risk, make faster progress, and avoid waste, I strongly recommend getting feedback on design artifacts before you start coding. This will allow you to be more confident in your hypotheses before you invest in coding. Once you have validated your mockups or wireframes with customers, it is time to start building your product. All the learning you gain in the Lean Product Process will help you better define the product to build. In the next chapter, I offer advice on how to go about building your product.

Part III

Building and Optimizing Your Product

Chapter 12
Build Your Product Using Agile Development

At this point, you have validated your target customer, their underserved needs, your value proposition, your MVP feature set, and your UX. As a result, you should feel confident about the blueprint you've developed. Validating product-market fit with prototypes is incredibly valuable, but now it's time to turn your blueprint into an actual working product that customers can use.

Building the product you've defined is obviously a critical step, and solid execution really matters here. There are many risks that could impede you while trying to build your blueprint. You may run into issues with technical feasibility, where what you've designed is impossible or too challenging to build, either in general, or with the resources you have available. Your product may be feasible but have such a large scope relative to your resources that it will just take too long to build. Good market opportunities only exist for so long before competition moves them to the upper right quadrant of the importance vs. satisfaction framework. An important part of product-market fit is having the right product at the right time (recall the product strategy discussion in Chapter 5). Even if you have an appropriate scope, poor execution can result in your actual product falling quite short of the promise of your prototype. You clearly want to minimize these types of risks—and the product development process you use can have a big impact on that. This chapter shares best practices in product development to help you deliver great products more quickly with less risk.

AGILE DEVELOPMENT

Just as you took an iterative approach to arrive at this point, you want to do the same in building your product. "Agile development" is the broad term used to describe a variety of iterative and incremental product development methodologies. Before the adoption of Agile development, most software products were built using the "waterfall" approach—one that proceeds sequentially through a series of steps. The team first defines all of the requirements, and then designs the product. They then implement the product, followed by testing to verify it works as intended. The key characteristic of waterfall is that the team does not progress to the next step until the previous step is 100 percent complete. In other words, no design happens until *all* of the requirements are defined, and no coding happens until the *entire* product is designed. Waterfall is also referred to as a "big design up front" (BDUF) approach.

In contrast, teams using Agile methodologies break the product down into smaller pieces that undergo shorter cycles of requirements definition, design, and coding. There are several benefits of Agile. First, because you are planning in smaller increments, you can react to changes in the market or other new information more quickly. Second, your product reaches customers earlier—which means that you start hearing feedback from customers on your actual product sooner, which helps guide your subsequent product development efforts. Third, teams can reduce their margin of error in estimating scope by working in smaller batch sizes.

I discussed the Lean concept of small batch sizes in Chapter 6, but let's explore why they are so beneficial in software development (or any development under conditions of high uncertainty). When developers estimate the amount of time it will take them to implement new functionality, there is a degree of uncertainty in their estimated values. This uncertainty results in estimation errors where the actual duration differs from the estimated duration. A good way to compare the actual duration and the estimated duration is to take the ratio of the former to the latter. If a project took twice as long as expected, the ratio would be 2×; if it took half as long as expected, the ratio would be 0.5×.

Steve McConnell created a diagram called the "cone of uncertainty" that characterizes the range of expected estimation error over the life of a software project. In McConnell's chart, the upper and lower bounds of the estimation error are symmetric curves, starting at 4× and 0.25×, respectively, at the outset of a project and decreasing throughout the project to converge at zero at the end. It makes intuitive sense and jibes with experience that the estimation error early in a project is larger than the estimation error near the end of a project.

However, in practice, I have not experienced estimation errors to be symmetric. In other words, I have not seen that developers are just as likely to finish tasks early as they are to finish them late. Most of the time, software development tasks take *longer* than estimated. And while it's true that some tasks do get completed early, the magnitude of positive surprises tends to be much smaller than the magnitude of negative surprises. Why is that? To help explain the asymmetric nature of software estimation errors, I'll quote epistemologist and former Secretary of Defense Donald Rumsfeld:

> There are known knowns. There are things we know we know. We also know there are known unknowns. That is to say, we know there are some things we do not know. But there are also unknown unknowns. The ones we don't know we don't know.

When developers are asked to estimate the effort for a task, they take into account the "known knowns." Skilled estimators will also account for the known unknowns in their estimates. It's true that some estimation error can come from an inaccurate understanding of the known knowns or the known unknowns. But I believe the biggest wild cards in estimate after estimate are the unknown unknowns, and that they are what make the distribution of estimation errors asymmetric.

Let's say I estimate that task A will take me five minutes and task B will take me five months. Both tasks could have unknown unknowns. But the uncertainty is nonlinear with increasing scope, as the top curve of the cone of uncertainty suggests. The chances that the five-minute task will spiral out of control are pretty low. The five-month task is over 30,000 times larger in scope, which is a lot more room for unknown unknowns to hide.

When developers go through the thinking and investigation required to break a large task into smaller ones, they reduce the unknown unknowns by converting them into known unknowns. You can't completely escape unknown unknowns, but by using smaller batch sizes, you can rein them in to be more manageable and ship product more predictably. In contrast, waterfall projects, which are typically large in scope, are notorious for taking much longer than original estimates.

Aside from these delays, some Agile zealots like to bash waterfall because they strongly object to the notion of a process having sequential steps that rely on prior steps. They act like Agile makes it okay to just jump in and start coding things. However, that perspective goes too far. Even in Agile, you should design before you code; you're just doing so in much smaller increments.

It's worth pointing out that waterfall *is* a better approach for some projects. For example, we wouldn't want to send humans into space with a minimally viable spaceship. I began my career designing nuclear-powered submarines. We definitely checked our requirements and reviewed our designs multiple times before starting construction. The risk of failure is just too high in these situations; that is, people would likely die. Also, unlike the code for a website—which can be quickly changed at will—it's much harder to make changes to a spaceship or submarine after it's built. When the risk of failure or the cost of making changes is too high, it's better to spend more time gaining a higher level of confidence before starting implementation.

Agile development's core principles were laid out in the Agile Manifesto, which was written in 2001 (you can view the manifesto and the principles at http://agilemanifesto.org.) Agile encourages early and continuous delivery of working software with a mindset focused on creating value for customers. A key part of Agile is defining your product in a customer-centric way with user stories. As Chapter 6 discusses, a user story is a brief description of the benefit that the particular functionality should provide, including whom the benefit is for, and why the user wants the benefit. Well-written user stories usually follow the template:

As a [type of user],
I want to [do something],
so that I can [desired benefit].

Agile also promotes strong cross-functional communication and collaboration, with business people and developers working together daily, ideally face-to-face. Instead of encouraging adherence to a rigid plan, Agile emphasizes flexibility to quickly respond to change. Teams can accomplish this by completing small batch sizes of work in short iterative cycles with feedback and learning, as opposed to trying to specify the entire set of detailed requirements upfront. Finally, Agile is about continuously improving your product development process via feedback and experimentation.

There are several different varieties of Agile development, including Extreme Programming (XP for short) and Lean Software Development. I'll provide a brief overview of two of the most commonly used Agile methodologies: Scrum and kanban.

SCRUM

Scrum is the most popular Agile framework. It's relatively easy to adopt because there is ample prescriptive guidance available on how to practice Scrum. A key aspect of Scrum is that the team works in *time-boxed* increments—that is, limited to a specific timeframe. This period of work, called a *sprint* or *iteration*, is a fixed length of time. Two-week sprints are very common, but you also see companies using one-week, three-week, and four-week sprints.

All work that the team completes comes from the *product backlog* of user stories. A backlog is a rank-ordered to-do list. User stories are written and placed on the product backlog by the *Product Owner*, one of the three roles specified in Scrum. The Product Owner, or PO for short, is responsible for using input from customers and stakeholders to create the prioritized backlog of user stories. The product manager on the team usually fills the Product Owner role. Some companies have a dedicated PO in addition to the product manager, and the two people coordinate closely. In smaller startups that don't have a dedicated product manager, one of the founders usually wears this hat.

The second role is "development team member." The Scrum guidelines say that the team should be multidisciplinary with all the skills required to complete the work. Scrum teams usually include several developers, whose job is to estimate the size of stories and build the product. Three other important team roles are UX designers, visual designers, and quality assurance (QA) testers. The traditional Scrum guidelines don't differentiate among team members, but it's fine to acknowledge distinct roles within the team. The designers bring the user stories to life by designing the user experience, which they convey through design deliverables. Well-written user stories include acceptance criteria, which are used to confirm when a story is completed and working as intended. QA testers help check to see if acceptance criteria are met and ensure the quality of the product.

The ideal size of a Scrum team is five to nine people. You may have heard of "the two pizza rule": if two pizzas aren't enough to feed your team, then it's too big. With this size, you should have enough people to accomplish a meaningful amount of work per sprint. Yet the team is small enough to feel like a cohesive unit and avoid the communication challenges that usually occur with larger groups.

The third role is Scrum Master, whose job is to help the team with the Scrum process and improve its productivity over time. Larger companies may have a Scrum Master that works with one or more Scrum teams, but a dev lead or dev manager often fills this role. Although it's not consistent with the Scrum guidelines, sometimes the role isn't explicitly filled by a single person—it's either ignored or the responsibilities of the role are distributed among the team.

The team carries out certain activities to prepare for the next sprint before it starts. The Product Owner will groom the backlog to make sure that stories being considered for the next sprint are well written and understood by the team. The PO usually does this with the dev lead or dev manager in a backlog grooming meeting (also called a backlog refinement meeting).

See Figure 12.1 for a visual depiction of the flow of work, meetings, and deliverables in Scrum.

At the start of each sprint, the team holds a *sprint planning meeting* where they decide which stories they plan to accomplish in the iteration and move those stories from the product backlog to the *sprint backlog*. Part of this process requires that the team estimate the scope of each story using *story points*, which are a relative measure of effort. Estimating points can often be more of an art than a science. You can find a variety of point systems in use. Some systems let the team assign any number of points to a story: 1, 2, 3, 4, 5, 6, and so forth. A common approach is to use the Fibonacci series for points, where the only valid values are 1, 2, 3, 5, 8, 13, and so forth. The benefit of this approach is that it forces distinct differences in estimated values. Another popular point system that forces even larger differences in

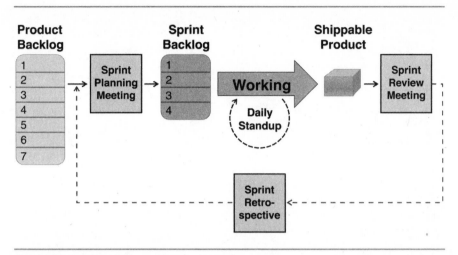

FIGURE 12.1   Scrum Framework

estimated values is the "powers of two" scale: 1, 2, 4, 8, 16, and so forth. *T-shirt sizing*, another popular technique, uses sizes such as small, medium, large, and extra large to estimate the scope of stories.

Stories with points at the high end of your scoring range have large scope and uncertainty and should be broken down into smaller stories, as discussed in Chapter 6. Stories that are too big to complete in one iteration are called *epics*, which *must* be broken down before they can be accepted into a sprint. Many Agile tracking tools enable the use of epics to organize related stories and manage them across multiple iterations.

If story points seem a bit abstract to you, it's because they are—at least at first. The goal is to determine a team's capacity for work by tracking how many story points they complete each iteration—which is called *velocity*. Once a team has calculated their average velocity, they can use that number of story points to plan their sprints. While story points start out a bit abstract, they provide a measuring stick for determining empirical values. In order to calculate velocity, story point estimates need to have a numerical value; so in the case of T-shirt sizing, the team would have to map each size to a relative number of points.

See Figure 12.2 for an example of how a team tracks their velocity over multiple iterations. The horizontal axis shows the iterations,

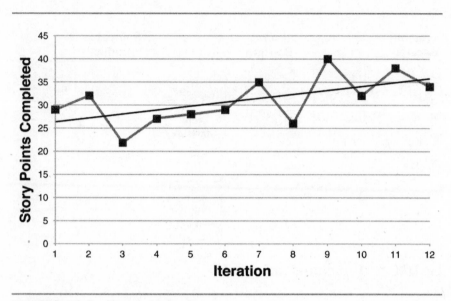

FIGURE 12.2 Team Velocity

numbered sequentially over time. The vertical axis shows the number of story points completed. Over these 12 iterations, the team's velocity has been variable (between 22 and 40 story points), which is normal. Despite this variability, the trend line shows that the team has been steadily improving their velocity over time.

Scrum teams use several techniques to reduce their story estimation error and achieve a more stable velocity. Teams will often discuss and estimate story points together, versus having only one team member size a given story. Some teams develop a reference set of user stories of different known sizes. Comparing stories to the reference stories helps them more accurately estimate scope.

Planning Poker is a popular technique for generating quick but reliable estimates as a group. Each team member receives a set of cards, with each card corresponding to one of the possible point values (e.g., 1, 2, 3, 5, and 8). After the team finishes discussing a story, each member privately selects the card with his or her points estimate, and then everyone reveals his or her card simultaneously. If the team has relative consensus, that gives higher confidence that the estimate is accurate. If there are material discrepancies in the estimates, they discuss the story further to try to reach a consensus estimate.

Teams will often break each story down into the set of coding tasks required to implement it. This helps ensure that they thoughtfully consider the work required for a story and that they don't overlook anything. Plus, it's usually easier to estimate the effort of each of these smaller tasks compared to the whole story. Some teams estimate the size of tasks with points, while others prefer to use hours of effort. Some teams identify tasks but don't bother estimating them, keeping their estimates at the story level.

When sprint planning is complete, the team should be clear on the set of stories they plan to accomplish in the sprint. They should choose the highest priority stories from the product backlog, and the total number of points for those stories should match the team's expected velocity for the iteration. In teams where the skill sets of developers vary, it's also a good idea to ensure each story has been assigned to a specific developer to ensure the team is properly load balanced for the sprint.

The team holds a daily Scrum meeting during the sprint, which is also called a *standup* because many teams stand up during the meeting to help keep it short. This meeting is usually held first thing in the morning so the team can discuss their plans for the day, and is generally time-boxed to 15 minutes. Team members each briefly describe what they did the previous day, what they plan to do today, and anything that is impeding their progress.

The team implements user stories starting at the top of the sprint backlog, collaborating as necessary. Many Scrum tools are available to help teams manage and track their work—some popular ones include JIRA Agile, Rally, VersionOne, and Pivotal Tracker. These facilitate product and sprint backlog management and sprint planning. Team members use them to track the state of each use story, changing states from "to be worked on," to "in development," to "code complete," to "done," for example.

Teams use a *burndown chart*—which shows how much work remains to be completed for the iteration—to track progress. The chart can display the remaining work in either points or hours, depending on the units your team uses for tracking. Figure 12.3 shows an example of a daily burndown chart, with the days of the sprint on the horizontal axis and the remaining story points for the sprint on the vertical axis. It starts on "day zero" of the sprint with the number of points to be completed, 45 in this case. This chart

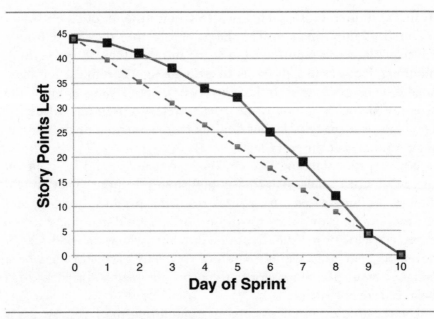

FIGURE 12.3   Burndown Chart

shows 10 working days, which corresponds to a two-week sprint (only weekdays are shown). Ideally, the team ends up with zero remaining story points at the end of the sprint.

QA testing is conducted during the sprint. To achieve a higher velocity, team members should test stories as developers complete them. If the story meets its acceptance criteria, then it is accepted; otherwise, it is rejected and kicked back to development. The team should also reserve some time at the end of the sprint to test the entire product after development is complete and to fix any bugs they find. I discuss testing later in the chapter.

The goal for the end of each sprint is to complete an "increment" of work that adds functionality to the product. The Scrum guidelines direct each team to define what "done" means for them. For many teams, "done" means a product that could be shipped, called a "shippable product" or a "potentially releasable product." Many teams release new product with the same frequency as their iterations, launching the output of their sprint to customers shortly after the sprint ends. Others have a separate release process with a longer cycle where the work from multiple sprints is released together at one time. Regardless of your deployment process, the goal is to ensure the product is in a shippable state at the end of the sprint. At the end of each sprint, the team holds a *sprint review meeting* (also called a sprint demo meeting) where they show what they have built. This helps ensure the product works as expected and lets everyone see the team's progress. Ideally, customers or stakeholders attend the demo to provide feedback to be considered for future sprints.

As with other Agile methodologies, Scrum also focuses on improving the team's process over time. To that end, teams hold *retrospectives* to specifically reflect on how the last sprint went. At these meetings, the team discusses what worked well, what didn't, and what improvements they want to make for the following sprint. Some teams hold retrospectives after each sprint; others do so after two or three sprints.

I've described the basics of Scrum here—if you want to learn more, see the latest version of the Scrum guidelines at http://scrumguides .org.

KANBAN

Another popular flavor of Agile development is kanban, a process adapted from the system Toyota developed to improve how they build cars. The Toyota Production System focused on just-in-time production and eliminating waste. I studied the original kanban system and Lean manufacturing, which inspired the Lean software development movement, in my graduate program at Virginia Tech.

Manufacturing workers use paper kanban cards to physically signal when additional work should be pulled into the system. These cards have been adapted in software development as virtual cards that each represent a work item but don't actually generate a pull signal. Instead, it's up to the team members to proactively pull the next work item forward.

A core principle of kanban is to visualize work. Each card is a user story or a development task that supports a user story. The cards are arranged on a kanban board, which consists of a set of columns, one for each different state of work. The columns are arranged left-to-right in the order in which work flows. See Figure 12.4 for an example of a kanban board. This kanban board has the following set of columns from left to right: "backlog," "ready," "in

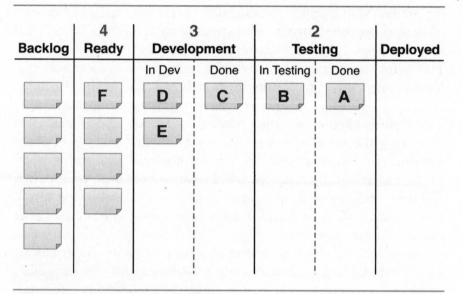

FIGURE 12.4   Kanban Board

development," "development done," "in testing," "testing done," and "deployed"—defined as follows:

- **Backlog:** Items to be potentially worked on, sorted in priority order.
- **Ready:** Items that have been selected from the backlog and are ready for development.
- **In development:** Items that a developer has started working on.
- **Development done:** Items that the developer has finished working on but which have not been tested yet.
- **In testing:** Items in the process of being tested.
- **Testing done:** Items that have successfully passed testing but have not yet been deployed.
- **Deployed:** Items that have been launched.

Some columns represent work being done (e.g., in dev, in testing) while others represent items waiting to be worked on (e.g., ready, development done). The latter type of columns are queues of work. When a team member frees up capacity after finishing work on one item, they pull the top item from the appropriate queue and start working on it.

As a work item progresses through each stage, its card is moved from one column to the next. It's easy to visualize the state of what the team is working on at any point in time by just looking at the board. It's also easy to see where the bottlenecks are by looking at which columns are accumulating the most cards.

You may have noticed that instead of having just a single state for "testing," Figure 12.4 has two: one state for items being tested ("in testing") and a second state for "testing done" items. "Development" similarly uses two states. This helps create a clearer picture of the status of the team's work and helps make bottlenecks easier to identify.

In kanban, the quantity of active work is managed by constraining the amount of "work in progress" or WIP. The team decides on the maximum number of cards each column can contain, which is called a *WIP limit*. Team members *pull* work items forward sequentially through each state of work. However, they can only move a work item to the next column if that column has spare capacity. This rule helps smooth out the work and achieve a steady flow. Teams should fine-tune their WIP limits over time to optimize their workflow. The WIP limit is displayed above each column. As shown in Figure 12.4, teams often use a single WIP limit to constrain the total number of cards across the two related "in progress" and "done" states (versus having separate WIP limits for each of the two columns). For example, the total number of "development" cards cannot exceed 3. This helps encourage the flow of cards to the right out of the completed states.

Looking at the work item cards in Figure 12.4, when the developer working on card D finishes, he would move it from "in dev" to "done." However, he would not be able to pull Card F forward from "ready" because "development" is at its WIP limit of 3. Likewise, when QA finishes testing Card B, they would move it to "testing done" but could not pull Card C forward because "testing" is at its WIP limit of 2. For work to progress, one of the "testing done" cards needs to be deployed. Once it is, Card C can be pulled forward to "in testing," which frees up "development" so Card F can be pulled from "ready" to "in dev."

You can further organize your kanban board with *swimlanes*—horizontal lines that separate cards into rows. There are a variety of ways to categorize cards with this technique. You can use swim-lanes to prioritize cards (the higher the row, the higher the priority). You can give each epic or each user story its own row. Swimlanes can also show each person's workflow more clearly, by having a row for each team member. You can also track multiple related projects on one board by putting each project in its own row.

The focus in kanban is on the flow of work. There is no time-boxed iteration as with Scrum. Work items move continuously from left to right on the kanban board as work progresses. The scope of user stories isn't necessarily estimated, so the Scrum concept of velocity (story points delivered per iteration) doesn't really apply. But you can measure the team's *throughput*, which is just the number of work items completed in a given timeframe, for example, 10 items per week. If you track your team's throughput over time, it should go up as they make process improvements and become more proficient.

Two commonly used metrics in kanban are *cycle time*—the amount of time on average from when work starts on an item to when the item is delivered to the customer—and *lead time*, the amount of time on average from when a work item is created (e.g., requested by a customer) to when it is delivered. It's important to note that cycle time and lead time aren't necessarily correlated with effort. A work item could take only an hour to complete but have a much longer lead time if it sat around for a while without anyone working on it.

You can visualize the flow of work in a kanban system with a *cumulative flow diagram* (Figure 12.5), a stacked area chart that shows how many cards were in each work state at the end of each day. For simplicity, Figure 12.5 only uses three work states: "backlog," "started," and "done." You can see the cycle time is the horizontal width of the "started" items, and the lead time is the combined horizontal width of the "backlog" and "started" items. The WIP is the vertical height of the "started" items.

The kanban mindset focuses on continuous improvement—so your team should be regularly identifying and discussing ways to work better and faster. The idea is that your lead time and cycle time should go down over time as your team makes process improvements and becomes more proficient.

Many teams have a constantly changing backlog; items that were considered important at one point in time become less important as

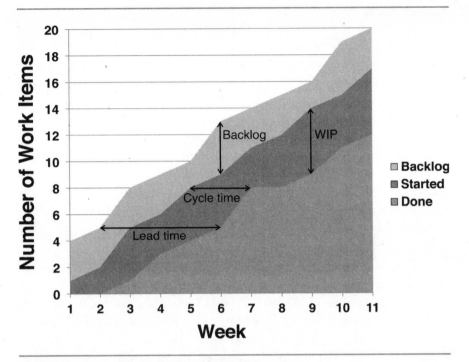

FIGURE 12.5   Cumulative Flow Diagram

they add new items. Unlike Scrum, where the sprint backlog is usually locked down within an iteration, team members can change a kanban backlog at any time. Cycle time may be the better metric on which to focus in such rapidly changing situations. You should still keep an eye on how long it takes to get backlog items ready for development to ensure that isn't decreasing team throughput.

If the scope of work items varies greatly, you can see a wide range in your cycle times, with smaller items having shorter cycle times and larger items having longer cycle times. Some kanban teams use the T-shirt sizing approach mentioned before (small, medium, large, etc.) for work items to enable more precise cycle time values. In that case, you would have a distinct cycle time for each T-shirt size.

Kanban does not have the level of process prescription that Scrum does; so no rituals are specified, but many teams practicing kanban hold daily standups and periodic retrospectives.

Kanban Tools

Many small product teams use a whiteboard for their kanban board, drawing a column for each work state and then using a sticky note for each work item. This makes it easy to move the items around and for anyone in the workspace to look at the board and see the status of the team's work.

There are many digital tools for managing kanban. Trello is a popular visual board application used to manage software development. In fact, many people use Trello to manage work outside of development. It's particularly popular with product managers and designers, who may maintain their own work boards that feed into the development board. Many teams use JIRA Agile for kanban, and other popular tools include SwiftKanban and LeanKit.

Although it's not a pure kanban tool, another application worth checking out is Pivotal Tracker. I used Tracker when I had the rewarding experience of working with Pivotal Labs to build a new product. Tracker uses a visual board of columns, one for each of the pre-defined work states. The tool supports an interesting blend of kanban and Scrum (there is actually an Agile methodology called "Scrumban" which you should check out if that idea sounds appealing).

Pivotal Tracker lets you estimate story points and calculate velocity if you want; if you don't, it feels more like kanban. If you do, it feels more like Scrum, except that the backlog for the current sprint is not fixed but rather determined dynamically. Stories are listed in priority order and automatically move in and out of the current iteration based on the estimate of story points that will be completed (using calculated velocity and the time remaining in the sprint). If you want Tracker to feel more like Scrum, you can use the "manual planning" mode (also called "commit" mode), which lets you lock down the set of stories in the sprint backlog.

PICKING THE RIGHT AGILE METHODOLOGY

You now have an overview of Scrum and kanban—how should you decide which one to use for your team? While devotees of each methodology may view them as vastly different, the two methodologies share many common Agile principles. I've found that Agile frameworks are like shoes: You really have to try them on to figure out how well they fit. It's often wise to just pick the methodology that sounds best to you and try it out for a few months. Many teams start by trying out either Scrum or kanban. If it's working well, then they stick with it. If not, they switch to the other methodology. After trying on both pairs of shoes, your team should be able to decide which one fits better.

That being said, here's some advice to increase your odds of starting off with the best fitting shoes: kanban tends to work best with smaller development teams. The lower process overhead and the lack of a predetermined iteration length can enable faster delivery of product. But as a development organization grows to multiple teams, kanban can start to become more challenging. The lack of a defined cadence to the work can contribute to this, since there is an increased amount of communication required to keep everyone on the same page. Teams that are strong at collaboration are able to scale kanban to larger sizes. If your organization has multiple development teams across which you need to coordinate work, then the predictable cadence of Scrum can be beneficial.

The idea of hard launch dates is tenuous with any Agile methodology. Most waterfall organizations are used to having a top-down roadmap that dictates what functionality they should launch each month or quarter, although those deadlines are often illusory due to delays. When these organizations transition to Agile, many still hold on to a waterfall mindset regarding their product backlog. I like using the term "Agilefall" to describe companies undergoing the awkward transition from waterfall to Agile, with a foot in both camps. If your organization would have a hard time letting go of the security blanket of hard deadlines, then Scrum is probably a better fit than kanban. At least with Scrum, you know you will have work done at the end of each iteration and can make high-level estimates for how many sprints a feature should take. Most kanban teams don't spend time estimating effort or completion dates. By carefully tracking your cycle time and using simple statistical techniques, it's possible to create projections with kanban that have relatively high confidence, but many teams don't achieve that level of tracking and precision.

Regardless of which flavor of Agile you choose, I highly recommend using a good tool to manage your work—and there are many available for each Agile methodology. One mistake some teams make is to use a general-purpose tool instead of one that is optimized for your development methodology. Again, I recommend you try out the tool you think will work best. If you're not happy with it after a month or two, then try another one.

I've encountered many dev teams that dislike a particular methodology or tool, which is to be expected. But I've also seen teams that have "the grass is greener" syndrome. They bash their current methodology or tool after trying it out for a short amount of time, switch to another one and use it for a month before complaining about that one and repeating the cycle. If your team goes through several methodologies or tools and doesn't seem to be able to find one that works well enough, you probably need to take a step back and reflect. It might be a sign that your team lacks the requisite level of commitment, training, or both.

Along those lines, having your team attend Agile training together can be very helpful. I've seen many a team adopt a new methodology without everyone on the team having an adequate level of understanding. Not surprisingly, many of those teams struggle. Before you adopt a new methodology, it's a good idea to assess each team member's level of knowledge with it. Even if several team members have worked with Scrum or kanban at prior companies, chances are that there are meaningful differences with how they practiced it there. If you don't set new expectations, team members will likely assume you are following the practices with which they are familiar. There is significant value in everyone on the team hearing the same thing at the same time about how the product development process should work. This ensures that everyone has the same expectations, reduces misunderstandings, and should enhance productivity.

SUCCEEDING WITH AGILE

Regardless of which Agile methodology you select, the additional advice below should help you succeed in building your product.

Cross-Functional Collaboration

Agile depends on strong cross-functional collaboration. There should be free and frequent communication among product managers, designers, developers, QA, and any other team members, who should speak daily. It's essential to avoid creating silos where each function throws their work product "over the wall" to the next function in the workflow. A certain amount of face-to-face real-time communication is critical to maximize shared understanding and team velocity. High-performing teams also employ communication tools such as chat, a development-tracking tool (e.g., JIRA Agile), and knowledge collaboration tools (e.g., a wiki or Google Docs) to work together effectively.

Every function should be involved throughout the process, though it's natural for a particular function to be more involved than others and take the lead during a certain phase. In a nutshell: product managers write the user stories, then designers create artifacts, then developers code, and then testers test. But product development is a team sport. Developers and testers should have some involvement early in the development process so that they understand the rationale behind product decisions, user stories, and UX designs. The team should encourage them to ask questions and make contributions at all stages. Similarly, product managers and designers should be in the loop during development and testing, especially since unforeseen questions or issues often crop up then. As we used to say at Intuit: good ideas come from everywhere. You can tell the level of collaboration by how often team members refer to one another as "we" instead of "they."

Effective collaboration helps the team achieve shared vision and avoid misunderstandings, and allows the team to move faster. Each team member makes numerous decisions about the product every day. If the team has shared vision and understands the objectives and rationale, members are more likely to independently make decisions that support that vision.

Ruthless Prioritization

You should maintain an up-to-date, prioritized backlog. It is important to be clear about the next set of user stories you plan to implement when resources permit. This allows you to act quickly. High-tech product teams usually operate in a dynamic environment where requirements and priorities change quickly. It's not enough to identify items as high, medium, or low priority. If a backlog has 15 high priority items, it won't be clear which of those items a developer should start on first when her time frees up. Priority levels are useful but not sufficient; you also need to rank order your backlog items within each level. I am a fan of *ruthless prioritization* (which, for the record, is the opposite of wishy-washy prioritization). Having your backlog rank ordered makes it clear which item should be done next. It also makes it much easier to determine where new requirements belong in the backlog when they come up.

The trick is to be both rigid and flexible when it comes to prioritizing your backlog. You must be clear on your rank order priorities at any point in time; but you must also be able to quickly incorporate new or changing requirements. I use the analogy of water and ice. Most of the time, your backlog is like ice; the rank order is frozen and fixed. But when new requirements come in or priorities change, you briefly melt the ice into liquid water so you can rearrange things. Once you're done reordering your backlog, you freeze it again. Following this approach means that your backlog will be up to date whenever anyone looks at it. A developer can reliably pull the item at the top of the stack and start working on it without having to confer with anyone.

Adequately Define Your Product for Developers

It's important to provide your developers with the information they need to build the desired product. A set of well-written user stories with accompanying wireframes or mockups usually does a good job of that. If the team already has a style guide in place and isn't introducing any new major UX components, wireframes are usually adequate. If, however, visual design details need to be conveyed, then mockups should be used. For features that are purely back-end with no UX component, wireframes or mockups aren't required. The team should ensure that it isn't just the happy path—that is, the expected path of user behavior—that they're defining. Rather, they need to think through the different conditions and states that could apply. There is a balancing act here. On one hand, you want to provide enough definition that developers can start building with confidence that you didn't fail to think through an important aspect. On the other hand, you don't want to experience analysis paralysis where you spend so much time fretting over every detail that implementation gets significantly delayed.

Stay Ahead of Developers

Many teams have struggled with integrating UX design into their Agile development process. The guidelines for Scrum don't explicitly deal with how best to handle this. It doesn't work well if the designer is creating wireframes for a user story at the same time that the developer is trying to code it.

In order for Agile teams to achieve their highest velocity, developers need to be able to hit the ground running when they start on a new user story—which means that the team must finalize the user stories and design artifacts beforehand. Because you want to achieve a steady flow of work, designers need to be at least one or two sprints ahead of the current sprint. In other words, by the end of sprint N, they should have finalized the design artifacts for sprint N + 1 or N + 2. Of course, the designers need solid user stories on which to base their designs—so product managers need to be working one or two sprints ahead of the designers.

The goal is to make sure that you never starve developers for work and always have at least one sprint's worth of fully groomed backlog ready to go. This requires some balance, because you don't want to specify too many sprints in advance, as things could change. And while I've described the situation in terms of Scrum, it also applies to kanban. Based on the designers' cycle time, PM should ensure there are enough cards in the "ready for design" queue. Likewise, based on the developer's cycle time, designers should ensure there are enough cards in the "ready for development" queue.

Neither the product managers nor the designers should be doing their work in a vacuum. The team needs to carve out a certain amount of time in the current sprint to review and discuss user stories and designs for future sprints.

Break Stories Down

Being Agile requires working in small chunks. I mentioned earlier that user stories should not be allowed to exceed some reasonable maximum size (i.e., number of story points). Beyond that, you should strive to break stories down into the smallest size possible. If you have a five-point story, try to find a way to break it into a three-point story and a two-point story. Better yet, try to break it into a couple of two-point stories and a one-point story. This may seem difficult at first, but like most things, you will get better with practice. If you're unable to break the story down any further, then the developers should try to break down the tasks required to implement the story. If they are having trouble doing that, start by enumerating the steps they plan to take to get the work done.

Smaller scope stories and tasks result in smaller estimation errors. Dividing user stories into smaller pieces usually requires that you think about them in more detail, which also reduces uncertainty and risk. You may realize when you break a story down that some elements of it are more important than others, which can help you refine your prioritization. The same advice applies for kanban, even if you're not using story points. Try to break each larger scope card into several smaller scope cards.

This chapter has covered a lot of ground on how to use Agile methods to build your product. Another important part of the product development process is testing, where you check the quality of what you've built before you release it to customers. Testing is part of quality assurance, the broader discipline of how companies ensure their customers receive a high quality product.

QUALITY ASSURANCE

Software products are inherently complex. They rarely work as expected 100 percent of the time, so you need to have some plan for assuring your product's quality before you release it to customers. Not having a good handle on your product quality can cause headaches like irate customers, lost revenue, and a disruptive drain on your team's resources.

Finding defects as soon as possible is a Lean principle that helps reduce waste. A major bug that you don't detect until after you launch your product is much more costly than one found during development. First, it negatively impacts customers. Second, it is usually more time consuming for the team to figure out the root cause of production bugs and fix them because they are no longer actively working on that code. Third, because the defect is live, the customer pain persists until the bug is fixed and you deploy the new code to customers.

QA testing should play a significant role, but there are also other ways to increase the software's quality. Coding standards help different developers on a team avoid arbitrary stylistic differences and achieve consistency in how they code, which helps eliminate inconsistencies that can result in quality issues. Coding standards also make it much easier for one developer to understand and modify another developer's code, which makes the code easier to debug and maintain and also improves developer productivity.

In a *code review*, one developer examines another's code—and can catch mistakes that the original developer missed. The reviewer also often has good ideas on how to improve the code. Code reviews allow defects to be found and fixed *before* testing, and are a great way for developers to learn from one another.

Going one step further than code reviews is *pair programming*—a technique where two developers work on creating the code together at the same time. They sit next to each other in front of a single computer and keyboard looking at the same screen. The developer in the "driver" role controls the keyboard and writes the code. The second developer plays the "observer" role and reviews the code as his or her partner creates it. The two developers switch roles frequently. Working in pairs promotes learning and usually results in better product designs and higher quality. Pair programming is a central tenet of Extreme Programming, another well-known Agile methodology.

Getting back to QA testing, there are two main types: manual and automated testing. In manual testing, one or more people interact with the product to verify it works as expected. Manual testing is also called "black box" testing because the tester doesn't have to have any knowledge of how the product was built or the technology behind it. Many companies have dedicated, full-time QA testers. In companies that haven't staffed QA, the testing burden falls on the other team members (such as developers and product managers). In those situations, developers are often testing their own code. One benefit of having dedicated QA testers is that they are more likely to find unforeseen problems than a developer checking her own code because they approach testing with a fresh perspective. Additionally, the testing is usually more thorough with dedicated QA resources. First, because it's QA's primary job, they have more time to test. Second, good QA people approach the testing systematically, which results in checking more conditions. Third, skilled QA people have a knack for being able to find ways to break software and are familiar with common issues that arise.

In automated testing, software is used to run tests on the product and compare the actual results with the predicted results. A person (usually the developer or the tester) has to initially define each automated test case, but once specified, they can be run whenever desired. Each time a set of tests is run, a report of which passed and which failed is generated. One benefit of automated testing is that it can save significant manual testing effort, especially for tests that are conducted repeatedly. However, there's a potential risk in that it is only as good as the set of test cases the team writes. If the team doesn't write test cases for certain functionality, then it won't get tested. By applying intelligence and creativity, a human tester hammering on a product will often test many conditions and combinations not explicitly called out in automated test cases. Such discoveries from manual testing should be used to add any missing automated test cases before the product is released. In addition, when the team makes functionality or user interface changes, they must revise the associated test cases accordingly.

The team should test two different aspects of the product when they build new functionality or make improvements to existing functionality. The first, called *validation testing*, checks to see if the new or improved functionality works as expected—that it is consistent with the associated user stories and design artifacts. Sometimes, the product is implemented differently from how it was designed, often due to a mistake or a misunderstanding. The developer might also do this deliberately because it wasn't feasible to implement the product as specified, or he or she chose a lower-effort solution. Even in cases where the product is implemented exactly as specified, the team might then realize that they missed something or didn't get something right. Any of those issues should get detected during validation testing.

The second aspect of product testing is to ensure that none of the other existing functionality was inadvertently broken during the process of building the new or improved functionality. In other words, you add Feature D to your product and want to make sure that Features A, B, and C still work as they did before you added Feature D. This is called *regression testing*. In this context, the word "regression" means "going back to a worse state"—that is, introducing a bug in existing functionality that wasn't present before.

Many companies use a combination of manual and automated testing, which can be very powerful. Manual testing is valuable for testing new functionality for the first time (validation testing), because the team probably hasn't thought of all the relevant test cases. A manual tester can try out different combinations and conditions to help identify corner cases. As you build more functionality and your product grows over time, the burden of regression testing grows with it. While you can conduct manual regression testing when the scope of a product is small, it's usually not feasible to scale a QA team as your product grows. That's why automated testing is a great fit for regression testing. As the team adds new functionality, they just need to add new test cases and update previous test cases as necessary.

TEST-DRIVEN DEVELOPMENT

Many Agile product teams practice *test-driven development*, a technique where developers write automated tests *before* they write code. Before coding a desired new functionality or improvement, the developer thinks about how to test it and writes a new test case. The test case *should fail* when the developer first runs it—because the code has not been changed yet. If the initial test doesn't fail, it indicates that the developer did not write the test correctly. The developer writes code until she thinks she is done and then runs the test again. If the test doesn't pass, the developer keeps working until the test passes. After a successful test, the developer will often *refactor* the code to improve its structure, readability, and maintainability without altering its behavior (while ensuring it still passes the test).

Test-driven development, also called TDD, has several advantages. First, it usually leads to higher *test coverage*, which is the percentage of your product's functionality that is covered by automated tests. As a result, you'll tend to miss fewer regression bugs—and enhance the team's confidence when they modify existing code (since automated testing lets them easily verify that they didn't break anything). TDD does require some overhead to maintain tests as the product changes over time. But if a team wants to scale their automated regression testing as the product grows, then they need to write new test cases as new functionality is developed—whether they decide to practice TDD or not.

CONTINUOUS INTEGRATION

Many product teams use *continuous integration* to iterate their product development more quickly. In order to explain continuous integration, I need to start with how software developers manage their code. Development teams use a *version control system* to keep track of every single revision made to the code; this makes it easy to see and manage changes. Version control also simplifies the process of restoring the code base to any prior state, so unwanted changes can be reverted. As of the time of this writing, Git is arguably the most popular version control system for Agile development.

When developers make changes or additions, they start with the current, stable version of the code base, called the *mainline* or *trunk*. Version control lets developers start with separate copies of the trunk (called branches), that they can modify without affecting the trunk. When developers are done building new functionality, they commit their changes to the version control system. Before doing so, each developer should perform *unit testing* of his or her code by writing the relevant test cases and ensuring they all pass. A team of developers all work in parallel, each committing their changes. Before merging the new code with the trunk and releasing it, all the changes are combined or "integrated" to build the new version of the whole product. *Integration testing* is performed at this point to ensure that the new product works as intended.

Historically, integration has typically been a manual process. Continuous integration uses an automated build process to create a new version of the product based on the latest code commits. The new build is automatically tested, and the team is notified about which tests passed or failed. They fix any issues and once the new code passes all the tests, clear it for deployment. Different teams conduct continuous integration with different frequencies: some daily, some multiple times a day, and some after each individual code commit. Continuous integration helps teams identify and resolve product development issues sooner than they otherwise would, which improves the speed with which the team can iterate. This is consistent with the Lean principle of detecting defects as early as possible to minimize waste. Instead of letting issues unknowingly pile up into a big mess between less frequent integrations, continuous integration lets the team deal with each issue as it arises. Another benefit is that your code is always in a shippable state, giving you more flexibility to deliver your updated product whenever you choose. Your test coverage impacts how beneficial continuous integration is: the higher, the better.

CONTINUOUS DEPLOYMENT

Many teams that practice continuous integration also practice *continuous deployment*, where code that successfully passes all tests is automatically deployed. Some companies automatically deploy to a staging environment (an internal environment that customers can't access), while others deploy straight to production. This requires automating your deployment process. Advances in automating operational tasks are being driven by the emerging field of *DevOps*, which focuses on building and operating rapidly changing, resilient systems at scale. A key part of a successful continuous deployment system is having the ability to quickly revert to the previous version of the code if any problems are detected, which is called automated rollback. Metrics that track the health of the product are used to trigger an automated rollback.

Let's walk through an example. A developer commits new code that implements a new feature on a website. The committed change goes through continuous integration, passes all the tests, and is automatically deployed to production. Right after the new code is deployed, the page load times on the website increase to unacceptably high levels, resulting in very slow performance for customers. The high page load times trigger an automated rollback that reverts the version of the product that is live back to the previous version of the code.

In order to work well, continuous deployment requires a robust analytics system. Technical metrics that track server health and performance are required to make sure the system is working properly, as are metrics that track product usage. The system needs to be able to tell if a new deployment prevents users from logging in or using some other key functionality. You also need analytics that track the health of the business. For example, if you had an e-commerce site and the number of orders being placed by customers suddenly decreased sharply after deploying some new code, you'd want that to automatically trigger a rollback.

This chapter covers a lot of ground related to product development. I've shared advice on and provided an overview of several important concepts. Many of the topics I discuss have entire books dedicated to them. These best practices—in the areas of Agile development, QA, and DevOps—have elevated the state of the art and made product teams much more effective. The common theme across these ideas is that they all help you build a great product more quickly with less risk.

Once you've launched your product, you can take advantage of the power of analytics. A robust analytics platform helps you understand how your business is doing and how customers are using your product. Analyzing your metrics over time and as you make changes gives you valuable insights that can help you drive improvements. The next two chapters cover how to use analytics to optimize your product and business.

Chapter 13

Measure Your Key Metrics

The customer research techniques available to you when you are building a new, v1 product differ before and after launch. Because you don't yet have a customer base before launch, you rely heavily on qualitative research with prospective customers for direct feedback on your product. While you can of course still conduct customer interviews to solicit feedback on your product after launch, your learning opportunities grow when you have a live product and a customer base using it. You can now take advantage of additional quantitative learning methods: namely, analytics and A/B testing. This chapter will explain how to use analytics to model and measure your product and your business. The next chapter builds on the lessons in this chapter by providing a structured process for using analytics to make improvements, and also includes a case study.

ANALYTICS VERSUS OTHER LEARNING METHODS

Before diving into analytics, I want to share a useful framework created by my colleague Christian Rohrer, a successful UX design and research executive. It categorizes the various ways you can learn from customers. Figure 13.1 shows a simplified version of Rohrer's framework. The vertical axis depicts the type of information you are collecting: attitudinal or behavioral. Attitudinal information is what customers say about their attitudes and opinions. Let's say you show a customer a mockup of a landing page. He tells you he likes the green color scheme, and that he would be very likely to click the big "buy" button. Those statements both convey attitudinal information.

In contrast, behavioral information has to do with what customers *actually do*. If you launch that landing page, you can conduct one-on-one user tests and see which customers click on the "buy" button. You can also use analytics to see what percentage of users

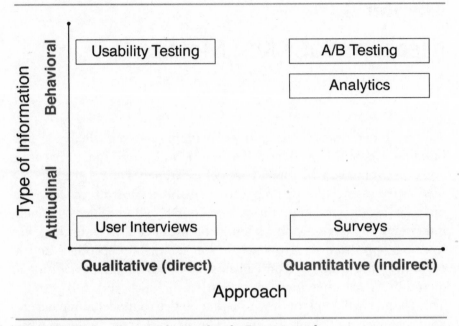

FIGURE 13.1   Research Methods Framework

visiting the landing page click the button. Those both provide behavioral information.

On the horizontal access of the Figure 13.1 framework is the approach for collecting the information, which is either qualitative or quantitative. Let's say you conduct one-on-one interviews with 10 prospective customers in an effort to understand their pain points and preferences. Or, you watch a customer use your website. Both are examples of qualitative tests, the kind of research that relies on direct observation of customers.

In contrast, you generate quantitative information by aggregating the results from many customers. You are not observing each individual customer but rather looking at statistical results for a large group. Say you track the conversion rate on your "buy" button to see what percentage of customers have clicked on it, or you email a survey to thousands of users to ask about their attitudes and preferences. In both cases, analyzing the results would yield quantitative learning.

OPRAH VERSUS SPOCK

Both qualitative and quantitative learning are important and actually complement each other. Quantitative research can tell you how many customers are doing (or not doing) something. But it won't tell you *why* the customers are doing it (or not doing it). On the flip side, qualitative research will help you get at the underlying reasons for why customers do what they do. But it won't tell you *how many* people do what they do for each particular reason. In market research, it's very common to start with qualitative research to understand the relevant questions to ask and the responses that customers give you (the "why"). Armed with this information, you then proceed to quantitative research to find out how many customers give each answer (the "how many").

I like to refer to the qualitative and quantitative methods as "Oprah versus Spock," respectively, to highlight the difference between the two. Popular television personality Oprah is purely qualitative; she talks to her guests one-on-one and conducts long, in-depth interviews where she gets to know them and what their opinions are. Spock, the logical character from *Star Trek*, is purely quantitative; he bases decisions strictly on what the objective data and numbers say. When you are validating product-market fit for a v1 product, the Oprah approach is most important. And while you can still use the Oprah approach after launch, you can then also start using the Spock approach to optimize your product.

USER INTERVIEWS

Each of the four quadrants in the Figure 13.1 framework represents a distinct type of learning. User interviews fall in the lower left quadrant of qualitative and attitudinal. In these interviews, you attempt to understand a user's needs and preferences. You want to determine how they think about the problem and the relevant context. You aren't trying to observe any behavior. You ask open-ended questions, but you are mainly listening to their thoughts and attitudes. See the advice in Chapter 9 about how to conduct effective customer interviews.

USABILITY TESTING

Usability testing falls in the upper left quadrant of qualitative and behavioral. Like user interviews, usability testing is also qualitative because you are paying attention to what each user has to say. However, usability testing is more concerned with behavior. Instead of having a user tell you if they would or wouldn't take a certain action in your product (attitudinal), you want to see if they actually do or don't (behavioral). The main goal is to gain behavioral learning by observing the customer use your prototype or your product. Conducting usability tests on a competitor's product can also yield valuable insights.

Even when the focus is on usability, most user testing inevitably yields a mix of attitudinal and behavioral information. In many user tests, you will want to explicitly ask customers some discovery questions, as I discuss in Chapter 9. It's important to keep straight in your head the type of information you're seeking from the customer and the type of information the customer is giving you.

SURVEYS

Surveys fall in the lower right quadrant of quantitative and attitudinal. They are quantitative because your goal is to obtain results from a large number of users to see the overall results, and they are attitudinal because customers are telling you what they think; you are not capturing behavioral data of them using your product.

I haven't spoken as much about surveys as the other types of user research—because I have seen them misused so often. A well-designed survey can generate useful information. But you have to know what you can use them for and not exceed those limits. If you survey 1,000 people and ask them to rate on a scale of 1 to 10 how likely they would be to use a new, easy-to-use photo-sharing app you plan to build, you're pushing it. Why? First, they know next to nothing about your product. Your product description, "a new, easy-to-use photo sharing app," conveys just eight words of information. It's not a live app, it's not a set of clickable wireframes, and it's not a mockup—so customers don't have much information to go on. How could people possibly predict with any accuracy if they would use it? Time and again, I see survey creators asking respondents to answer questions about which they certainly do not have enough information.

Second, because surveys provide attitudinal data, you have to take the results with a grain of salt. People can give optimistic or pessimistic answers to how likely they would be to use a new product; but their opinions often don't end up matching behavior. I'd rather do a smoke test with a landing page for the new product. I'd include a "buy" button or ask people to provide their email address to be placed on the beta wait list and observe the conversion rate. This behavioral data would answer the same question in a more reliable manner than a survey.

Third, survey question results can be highly sensitive to the specific wording of the question and the answers you allow the respondent to select. If you're relying on survey data to make some important decisions, it's a little scary to think that you could get quite different results depending on *how* you ask things. If you can't tell the difference between high-quality and low-quality question design, you could be setting yourself up for that. There are people who earn PhDs in market research for a reason. Don't get me wrong; you can and should use surveys. Just make sure a survey is the right tool for the learning you want and apply good survey design skills (or find someone who can).

So if surveys are bad for certain kinds of questions, what are they good for? Well, they are good for simple questions about the respondent's attitudes where they have the information required to answer. Chapter 4 discussed the use of surveys to measure importance and satisfaction, for example. Surveys can help you see how people feel about your product and brand. You can also use them to see how customers perceive your product relative to competitors. Tracking surveys, where customers are asked the same questions at periodic intervals, can be useful to identify trends over time.

Net Promoter Score

One of the mostly widely used survey-based metrics is the Net Promoter Score, or NPS for short. This metric is based on the results of a single question, "How likely are you to recommend [product X] to a friend or colleague?" A "likelihood to recommend" scale from 0 to 10 is provided, with 10 being "extremely likely" and 0 being "not at all likely." Customers that give you a 9 or 10 are called promoters; those that give you a 7 or 8 are called passives; and those who answer 0 through 6 are called detractors. To compute your NPS, you take the percentage of promoters and subtract the percentage of detractors. NPS can range from −100 to 100.

NPS is an attitudinal measure of customer satisfaction with your product, and is a proxy indicator of product-market fit. Customers are only going to recommend a product with which they are very satisfied. The average score from a single wave of NPS surveys is somewhat useful. But the main value comes from tracking your NPS over time with periodic surveys—since it should increase as you improve product-market fit. Of course, your NPS can also decrease as issues arise. Because it measures overall customer sentiment, it can alert you to issues in a wide range of areas beyond just your product, including customer service or support. This is why it's important to include in your survey an open-ended question asking customers *why* they gave the score they did. You can also compare your NPS to your competitors' scores and to benchmarks for your product category.

Sean Ellis' Product-Market Fit Question

Sean Ellis is a talented marketer and Lean Startup practitioner—he coined the term "growth hacker" and runs the community site http://growthhackers.com. Ellis is also CEO of customer insights company Qualaroo http://qualaroo.com. He has helped many companies achieve high customer growth.

Ellis advocates, as I do, that you should not invest in trying to grow your business until *after* you have achieved product-market fit. So he developed a survey question to assess your level of product-market fit. In the survey, you ask the users of your product the question, "How would you feel if you could no longer use [product X]?" The four possible responses are:

- Very disappointed
- Somewhat disappointed
- Not disappointed (it isn't really that useful)
- N/A—I no longer use [product X]

After conducting this survey with many products, Ellis found empirically that products for which 40 percent or more of users reply "very disappointed" tend to have product-market fit. There can be some variability in that threshold based on the product category, but it is a good general rule of thumb. For an accurate read, Ellis recommends sending the survey to a random sample of customers who have used your product at least twice and have used it recently. When this survey question is asked, it should also be followed by the open-ended prompt, "Please help us understand why you selected this answer," as I recommended for NPS.

ANALYTICS AND A/B TESTING

The upper right quadrant in Figure 13.1 is quantitative and behavioral. This is where analytics and A/B testing live. Analytics allow you to measure real customer behavior—so you don't have to worry about any disconnect between what customers say they will do and what they *actually* do. And unlike qualitative research on user behavior, analytics aggregate many customers' behavior—thereby enabling you to reach statistically significant conclusions.

For example—let's say you have a landing page. You see from your analytics that your conversion rate is only 5 percent, much lower than you think it should or could be; so you design a new, improved version of the landing page. You conduct usability tests and ask customers for their feedback on the new page. The feedback is generally positive; 9 out of 10 users indicate that they would click the "sign up" button. So you decide to launch the page. Before launching, you aren't really in a position to estimate the impact of the new design. The real conversion rate is not likely to be 90 percent. That value is artificially high because of the nature of moderated usability testing. You may expect the conversion rate to go up, but it would be hard to quantify by how much from just the usability test results.

A/B testing allows you to send a portion of your customer traffic to the new version and the rest to the old version, while tracking the results for each. This way you *can* know the difference in conversion rate. If you have a high volume of traffic, you will be able to quantify the difference with a high degree of confidence.

Analytics are critical for any product team to fully understand how their customers are using the product. Analytics can't give you the entire picture; you also need qualitative research to know your customers. But you are flying blind without analytics. To paraphrase Peter Drucker, you can't manage what you don't measure. A/B testing builds on analytics to give you a way to confidently know the impact of changes you make. It provides a platform for experimentation and is a powerful tool that enables Lean teams to innovate rapidly.

It's worth mentioning that the full version of Rohrer's framework also includes a third dimension for "context of use." He distinguishes between the different contexts of product use for each research method: "natural use" (e.g., analytics), "scripted use" (e.g., usability tests), and "not using the product" (e.g., discovery interviews). I encourage you to explore his full framework, which categorizes 20 different UX research methods. You can find it on the Nielsen Norman Group website at http://nngroup.com/articles/which-ux-research-methods. You can see Rohrer's other publications and blog posts at http://xdstrategy.com.

Now that it's clear where analytics and A/B testing fit in, let's discuss some frameworks for using these powerful tools.

ANALYTICS FRAMEWORKS

For any business, there are a multitude of metrics that you could track to describe how it's performing. Because there are so many different metrics that you *could* try to improve, it's very helpful to have a holistic analytics framework that encompasses your entire business. This allows you to be clear about how the various metrics fit together and can help you identify where you should focus.

Analytics at Intuit

After launching a new web product at Intuit, I wanted to track and improve our product and business. I created an analytics framework that covered the four main elements of our business:

1. **Acquisition:** How many prospects (new visitors) are our marketing programs driving to our website?
2. **Conversion:** What percentage of prospects that come to our website sign up as customers?
3. **Retention:** What percentage of our customers remain active over time?
4. **Revenue:** How much money do our customers generate?

After we launched, customers were signing up for our product and we were generating revenue. So we were feeling pretty good about product-market fit. But we realized that we had a conversion problem: The percentage of prospects signing up was lower than we had expected it to be. The nature of our product required a sign-up process that was several pages long. Using analytics, we measured how many prospects were dropping off at each point in the sign-up process. We then conducted usability testing with users focused on the biggest problem areas we found. We discovered several UX design issues. We then used these insights to quickly make targeted UX design improvements. When we rolled out the improvements, we saw a 40 percent improvement in our conversion rate. The funny thing is, because we had built such a detailed model of the different use cases and usability issues and had such accurate metrics data, we were able to predict the improvement within a couple percentage points.

This example is a great illustration of how quant and qual can work together. Quant was the smoking gun that told us we had a conversion problem and identified where people were dropping off the most, but it couldn't tell us *why*. Qual gave us the insights we needed to understand and address the issues. After we rolled out the improvements, quant showed us the impact of the changes we made.

Analytics at Friendster

Two years later, I joined Friendster, the pioneering social network. I again wanted to use analytics to track and improve the product and business, so I developed a framework to do that. The company agreed that the main metric that mattered was our number of users. Social products benefit from network effects, where their value grows exponentially with the number of users. Plus, we were in the early days of social networking with market leadership still up for grabs. The best way to grow our user base was to have our existing customers invite as many noncustomers to join Friendster as possible. If, on average, each customer generates enough prospects that subsequently convert into more than one new active customer, then you have *viral growth*. Social products have high potential for viral growth (as well as high, nonviral growth rates). The detailed steps by which an existing customer generates a new customer are called your *viral loop*.

At Friendster, I built an analytics framework for our viral loop so I could optimize our virality. My framework included viral acquisition but not nonviral acquisition. It also included conversion, since prospects had to go through our registration flow to become customers. And since only active customers invited their friends to join, my framework also included retention. It did not include revenue (which we tracked separately). I share a detailed case study about my Friendster analytics framework in the next chapter.

The business goals for the two analytics frameworks I just discussed are certainly not unique to those two businesses. In fact, they are widely applicable to all businesses. At a high level, almost every company has these five common goals:

1. It wants to make prospective customers aware of its product.
2. It wants to convert those prospects into customers.
3. It wants to retain as many of its customers as it can over time.
4. It wants to generate revenue from its customers.
5. It wants its customers to spread the word about the product to generate prospects.

Startup Metrics for Pirates

In 2007, I had the good fortune of meeting Dave McClure. Chances are you've heard of Dave—but for those of you who haven't, he describes himself as a "geek, marketer, investor, blogger, and troublemaker." He is the founding partner of 500 Startups (http://500.co), a startup seed fund and accelerator. That year, Dave gave a talk where he shared his "Startup Metrics for Pirates" framework. I was excited to see that his framework was very similar to the ones I had developed working at Intuit and Friendster. Dave presented his ideas in such a simple, effective way that the value and wide applicability of his framework was readily apparent.

Dave and I just had two minor differences in terminology. First, Dave used the term *activation* instead of conversion. For Dave, the term activation is a slightly broader term that includes conversion as I've defined it; however, it also includes other ways in which a prospect can engage with your product short of becoming a customer. For example, a prospect may not sign up for your service, but may give you his or her email address to be notified about product news. That action wouldn't qualify as conversion to a full customer but could be measured as an activation metric. Second, Dave used the word *referral*—an excellent, catch-all term—to describe the concept of your existing customers taking actions that lead to new prospective customers learning about your product. Dave called his framework "Startup Metrics for Pirates" because if you make an acronym for his five metrics—acquisition, activation, retention, revenue, and referral—it spells "AARRR!" (with an exclamation point added for good measure).

In his talk, Dave recommended tracking two or three key metrics for each of the five elements of his framework. That is a good idea because your conversion funnel, for example, isn't really just one overall metric; you can (and should) track the more detailed metrics. So we can make a distinction between the macro-metrics and the micro-metrics that relate to them. Identifying the best micro-metrics to track for a given macro-metric is part of what I call "peeling the analytics onion," which I will discuss later.

KISSmetrics created an excellent diagram to depict the AARRR framework, which I modified slightly (see Figure 13.2). This isn't too surprising—since KISSmetrics CEO and founder Hiten Shah is one of the top Lean Startup and analytics thought leaders.

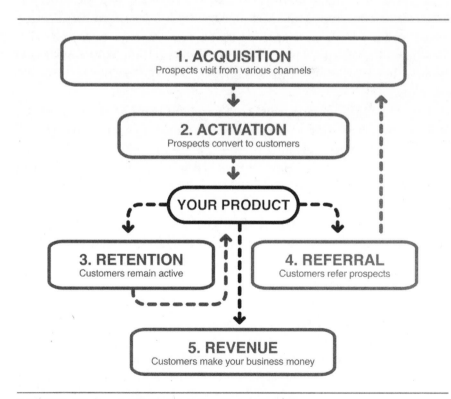

FIGURE 13.2   AARRR Metrics Framework

IDENTIFY THE METRIC THAT MATTERS MOST

At any point in the life of your business, one of the five macro-metrics in the AARRR model will be more important than the others. I call this the "metric that matters most"—or the MTMM for short. You could improve your business by improving other metrics. But your MTMM is the metric that offers the *highest* ROI opportunity for improving your business right now—and the "right now" is an important aspect. At some point, after you make significant progress on your MTMM, it will no longer be the MTMM—since a different metric will now offer higher ROI opportunities. For example, let's say after launching your product you realize that only 10 percent of customers who start your sign-up process actually complete it. You decide your sign-up conversion rate is the MTMM for your business right now, so you conduct user testing of your sign-up process and discover several usability issues. You also discover the form doesn't work with one particular browser. You check your server logs and realize that sometimes an error occurs, causing the form not to work as expected. You work hard with your team to fix all these issues and see your sign-up conversion rate improve to 90 percent. At this point, the sign-up conversion rate is no longer your MTMM. Some other metric now offers higher ROI opportunities to improve your business.

The MTMM changes due to the phenomenon of diminishing returns. When you first focus on optimizing a particular metric for your business, you will quickly find the low-hanging fruit: the ideas that can lead to a large improvement without much effort. After you make these improvements, the ROI on the next set of opportunities is lower, and continues to decrease as you make more progress.

With a new product, there is often a natural order in which it makes sense to optimize your macro-metrics. A common scenario is for the MTMM to start out as retention and then change to conversion, followed by acquisition. Let's explore why.

Optimize Retention First

When you are working on a new product, you need to first achieve product-market fit. Until you know that customers find your product valuable, it doesn't make sense to spend lots of resources trying to acquire customers. Nor does it make sense to optimize conversion. Not only will spending time on those areas have less of an impact on your business, but doing so would take valuable time away from what is most important right now. If customers find value in your product, they will continue using it; otherwise, they won't. Retention is the macro-metric most closely related to product-market fit. For this reason, it is typically the first MTMM for a new product.

Optimize Conversion before Acquisition

Once you confirm strong product-market fit with a healthy retention rate, you know that a high enough percentage of customers that get through your front door and use your product will stick around. It usually makes the most sense to focus next on making sure the highest percentage of prospects who show up at your front door make it inside. Conversion, the macro-metric that tracks this, has now become the MTMM. Why not focus on acquisition instead? That would mean sending a lot more prospects to your front door. However, many of those prospects aren't going to become customers if your conversion rate is lower than it should be. By optimizing conversion first you will see a much higher return on your investment when you *do* focus on acquisition, because a higher percentage of prospects will turn into customers.

Optimizing Acquisition

Once you have optimized retention and conversion, it often makes sense to focus on acquisition—that is, identifying new and better ways of attracting prospects. You can explore new and different acquisition channels, segments within your target market, messaging, pricing, promotions, and so forth. You usually undergo this kind of exploration with a series of experiments to test out each new idea with a small sample size. Once an experiment shows that a particular new idea works well, you then roll it out at a larger scale.

At a high level, you can divide acquisition into "paid acquisition" and "free acquisition." Paid acquisition requires you to pay money to attract prospects—for example, advertising your product on Google or Facebook. Viral marketing is free. Your users' actions drive other people to try your product, but you're not paying them anything. Organic search is another free acquisition channel.

The distinction between paid and free acquisition is important because it impacts whether it makes sense to focus on acquisition or revenue first. If your acquisition is largely free or inexpensive, then you can optimize acquisition and worry about revenue separately because you're not relying on the revenue to fund your acquisition efforts. If, on the other hand, your business relies on expensive paid acquisition, you may decide that it's important to focus on optimizing revenue before acquisition to reduce your risk. Once you know that each customer is going to generate a certain amount of revenue, you can more confidently spend money on acquiring more.

There are countless metrics that you can track and optimize. Since building a successful new product starts with achieving product-market fit, it would be valuable to identify the best way of measuring it. In my talks and workshops, I often ask my audience, "If you could only track one metric to measure your product-market fit, which would it be?" I usually get a variety of answers. Some people argue that revenue is the ultimate measure. Others think that the growth rate of your customer base is most important. Those two metrics *could be* the MTMM for a business, depending on its situation. However, I deliberately word my question very carefully by including "to measure your product-market fit." Retention rate is the single best metric to measure your product-market fit. Let's dig deeper into retention and how to measure it.

RETENTION RATE

Retention rate measures what percentage of your customers are actively using your product. To calculate it, divide the number of active customers by the total number of customers. You want to track retention rate over time to see what percentage of customers keep using your product—and do this in an aggregate way to understand what's going on across *all* users. One complication that doesn't exist with other metrics is that different customers start using your product on different dates, so you can't just think of retention in terms of calendar dates (as you can with most other metrics). For retention, it's most intuitive to aggregate the data using "relative days," where you count the number of days since each user signed up.

Retention Curves

Retention curves are an intuitive way to visualize your customer retention. See Figure 13.3 for a sample retention curve. The vertical axis is the percentage of users returning. The horizontal axis is the number of days (or weeks or months) since first use. The value for each point on the curve has been calculated based on sign-up and usage data for a population of users. Retention curves always start at 100 percent on day zero (the day each user signed up) and then tend to decrease over time as more and more customers fail to return to use your product. There can be quite a drop-off in retention on day 1 (the day after sign up). As a result, day zero is usually not

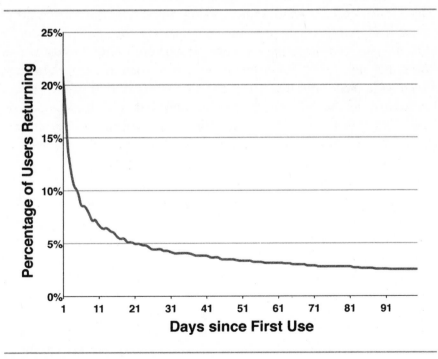

FIGURE 13.3   Retention Curve

shown on the graph, and day 1 is the first day displayed; this makes the graph more readable.

In this particular retention curve, notice how the value at day 1 is around 20 percent. That means around 80 percent of customers that used this product never came back. This "initial drop-off rate" is one of the key distinguishing parameters of a retention curve. Different product categories have different initial drop-off rates. This retention curve is for a mobile application, a product category that has very high initial drop-off rates. Think about it: people install and use new mobile applications all the time. But after they finish using an app for the first time, they often don't go back and use it because it's not front-and-center in their mind. The application icon is usually buried in a sea of other icons on their phone. Unless there is some trigger to remind users about the existence of that app they used, they are likely to forget about it. That's why notifications are so important for mobile apps in order to combat this "out of sight, out of mind" problem.

The second distinct parameter of a retention curve is the rate at which it decreases from that initial value. Some retention curves drop very quickly while others descend more slowly over time. The curve can either keep descending towards zero or eventually flatten into a horizontal line (an asymptote). If the curve goes to zero, then that means you eventually lose all of the customers in that group. If the curve becomes flat at a certain value, then that is the percentage of customers you eventually retain. The terminal value for retention curves that flatten out is the third distinct parameter. One product may flatten out at 5 percent while another flattens out at 20 percent.

Those three distinct retention curve parameters I mentioned— initial drop-off rate, rate of descent, and terminal value—are direct measures of product-market fit. The stronger your product-market fit, the lower your initial drop-off rate, the lower your rate of descent, and the higher your terminal value. The weaker your product-market fit, the higher your initial drop-off rate, the higher your rate of descent, and the lower your terminal value. Terminal value is the most important of these three parameters, since it answers the question, "What percentage of customers who tried your product continue to use it in the long run?" If you told me product A had a terminal value of 1 percent and product B had a terminal value of

50 percent, I could tell you which one had better product-market fit (product B) without knowing *anything else* about the two products.

Product-market fit seems like a somewhat fuzzy and difficult-to-measure concept. So it's great that retention curves give you hard numbers you can use to measure product-market fit. And while that's the main reason retention rate is the ultimate metric of product-market fit, there are several other reasons. Another benefit of retention rate is that it is a pure measure of product-market fit that is not conflated with any other components of the macro-metrics framework (e.g., acquisition). What do I mean by this? Well, let's say you were using the number of active users as your measure of product-market fit, and let's say your number of active users is trending up and to the right, as we all hope. That can only happen if you are adding new users (via acquisition and conversion). The trend you're seeing in active user growth could be due to modest new user growth with decent retention. However, the same trend could also result from very high growth and very poor retention. By only tracking active users, you wouldn't be able to tell the difference between these two scenarios.

This is why it is critical when tracking your user counts over time to distinguish between new users and *returning users*, the latter being the metric used in the numerator when calculating the retention rate. New users are customers who use your product for the first time (during a certain time period). Returning users are customers who use your product during a certain time period who first became users *before* that time period. Tracking returning users over time is valuable. You'd obviously like the graph of returning users to be trending up and to the right with the highest slope possible. Be mindful, however, that unlike retention rate, returning users isn't a pure measure of retention. It is conflated with acquisition and conversion. The number of returning users represents the total number of customers you have captured and managed to keep at a given point in time. In contrast, because of the way it's calculated, retention rate answers the question "of the customers that I captured, what percentage are still active?" at a given point in time.

Since retention curves measure product-market fit, they give you a way to measure how much you're improving your product-market fit over time. You can see how your retention changes over time by generating multiple retention curves: one for each slice of time. For example, you might generate a new retention curve monthly. This would give you a set of retention curves, with a curve based on the data for the customers that signed up each given month.

Cohort Analysis

A group of users that share a common characteristic—such as the month that they signed up—is called a *cohort*. *Cohort analysis*—the analysis of metrics for different cohorts over time—is a powerful tool. Figure 13.4 depicts a graph with three cohort retention curves. The horizontal axis is the number of weeks since sign up (instead of days, as in Figure 13.3). As you can see, Cohort A has the lowest initial drop-off, highest rate of decay, and lowest terminal value. Cohort C has the highest initial drop-off, lowest rate of decay, and highest terminal value. The parameters of Cohort B's curve are in between those of Cohorts A and B. So which of the three cohort retention curves would you prefer to have? I'd choose the Cohort C curve

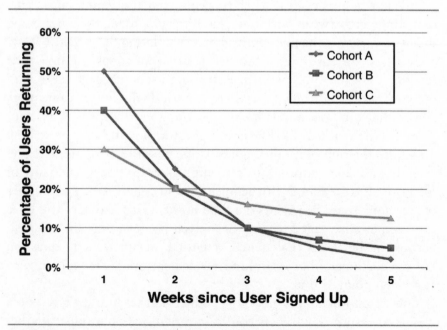

FIGURE 13.4   Cohort Retention Curves

because it has the highest terminal value. From week 3 on, Cohort C has a higher percentage of active users than the other two curves. That translates into more revenue. As an aside, once you have more than five cohort curves on the same graph, it becomes difficult to read—especially since cohort data can be noisy, with curves crossing one another.

Table 13.1 shows the standard format for storing the data used to generate retention curves for multiple cohorts. From the first column, you can see that each row is a cohort. This example shows monthly cohorts for January through May—this would be the snapshot as of June. For each cohort, you capture the initial number of users in the second column. In each subsequent column, you capture the number of active users for the cohort as a function of the number of months since they signed up. The older the cohort, the more data points you will have for that curve.

The data in Table 13.1 is used to calculate the values in Table 13.2. The percentage in each cell of Table 13.2 is the retention rate for the combination of that row's cohort and that column's timeframe. Each

TABLE 13.1   Raw Data for Cohorts

Cohort	New Users	Active Users				
		Month 1	Month 2	Month 3	Month 4	Month 5
Jan	10,000	3,000	2,000	1,000	500	300
Feb	8,000	2,700	2,000	1,000	700	
Mar	9,000	3,200	2,500	1,500		
Apr	11,000	4,200	2,500			
May	13,000	5,200				

TABLE 13.2   Cohort Retention Rates

Cohort	Retention Rate					
	Month 0	Month 1	Month 2	Month 3	Month 4	Month 5
Jan	100%	30%	20%	10%	5%	3%
Feb	100%	34%	25%	13%	9%	
Mar	100%	36%	28%	17%		
Apr	100%	38%	23%			
May	100%	40%				

retention rate is calculated by dividing the number of active users (for that cohort and timeframe) by the cohort's initial number of users. Each row of Table 13.2 is plotted as a separate cohort curve on the retention graph.

Watching Your Product-Market Fit Improve

If you are improving your product-market fit over time, your cohort retention curves will be moving up, reaching higher terminal values for newer cohorts. Figure 13.5, which shows the retention curves for three cohorts using our product, shows an example of how this would ideally look. Cohort A users signed up when we launched our MVP 24 months ago. Cohort B users signed up 18 months ago, and Cohort C users signed up 12 months ago. As you can see, we've improved our product-market fit over time, with our retention curve moving up. Each subsequent cohort has a lower initial drop-off, lower decay rate, and higher terminal value than the previous one.

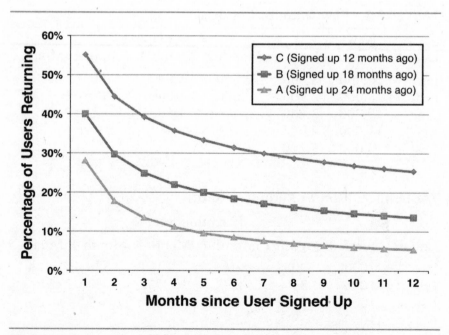

FIGURE 13.5   Improving Retention Rate over Time

THE EQUATION OF YOUR BUSINESS

It's great that the AARRR framework applies to all businesses at a high level and helps you focus on the right metric at the right time. But at some point, you need to take into account your specific business model to further optimize your business. There are several common business models, including e-commerce, subscription, and advertising. I've helped my consulting clients use analytics to optimize their results across all of those business models. I've used the same powerful tool to do so in each case: the equation of your business.

When there's something I want to optimize, my engineering and math training make my first instinct to express it as an equation. Countless times in school, one variable Y would be expressed as a function of another variable X and the goal was to find the value of X that resulted in the maximum possible value of Y. More advanced versions of this exercise involved multiple variables. The starting point was always an equation that told you how Y was calculated from X (or the multiple variables). That's the theoretical world of mathematics—and you can apply a similar technique in the real world of business.

Every business can be expressed as an equation. The goal is to come up with a quantitative representation of your business constructed from a set of metrics that you can use to optimize your business results. If it isn't entirely clear how to do that just yet, let me walk through an example.

There's one equation you can start with that applies to every business:

$$\text{Profit} = \text{Revenue} - \text{Cost}$$

This equation tells you that you can increase profit by increasing revenue or decreasing cost. You can apply it to any given period of time (e.g., day, week, or month). The metrics of revenue and cost are too high level to be actionable, but this is a good starting point. You are going to break down these higher-level metrics into formulas of more detailed metrics to go several levels deeper. This is what I call "peeling the analytics onion."

Most high-tech companies, especially those trying to achieve product-market fit, are much more focused on increasing revenue than reducing cost. That is because the economics of most high-tech products are such that as you achieve a higher volume of sales, the incremental revenue from each additional unit (called marginal revenue) exceeds the incremental cost to produce that additional unit (called the marginal cost). And the gap between marginal revenue and marginal cost grows larger as the volume grows larger.

Facebook is a good example to illustrate this. They have over 1 billion users. Serving up the Facebook website and mobile app in a timely manner to so many users requires a lot of servers, storage, networking hardware, and bandwidth to run Facebook's software. Does Facebook need to develop any additional software for each new user? Do they need to add an additional server when a new user joins? No. The only real incremental resources required would be a tiny amount of storage to save the user's data and a tiny amount of additional bandwidth. For all intents and purposes, the marginal cost of a new Facebook user is zero.

Facebook mainly makes money from advertisements it displays in its products. That new user will generate some small amount of incremental ad revenue. So a marginal cost of almost zero and a small marginal revenue result in a small marginal profit.

Let's return to the equation to break revenue down into actionable metrics. There are different ways to do this, but doing so on a "per user" basis usually works best:

$$Revenue = Users \times Average\ Revenue\ per\ User$$

This equation tells you that there are basically two ways to increase revenue: increase the number of users or increase the average revenue per user (ARPU). Perhaps you've heard the term ARPU before; it's a key metric tracked by many businesses.

The Equation of Your Business for an Advertising Revenue Model

The best way to break users and ARPU down further into more detailed metrics depends on the revenue model. For this example, let's assume we have a business that generates revenue from display advertising. With many ad-based products, the people who see the ads don't have to be registered users. Think of most popular content sites, such as YouTube or the *New York Times* website: We use the term *visitors* in these cases. Given the nuances of how web analytics tracking works, the term *unique visitors* makes it clear we are only counting each visitor once during the particular time period. So, for an advertising business:

$$Revenue = Visitors \times Average\ Revenue\ per\ Visitor$$

Display advertising is sold to advertisers on the basis of ad *impressions*, a term that just means that an ad was served on a page that a person visited. It doesn't necessarily mean that the visitor actually saw the ad. Let's say an advertiser buys a campaign of 100,000 impressions. The media site that sold the impressions would serve the ads, keeping track of how many they've served, and end that ad campaign once 100,000 have been served. The cost of the ads is specified in units of "CPM," or cost per thousand impressions (here "M" is the Roman numeral for 1,000). The CPM for this campaign was $10, making the total cost of the campaign $1,000 for 100,000 impressions. CPM can be a good way to compare different types of advertising on an apples-to-apples basis. As a result, you will often hear "effective CPM" used as a broader, catchall term. We can now expand average revenue per visitor:

$$Average\ Revenue\ per\ Visitor = Impressions\ per\ Visitor \\ \times Effective\ CPM \div 1,000$$

We can't really break down effective CPM any further. As we can see from our equations, it's a detailed metric that has a proportionate impact on revenue. If you double effective CPM, you will double revenue.

How can we break down impressions per visitor further? Remember, each of these equations applies for a particular time period. So, what factors determine the number of ad impressions served to a visitor in a given time period? Since visitors may visit our site multiple times in the same time period, we can model that. Ads are displayed on web pages, so the more web pages the average visitor visits (called pageviews), the more impressions. Finally, we control how many ad impressions are served on each page, so we can account for that. So we can expand impressions per visitor as follows:

$$\text{Impressions per Visitor} = \frac{\text{Visits}}{\text{Visitor}} \times \frac{\text{Pageviews}}{\text{Visit}} \times \frac{\text{Impressions}}{\text{Pageview}}$$

Each of the three metrics in this equation is a variable that we control or can try to influence. A change in the value of any of these metrics will result in a proportional change in revenue. We can drive more frequent visits to our site, for example, by updating our content often or sending emails enticing visitors back to our site. And we can try to get visitors to view more pages each time they visit by spreading articles across more than one page or including links to related articles. We can try to cram more ads per page, although at some point that will likely negatively impact the user experience enough that it will affect our retention metrics.

Now that we've expanded average revenue per visitor as much as we can, we can go back and expand visitors. As I mentioned earlier, it is beneficial to distinguish between new and returning users (or visitors).

$$\text{Visitors} = \text{New Visitors} + \text{Returning Visitors}$$

New visitors are people who visit your product for the first time (during a certain time period). The total number of new visitors can be broken down in a variety of ways—one of which is via the channel or source from which they came. Many businesses categorize new users by those who come via free versus paid channels, for example, organic search versus pay-per-click advertising. If your product has a viral loop, you can split new users into those who were acquired virally versus those who weren't. You could further break down the number of viral new users into a formula of viral loop metrics.

Returning visitors are people who visit your product during a certain time period who had already visited your product *before* the current time period. We can express returning visitors in terms of the total number of visitors we had in the prior time period multiplied by a retention rate. This retention rate is a little different from the one we discussed earlier because its context would only be from period-to-period (e.g., one month to the next) and not the entire life of the visitor. So let's call it "return rate" to avoid confusion. We express returning visitors as follows:

$$\text{Returning Visitors}_T = \text{Visitors}_{T-1} \times \text{Return Rate}$$

I've added the subscript T to denote the current time period and $T-1$ to denote the previous time period. Returning visitors and visitors are just values that you measure; you're not trying to influence them directly. Return rate would be the variable we would try to improve. For example, we could add a weekly or monthly email with links to popular or recommended stories to try to lure visitors back. We would calculate return rate from the other two numbers.

$$\text{Return Rate} = \frac{\text{Returning Visitors}_T}{\text{Visitors}_{T-1}}$$

If we take a step back, we can see that we started out with a very high level equation but managed to keep breaking the equation terms down until we had actionable metrics. That is what I mean by "peeling the onion." We happened to do it for an advertising-based business, but you can do it for any business.

The Equation of Your Business for a Subscription Revenue Model

Without going through the same level of detailed explanation, here is how I would peel the onion for a subscription-based business.

$$\text{Profit} = \text{Revenue} - \text{Cost}$$

We will again focus on increasing revenue and not break down cost.

$$\text{Revenue} = \text{Paying Users} \times \text{Average Revenue per Paying User}$$

I've used the term *paying users* instead of *users* to allow for the fact that not all of our users are paid subscribers. This would be the case if we offered a 30-day free trial, for example. It could also be the case if we had a *freemium* business model, where we offered both free and paid subscription levels. For this example, I am going to assume we are not freemium (all of our services require a paid subscription), but we do offer a free trial.

$$\text{Paying Users} = \text{New Paying Users} + \text{Repeat Paying Users}$$

As with the previous example, we break down the number of paying users into the new ones we acquired in this time period plus the paying users we retained from the past.

$$\text{Repeat Paying Users}_T = \text{Paying Users}_{T-1} \times (1 - \text{Cancellation Rate})$$

As with the previous example, we express repeat paying users for this time period (denoted with the subscript T) in terms of the number of paying users from the previous time period (denoted with the subscript $T - 1$). The cancellation rate is the percentage of paying users who cancel from one time period to the next. This is a very important metric for a subscription business to track and try to improve. We've broken down the metrics far enough in this direction, so let's return to new paying users to break down that metric.

$$\text{New Paying Users} = \text{Free Trial Users} \times \text{Trial Conversion Rate} + \text{Direct Paid Signups}$$

Some prospects who show up at our site may subscribe to one of our paid offerings right away (direct paid sign ups). Other prospects may sign up for the free trial first (free trial users). Only a certain percentage of free trial users convert to a paid subscription, measured by the trial conversion rate.

I won't write out the equations, but we could further break down the number of free trial users to account for the various channels through which we acquire prospects. Our breakdown should also include a metric for our conversion rate from prospect to free trial user. This would help us measure the effectiveness of our marketing efforts (landing pages, email campaigns, etc.)

This second example of the equation of your business for a completely different revenue model shows you how versatile a tool it is—one that can be applied to any business. You should sit down with your team to determine the equation of your business. The goal is to identify the key metrics that you want to measure and try to improve. The equation of your business helps you understand how much a change in each metric will affect your overall business results, so that you can prioritize where to make improvements.

ACHIEVING PROFITABILITY

I explained the equation of your business as it applies to a certain time period (e.g., day, week, or month). Another way to apply the equation of your business is to ignore time and look at it on a *per customer* basis.

$$\text{Profit} = \text{Number of Customers} \times \text{Profit per Customer}$$

This way of looking at profit wouldn't be as relevant if you were still seeking product-market fit. But if you've achieved product-market fit and are trying to reach profitability, it is very valuable. In the above equation, profit per customer is the metric to improve. Let's peel the onion another layer.

$$\text{Profit per Customer} = \text{Revenue per Customer} - \text{Cost per Customer}$$

There is a very powerful way to break this down further that provides insights into the "per customer" economics of your business. Unlike the last example, which was completely focused on revenue, when you are trying to achieve (or improve) profitability, you have to look at costs. But you should focus on one particular set of costs: the costs associated with acquiring a revenue-generating customer. This can be done by rearranging things a bit in the equation and introducing some new metrics. I'll share the equation, and then explain it.

$$\text{Profit per Customer} = \text{Customer Lifetime Value}$$
$$- \text{Customer Acquisition Cost}$$

Customer Lifetime Value

This equation is an alternate expression of profit per customer that is very useful. *Customer lifetime value* (LTV) is the profit that a customer generates for you *without taking into account the cost to acquire the customer*. Customer acquisition cost is the amount you pay on average to obtain a new customer. Breaking this cost out as a separate metric allows you to track and improve it. When your LTV is greater than your customer acquisition cost, then each new customer generates profit for your business. In order to have actionable metrics you can use to improve LTV, the onion needs to be peeled another layer.

$$LTV = ARPU \times \text{Average Customer Lifetime} \times \text{Gross Margin}$$

There's ARPU again—exactly the same metric discussed earlier—average revenue per user (per time period). For example, if all of your subscribers are paying you $10 per month, your ARPU would be $10 per month. The average customer lifetime is how many time periods your average customer stays with your business. If you multiply ARPU by the average customer lifetime, that tells you how much revenue your average customer generates for you (throughout the entire time they are a revenue-generating customer). Let's say you analyzed your customer data and found that your average customer lifetime was 10 months. Then average lifetime revenue would be $10 per month times 10 months, or $100.

Gross margin is a percentage that accounts for the cost of providing the product or service to the customer. Many high-tech companies have high (over 80 percent) gross margins and therefore ignore this term for simplicity.

There are more complex LTV models that account for the fact that the customer revenue isn't generated all at once but rather over time by discounting the cash flow stream using a cost of capital discount rate. However, you don't need that extra complexity, since the goal is not to have the most accurate measure of LTV, but simply to break it down into actionable metrics that you can track and improve.

The equation shows that you can increase LTV by increasing ARPU. You could increase ARPU by raising your prices, selling more to your existing customers, or adding new higher-priced products, for example.

You can also increase LTV by increasing your average customer lifetime, which you can do by decreasing your cancellation rate: the percentage of paying customers that stop paying you each time period.

This is more broadly called *churn rate* to include revenue models where the customer doesn't pay you directly. You can also think of it as one minus your retention rate (from one time period to the next). The average customer lifetime can actually be calculated from the churn rate using a simple formula:

$$\text{Average Customer Lifetime} = \frac{1}{\text{Churn Rate}}$$

For example, if your churn rate is 5 percent per month, then your customer lifetime is 20 months. You can reduce your churn rate by providing better customer service and support, by improving product quality and reliability, and by ensuring your product continues to meet customer needs. Since churn rate is the metric you are going to measure and try to improve, you can restate LTV in terms of it. Setting gross margin aside, this formula makes it very clear that the two ways to increase LTV are to increase ARPU and to decrease churn rate:

$$\text{LTV} = \frac{\text{ARPU} \times \text{Gross Margin}}{\text{Churn Rate}}$$

Customer Acquisition Cost

Let's return to customer acquisition cost (CAC), which you can calculate if you know the number of new customers you added in a given time period and your sales and marketing costs for the same time period:

$$\text{CAC} = \frac{\text{Sales and Marketing Costs}}{\text{New Customers Added}}$$

That equation is a convenient way to calculate CAC, but isn't really actionable. To use more actionable metrics, you can break it down as follows:

$$\text{CAC} = \frac{\text{Cost per Acquisition}}{\text{Prospect Conversion Rate}}$$

The cost per acquisition (often shortened to CPA) is how much it costs on average for each prospect. Let's say you advertise on Google AdWords and pay a cost-per-click (CPC) of $1.00. Then your CPA is $1.00 because each person who clicks on your ad will go to your website. To increase profit per customer, you want to decrease CAC—which you can do by decreasing CPA. You can achieve a lower CPA by finding lower-cost marketing programs and channels. Perhaps you can find other keywords with lower CPCs, or find some inexpensive ad inventory to buy. For impression-based advertising (such as display ads), you can decrease your CPA by improving the effectiveness of your ads (i.e., increasing your ad clickthrough rates).

When people click on your Google ad, they arrive at your landing page or home page and become prospects. From here, they can learn more about your product and become customers. The percentage of prospects that convert into customers is your prospect conversion rate. You can improve this metric by optimizing your landing pages for conversion, which includes improving the messaging and UX design. A/B testing is a great tool for doing that.

To generate a profit, you want your LTV to exceed your CAC, and the larger the difference, the larger your profit. Instead of looking at the difference, some businesses prefer to look at the ratio of LTV to CAC. For example, a general guideline for successful SaaS businesses is that your LTV-to-CAC ratio should be greater than three.

In this chapter, I show how you can leverage analytics to measure your business and to create a framework for optimization. Before you launch your product, you rely more heavily on qualitative learning; but once you launch a live product, you have a wealth of analytics at your disposal. You can assess how you're doing on product-market fit by using cohort analysis to track your retention rate over time. In addition, you can use the AARRR framework and the equation of your business to identify the key metrics to improve. You can use LTV and CAC to achieve and improve your profitability. In the next chapter, I build on what you learned in this chapter and share the Lean Product Analytics Process: a repeatable process you can follow to optimize the metrics of your business. I also share a case study that applies that process and the principles from this chapter.

Chapter 14

Use Analytics to Optimize Your Product and Business

Chapter 13 covers how to define and measure your key metrics, providing the foundation for using analytics to improve your product and business. The great thing about a live product is that analytics let you clearly see the results of changes that you make. With a good A/B testing framework, you can easily conduct experiments and make improvements rapidly. Companies that do this well have an advantage over their competitors. The size of your current business becomes less relevant; instead, how quickly you can learn from customers and iterate becomes the basis of competition. Speed is a weapon—in today's fast-paced world, David can unseat Goliath overnight. This chapter shows you how to harness the power of analytics to optimize your product and business.

THE LEAN PRODUCT ANALYTICS PROCESS

I've worked with many companies to define and implement their analytics framework, which I then used to optimize their product and business. Along the way, I developed a simple, repeatable process for how to use analytics to drive improvements—the Lean Product Analytics Process, illustrated in Figure 14.1.

The first step in the Lean Product Analytics Process is to define the key metrics for your business, which I covered in the prior chapter. Next, you need to start measuring these metrics so you can establish a *baseline* value for each one so you know where you stand today. This step may sound relatively trivial, but a lot of companies stumble here. Setting up metrics tracking for—or instrumenting—your product takes work. After the initial setup, it usually takes additional effort to ensure that the metrics data you're collecting are accurate and match what you intended to track. Analytics packages such as

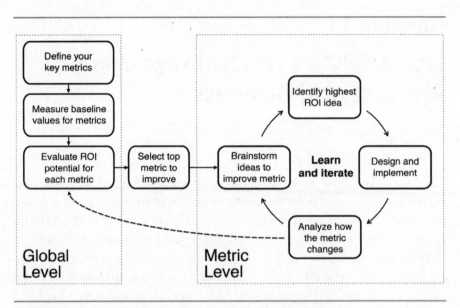

FIGURE 14.1 The Lean Product Analytics Process

Google Analytics, KISSmetrics, Mixpanel, and Flurry can make this task easier. The data for many key metrics often reside in your product's database, so many companies use a combination of third-party packages and homegrown analytics code. The goal is to have a set of analytics dashboards that make it easy to see how each metric is performing over time.

Once you have accurate baseline values for your metrics, you can proceed to the next step: evaluating each metric's upside potential. This is where you assess each metric through an ROI lens. I find it helpful to think of each metric as a dial on a gauge, as you might see on a car dashboard or an air pump. The value on the dial that the needle is currently pointing to is the baseline value for that metric. You want to evaluate how easy or hard it would be to move the needle— that is, to improve each metric. There will be a diminishing returns curve, and you want to roughly estimate where you are on that curve.

Figure 14.2 shows ROI curves for three different metrics. On each chart, the vertical axis shows the value of the metric (where higher is better). From the equation of your business, you should know how much an increase in the value of each metric translates into an improvement in the higher-level metric you are trying to improve

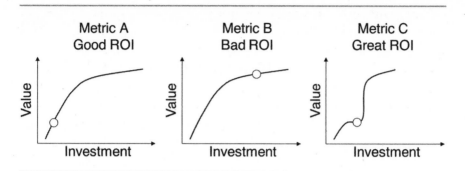

FIGURE 14.2   ROI Curves for Three Different Metrics

(e.g., revenue). The horizontal axis shows the level of investment required. Each ROI curve shows the improvement opportunities for that metric, and the circle shows the baseline value of where each metric currently is on its curve.

Metric A is near the bottom of its ROI curve where the slope is still steep. Therefore, you should be able to make a meaningful improvement in the value of this metric with relatively little effort. This could be the case if you haven't yet worked on improving metric A. In contrast, metric B is near the top of its ROI curve where the slope has flattened out. Even if you put in a lot of effort, you would only see a small improvement in the value of the metric. This could be the case if you have already spent a lot of effort improving metric B.

Most metrics offer the typical diminishing returns curve shown for metrics A and B. However, there are some opportunities where just a small amount of effort can cause a major improvement in a metric's value. I call these "silver bullets," and metric C in Figure 14.2 illustrates such an opportunity. These are special cases where a small but profound change can cause some aspect of your product or business to work much better than before. You usually discover these silver bullet opportunities through careful analysis.

Once you've assessed each metric's upside potential, you move on to the next step in the process: selecting the metric that offers the most promising opportunities for improvement. This is the "metric that matters most" (MTMM) discussed in the previous chapter. As Figure 14.1 indicates, this is the point where you transition from a global perspective across all your metrics to focus on just the MTMM.

You want to brainstorm as many improvement ideas as you can for this top metric. Then you want to estimate how much each idea will improve the metric. When you do so, you are forming hypotheses, such as "Creating a mobile optimized version of the registration page will improve the conversion rate from 20 to 30 percent." You also want to estimate the effort for each idea so you can evaluate ROI (as discussed in Chapter 6). You then pick the highest ROI idea to pursue.

Next, you design and implement the top improvement idea. Ideally, you would use an A/B testing framework to roll out the improvement to a fraction of your users. This gives simultaneous metrics results that you can compare to assess the relative performance of your improvement versus the status quo. If you don't have an A/B testing framework and the metric you're trying to improve has had a relatively stable value, you can roll out the change and do a before-and-after comparison. However, A/B testing is better because it reduces the risk of other unknown factors causing a difference in the results.

Of course, you hope your target metric improves. But you've made progress even if it doesn't because you've gained valuable learning that you can apply to create better hypotheses as you iterate in the future. You now revisit your list of ideas to improve the metric and select the next best idea, repeating the loop shown on the right side of Figure 14.1.

Eventually, you should see the target metric improving after trying several ideas. You can continue to iterate and improve this metric and should experience diminishing returns as you do. At some point, a different metric will offer greater opportunities for improvement. As shown in Figure 14.1, that is when you jump back to the global metrics perspective and identify the next top metric for improvement (MTMM). You then apply the iterative improvement loop on that metric.

Repeatedly following this process allows you to systematically drive improvements to your business. Having a robust analytics framework and set of dashboards lets you easily track how your business is doing. Having an A/B testing platform lets you continuously experiment to see if new ideas can outperform the current champion. Once you have the critical elements in place—the analytics framework, the dashboards, the A/B testing platform, and a continuous improvement process—the limiting factor just becomes how quickly you can identify and implement good, creative ideas to throw into the machine.

Avoiding a Local Maximum

That brings up a good point, which is to be careful not to get stuck at a *local maximum*. In the process of improving a metric, you may reach a point where it seems that you can't improve it any further. Sometimes, it's true that you've fully maximized the metric and aren't able to improve it any further. However, sometimes you are stuck at a local maximum but actually *could* improve the metric further by considering a completely different alternative or approach.

For example—if you have a landing page, you could A/B test different colors for your primary call-to-action button to find which yields the highest conversion rate. Google famously A/B tested 41 different shades of blue for a toolbar to see which color resulted in the highest clickthrough rate. However, if you stop iterating after you find the best color for the button, you'll probably be stuck at a local maximum. You should also experiment with different messaging, images, page layouts, and so forth, to see if you can achieve an even higher conversion rate. Your rate of improvement depends on how quickly you can identify and implement good ideas. A/B testing makes experimentation easy, but it's up to you to determine the hypotheses to test. To avoid getting stuck at a local maximum, you want to make sure you cast a wide net in coming up with potential improvement ideas.

A LEAN PRODUCT ANALYTICS CASE STUDY: FRIENDSTER

To reinforce the Lean Product Analytics Process and help bring it to life, I'll walk through an end-to-end case study of the process in action. This is a real-world example from Friendster where I more than doubled a key metric in just one week by applying this process.

When I joined social networking startup Friendster as the head of product, it was clear that viral customer acquisition was important. We had a large user base and were generating some advertising revenue, but the average revenue per user was too low to justify spending money to acquire customers (as is often the case with large-scale consumer businesses). Fortunately, we didn't have to—viral marketing allowed us to acquire users for free. Because of network effects, the value of a social networking product like Friendster increases exponentially with the number of active users. We knew that rapidly growing our user base was critical to success, and viral marketing offered the best way to do that. Therefore, I made improving our viral growth one of my top objectives. Everyone in the company shared this perspective, but no one had actually *measured* how our viral growth was doing. So I started with the first step of the Lean Product Analytics Process: defining our key metrics.

Define Your Key Metrics

We were tracking new users, and were also able to track which new users had been *invited* to join versus those that hadn't. While "new users from invites" was a high-level metric we cared about, it wasn't actionable. So I applied my equation of the business technique to break this high-level metric down into more actionable metrics that we could try to improve.

I started by defining our viral loop: the steps by which we acquired a new customer from an existing customer, shown in Figure 14.3. The process starts with our current users in the bottom left box. However, not all users generate new customers through viral marketing. While we have a larger number of registered users, only our active users invite their friends to join Friendster (the inactive ones don't). So I broke out active users separately. Using our product, active users

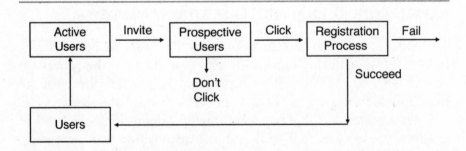

FIGURE 14.3   Friendster Viral Loop

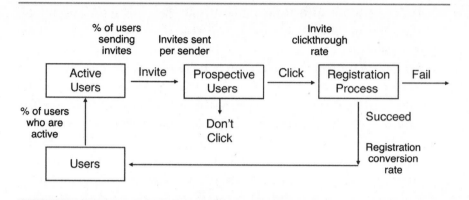

FIGURE 14.4   Friendster Viral Loop Metrics

send email invitations to their friends who aren't yet using Friendster (prospective users). When a prospective user receives the email invitation, they either click on the link in the email to sign up for Friendster or they don't. The ones that do end up going through our registration process, which some people complete and some don't. The invitees that successfully complete registration become users, who can go on to be active users and repeat the loop again.

Having defined the viral loop, I next wanted to determine the metrics I would use to track it. I didn't want to track "atomic" metrics, such as the number of active users, because the values would fluctuate with the size of user base. Instead I wanted to identify "normalized" ratio metrics that enabled apples-to-apples comparisons over time. I came up with a set of five metrics that met that criterion and that, taken together, fully captured all aspects of our viral loop, shown in Figure 14.4:

1. **Percentage of users who are active:** This metric was calculated by dividing the number of active users by the total number of registered users.
2. **Percentage of users sending invites:** Not all users sent invites, so this metric let us isolate that factor. It was calculated by dividing the number of users who sent invites by the number of active users.
3. **Average number of invites sent per sender:** When users sent invitations to their friends, they could invite just one friend or

several friends at a time. This metric was calculated by taking the total number of invites sent divided by the number of users who sent invites.

4. **Invite clickthrough rate:** The percentage of prospective users who clicked on the link in the email invitation, calculated by taking the number of prospective users who clicked on the link divided by the number of prospective users who were sent an invitation.

5. **Registration conversion rate:** The percentage of prospective users arriving at the registration page that actually completed the registration process. This metric was calculated by dividing the number of prospective users who registered by the number of prospective users who visited the registration page.

These metrics apply to and can be calculated for any given timeframe (e.g., past 30 days). Multiplying these five factors together gives the *viral coefficient* of the loop. If your coefficient is greater than one, then your product is officially "viral," which means that each current user generates more than one new user, resulting in exponential growth—like a nuclear reactor that goes supercritical. Products don't remain viral for long periods of time (if they did, everyone with Internet access would become a user). When a viral product achieves high market penetration, there just aren't as many prospective users left to join. Facebook is in this enviable position. That being said, a viral coefficient that's less than 1 but still high—say 0.4—is nothing to sneeze at. That still means you're growing your user base by 40 percent per time period for free through viral marketing.

Measure Baseline Values for Metrics

After identifying these five metrics, the next step in the process is to establish the baseline value for each one. There is no comparison between today's third-party analytics packages and those available when I worked at Friendster. We wrote our own code to track and calculate these metrics. We started by capturing the data for each atomic metric, such as registered users, active users, email clicks, and so forth. We then calculated the five ratio metrics from these atomic metrics.

For the sake of simplicity, I'll continue the case study by focusing on just three of the five metrics and their baseline values:

- Percentage of users sending invites = 15 percent
- Average number of invites sent per sender = 2.3
- Registration conversion rate = 85 percent

Evaluate ROI Potential for Each Metric

The next step in the Lean Product Analytics Process was to select which metric we thought offered the greatest opportunity for improvement. Imagine for a minute that you were in my shoes. Recognizing that you only have the limited information I've shared here, which of these three metrics would you choose to focus on improving first? How would you decide?

I realize you don't have specific information about potential improvement ideas for each metric. Taking an ROI approach, it's difficult to estimate the return, or increase in value, that could realistically be achieved for each metric. A hack you can use when you don't have much information is what I call the *upside potential* of a metric—that is, what the maximum possible improvement *could* be. You estimate this by considering the metric's current baseline value and its maximum possible value. See Figure 14.5, which illustrates the concept using our three metrics.

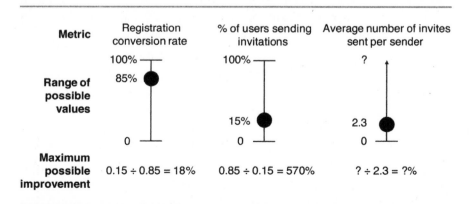

FIGURE 14.5   The Upside Potential of a Metric

Let's start by looking at registration conversion rate. It's a percentage, so it can range from a minimum of 0 percent to a maximum of 100 percent. The current value is 85 percent. So no matter what improvements we make, we can only increase the metric an additional 15 percentage points (to 100 percent). To express this upside potential as a percentage, we take 15 percent and divide it by 85 percent, which is 18 percent. So the maximum upside potential for registration conversion rate is 18 percent.

The second metric—the percentage of users sending invitations—can also range from 0 to 100 percent. Its current value is 15 percent, so we could theoretically improve this metric by as much as 85 percentage points. To express this upside potential as a percentage, we take 85 percent and divide it by 15 percent, which is 570 percent. So the percentage of users sending invitations has significantly more upside potential than the registration conversion rate.

Now let's turn to the third metric: average number of invites sent per sender. That metric is *not* a percentage. Its minimum value is 0. Its current value is 2.3. What is its maximum possible value? Offhand, it's seems hard to say exactly. But we need to have at least an estimate of the maximum value to calculate the upside potential of this metric. Could it be infinity? No, because there are a finite number of people in the world. Each user could invite *all* of his or her friends to join Friendster. So the maximum value would be the average number of friends that a Friendster user has. What is that number? I didn't know exactly, but I thought a reasonable estimate was between 100 and 200. In the 1990s, psychologist Robin Dunbar conducted research on the maximum number of people with whom a person can maintain stable social relationships. He concluded this limit—called Dunbar's number—is 150, which is the middle of my estimated range. If we use 150, we see that the upside potential of the average number of invites sent per sender is $150 \div 2.3 = 6,520\%$. Even using the more conservative value of 100, the upside potential of this metric far exceeds that of the other two metrics.

When you saw Figure 14.5, you may have experienced déjà vu. Take a look at the three metric ROI curves in Figure 14.2 again. Do you sense a similarity? The percentage of users sending invites is like metric A, offering a good ROI. The registration conversion rate is like metric B, offering a bad ROI. The average number of invites sent per sender *could* be like metric C. We won't know for sure until we see how much we can move the needle and how much effort that takes.

Select Top Metric to Improve

I decided to focus on trying to improve the average number of invites sent per sender, mainly due to its much larger upside potential. I also chose to focus on this metric because improving it didn't necessarily involve trying to change human behavior. Fifteen percent of our users were already sending invites; we were just going to try to get them to send more. In contrast, trying to increase the percentage of users who invited friends *would* require behavior change. For whatever reasons, the other 85 percent of users had chosen *not* to invite their friends, despite our best efforts to get them to do so. It was harder to envision how we would move the needle much on that front. I also knew that our current user experience for inviting friends required too much manual effort and was confident that we could improve the user experience to make it easier.

The Metric Optimization Loop

Now that I had selected the average number of invites sent per sender as the top metric to improve, I moved on to the next step in the Lean Product Analytics Process. At this point, I entered the metric optimization loop shown in the right side of Figure 14.1. I brainstormed potential improvement ideas with the team. We then discussed for each idea how much we thought it would improve the metric and how much effort it would take. After doing so, we concluded that our highest ROI idea was an address book importer. Though address book importers are commonplace now, they weren't back then. Many of our users had stored their friends' email addresses in an address book that was tied to their email account at providers such as Gmail and Yahoo! Mail. The address book importer would let users enter the credentials for their email website and then import their friends' contact information into Friendster. The address book importer we designed displayed the list of imported contacts and let users select the ones they want to invite. We hypothesized that building such an importer would help us to significantly improve the average number of invites sent per sender.

On the technical implementation side, we could leverage some of the initial development work across all of the various email providers, but there was a certain amount of work required for each different email service. At this point, I realized it would be beneficial to break the feature into smaller pieces (as discussed in Chapter 6), with a feature chunk for each email provider. To test our hypothesis with the least amount of effort, I decided to pursue an MVP address book importer that only worked with one email service. After analyzing our user information, I found that Yahoo! Mail was the most popular email service among our users. So that feature chunk offered the highest ROI. The next step in the process was to design and implement the solution, which took about one week of work for a product manager and a developer.

Silver Bullet or Not?

We launched our improvement and proceeded to the next and most exciting step in the Lean Product Analytics Process: watching how our metric changed. Figure 14.6 shows a chart of the metric before and after we launched our improvement. The vertical axis shows the average number of invites sent per sender and the horizontal axis shows the date. Like many websites, we had seasonality in our usage patterns; many metrics varied quite a bit from weekday to weekend. As a result, we tracked seven-day averages for most metrics to more easily see trends. The data point for each day in Figure 14.6 actually displays the average of the metric's value for the trailing seven days.

Looking at the chart, we had over a month of baseline data where the value of the metric was quite stable, staying between 2.2 and 2.4. Where the graph changes from the smooth horizontal line and starts to shoot up and to the right corresponds with the date we launched our improvement. Because we plotted the seven-day average, it took several days for the chart to catch up with the new average value after launching the address book importer. The new value for the average number of invites sent per sender kept growing each day and then settled out around 5.3. I was ecstatic!

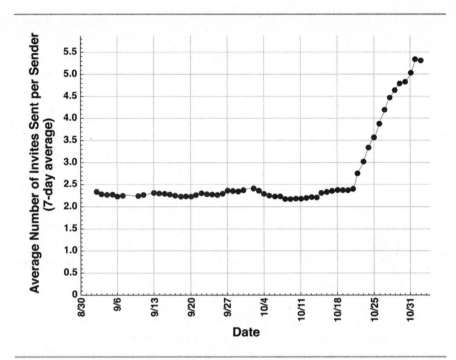

FIGURE 14.6   Average Number of Invites Sent per Sender: Before and After

This was a silver bullet improvement: Just a week's worth of work had more than doubled this key metric ($5.3 \div 2.3 = 2.3 \times$)! Going back to the equation of the business, a 2.3× improvement in this metric directly translated into a 2.3× improvement in the number of new customers we were acquiring from viral growth. And we had only built the importer for *one* email provider. With this clear quantitative evidence that validated our hypothesis, we proceeded to complete the incremental work required to add additional email providers to our importer, which yielded additional gains in this key metric.

We continued to improve the average number of invites sent per sender for a while longer but then exhausted all the high ROI improvement ideas we could identify. At that point, we exited the improvement loop for that metric and switched our focus to a different viral loop metric that offered a higher ROI.

This example shows how easy it can be to use analytics to improve your business. By applying the Lean Product Analytics Process, you can achieve similar results. As with the MarketingReport.com case study in Chapter 11, I didn't do anything extraordinary; I just followed the process and principles I've described in this book.

OPTIMIZATION WITH A/B TESTING

As Chapter 7 discusses, A/B testing, also called split testing, is a quantitative technique where you test two (or more) alternatives simultaneously to compare how they perform. At the time that I worked at Friendster, A/B testing tools were not readily available and building an in-house tool would have required a large amount of valuable engineering resources. That's why I did a "before and after" comparison of the metric I was trying to improve, which worked out fine. Nowadays, you would ideally run an A/B test for each improvement idea you implement. Running the new version concurrent with the old one helps avoid other potential sources of variation.

An important concept in A/B testing is statistical significance, which is determined by the difference in performance and the sample size. There are online tools to help you calculate the statistical confidence level for your test. So you don't necessarily need to know the formula, but it's important to know that statistical significance is higher for larger differences in performance and for larger sample sizes. If your sample size is too low, you won't achieve statistically significant results. If you have two alternatives with very similar performance, it may take a very large sample size to discern any statistically significant difference.

There are numerous third-party A/B testing tools available, including Optimizely, Unbounce, KISSmetrics, Visual Website Optimizer, and Google Content Experiments (part of Google Analytics). Many companies also choose to create their own in-house A/B testing platform. These tools let you specify one or more variations and then randomly distribute traffic among the variations. They keep track of the results for the metric you care about and show you how each variation is performing, along with statistical confidence levels based on the sample sizes.

Many companies have incorporated A/B testing into their product release process, especially when making major changes. Instead of instantly switching from the old version of their product by launching the new version, they keep the old version running for almost all users and "launch" the new version to a small percentage of users. Then, they compare key metrics across the new and old versions. Before ramping up the percentage of users who see the new version, the product team wants to make sure the metrics targeted for improvement are performing better and that other key metrics aren't materially worse. This process, called throttling, is a great way to apply Lean principles to reduce risk *after* you've launched your product. Eventually, if the metrics look good, 100 percent of users are switched to the new version and the old version just goes away.

Netflix is known for its robust A/B testing on both the marketing and product fronts. In response to the question, "What types of things does Netflix A/B test aside from member sign-up?" on question and answer website Quora, Netflix Chief Product Officer Neil Hunt replied: "Short answer—almost everything." Hunt explained how Netflix tests different user interface variations, recommendation algorithms, button placements and sizes, page load times, and quality levels of video streaming encoding. Hunt closed his response with:

> We are very proud of our empirical focus, because it makes us humble—we realize that most of the time, we don't know up-front what customers want. The feedback from testing quickly sets us straight, and helps make sure that our efforts are really focused at optimizing the things that make a difference in the customer experience.

Is A/B Testing All You Need?

A/B testing is the ultimate evidence-based product decision-making tool. You are generating data from the real-world behavior of many users, so there is no risk of a disconnect between what users tell you and what they do. You are not by their side as they experience the test, so there is no risk of you perturbing the results. Of course, a product team cannot live on quant alone—don't forget about Oprah. There will be times when you need to complement your quant testing with qualitative learning to understand the whys behind the behavior.

Product teams that reach the point of enjoying rapid, iterative A/B testing have come a long way from their pre-MVP days, when there was less hard data available to make decisions. Some people might be tempted to skip all the qualitative testing and learning, just launch an MVP candidate and attempt to A/B test their way to product-market fit. That approach would almost certainly waste resources and fail. In that scenario, A/B testing would most likely guide you to an inferior local maximum that leaves you far from product-market fit.

Let's refer back to the Product-Market Fit Pyramid, shown again in Figure 14.7. The hypotheses you make in one layer affect all the layers above it. Your UX is the easiest layer to change. You can also change your feature set, but it takes more effort. But the foundational elements of product-market fit—your target customers, their underserved benefits, and your value proposition—are difficult to change once you've built your product. Once you've locked in your hypotheses for these layers, they are like a set of interconnected tectonic plates. If you move one of them after you've already built your product, much of the product you've built will no longer be relevant—like an earthquake that reduces a building to rubble. When that happens, human nature can make you want to salvage and reuse as much as of your work as you can. But doing so can add onerous constraints to your solution space, which is suboptimal when you

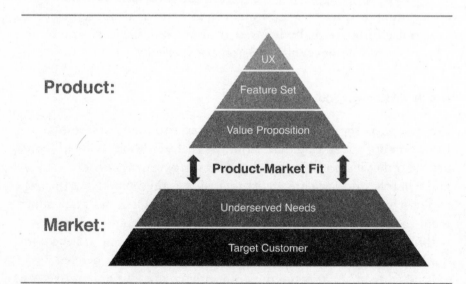

FIGURE 14.7   Product-Market Fit Pyramid

are changing your problem-space hypotheses. You would be better off building again from scratch on top of the new foundation.

The Lean Product Process follows the sequence it does so that you validate your key hypotheses in the order that most reduces risk and increases your odds of achieving product-market fit. The problem space is not as amenable to A/B testing as the solution space. The three lower layers of the Product-Market Fit Pyramid require qualitative research for you to create, test, and improve your hypotheses. There is a natural progression from more qualitative learning to more quantitative learning after you launch your product. In a nutshell: qualitative helps you define your product and quantitative helps you optimize your product. You need both Oprah and Spock to create a successful product.

Chapter 15

Conclusion

My goal for this playbook is to help you create products that customers love. It began with the Product-Market Fit Pyramid—an actionable model that defines the components of product-market fit and how they are connected. Your market consists of your target customers and their needs, and your product is the combination of your value proposition, feature set, and user experience. When you try to achieve product-market fit, you make critical hypotheses at each of these five layers.

The Lean Product Process guides you through the formulation and testing of your hypotheses with these six steps:

1. Determine your target customers
2. Identify underserved customer needs
3. Define your value proposition
4. Specify your minimum viable product (MVP) feature set
5. Create your MVP prototype
6. Test your MVP with customers

The process starts in the problem space and progresses to the solution space. You begin by determining your target customers, which you describe using personas. To create the most value for customers, you use the importance versus satisfaction framework to identify their important but underserved needs. Using the Kano model, you define a differentiated value proposition that better meets those needs for your target customers. You then take an MVP approach, trying to identify the minimum set of functionality required to deliver the key parts of your value proposition. You bring your MVP feature set to life by applying the principles of great UX design to create a prototype with a usable and delightful user experience.

To assess product-market fit, you test your MVP candidate with your target customers, who can give you better feedback in the solution space than in the problem space. To save resources and iterate more quickly, you ideally test with design deliverables such as clickable or tappable mockups before actually building your product. You use the knowledge you gain to revise your hypotheses and your MVP candidate. You continue to iterate through the hypothesize-design-test-learn loop with additional waves of user testing, hopefully achieving higher and higher levels of product-market fit. As you test, you may decide to pivot to a more promising opportunity by changing one or more of your fundamental assumptions.

Once you have validated your product-market fit, it's time to build your MVP. To reduce risk and deliver customer value more quickly, you should build your product in an incremental, iterative manner using Agile development. QA and test-driven development help achieve higher product quality; continuous integration and continuous deployment help improve the speed of your development process.

After you've launched your product, you employ analytics to understand how customers are using it. Your retention rate gives you a quantitative measure of product-market fit, and cohort analysis shows you how it changes over time. Once you have good retention, you can focus on improving other macro-metrics in Dave McClure's AARRR framework (acquisition, activation, retention, revenue, and referral). Defining the equation of your business helps you identify the key metrics for your particular business, and the Lean Product Analytics Process provides a systematic way of optimizing your metrics, resulting in greater revenue and profitability.

I hope you find the Lean Product Process and the other guidance in this book valuable. In addition to the advice I've shared throughout the book, I want to leave you with this list of 10 best practices for creating successful products.

1. **Have a point of view but stay open-minded.** As you probably realize, building products is not for the faint of heart. You constantly have to make decisions under conditions of uncertainty. Therefore, it's important to have a point of view and be decisive. At the same time, you should identify how to test the areas of greatest uncertainty and risk. As you test, you should avoid anchoring on your initial point of view and instead be objective and evidence-based. By listening with

an open mind, you will gain the most learning, which you should use to revise and improve your thinking.

2. **Articulate your hypotheses.** Creating a product requires that you make a lot of decisions and assumptions. An interesting way to think of a product is to view it as the collection of all the hypotheses that led to it becoming what it is. You should try to be as explicit as possible about the hypotheses you are making. Writing down your hypotheses is incredibly helpful. As Admiral Hyman G. Rickover said, "Nothing so sharpens the thought process as writing down one's arguments." Your teammates should do the same, and you should make your team's hypotheses transparent. By posting your hypotheses where everyone on the team can review them and by openly discussing them, they will only get better.

3. **Prioritize ruthlessly.** There are many ideas contending for resources when you are creating a product, and tradeoffs are unavoidable. Being vague about your priorities usually leads to inefficiency and indecision. That's why I recommend rank ordering your backlog and all other to-do lists. Clearly identifying what is most important helps you spend your valuable resources and time wisely. As Peter Drucker said, "Time is the scarcest resource and unless it is managed nothing else can be managed."

4. **Keep your scope small but focused.** Related to prioritization is the idea of deliberately keeping your scope small. As discussed in Chapter 6, smaller batch sizes encourage focus and are completed more quickly, enabling faster feedback from customers. Be careful not to bite off more than required to accomplish your objective. This doesn't mean that you should avoid tackling large tasks altogether—just that you should try to split them up into smaller items to reduce risk and iterate more quickly.

5. **Talk to customers.** Your customers are the judges of product-market fit; they help you obtain the learning that you need to achieve it. The sooner and more frequently you talk with customers, the better. It's worth investing the effort to establish systems that make your user testing easier to schedule and conduct, so that you talk to more users over time. Don't allow too much time to pass since your last user test; customers will always surprise you with unexpected learning.

6. **Test before you build.** Many teams rush to build their product without testing any of their hypotheses. But building before you've

validated product-market fit will almost certainly waste resources. It is faster and less costly to iterate with design deliverables than with an actual product. Plus, once a team builds a product, they naturally grow attached to it, which can cause them to be less open-minded and less willing to make major changes.

7. **Avoid a local maximum.** As you'll recall from Chapter 14, a local maximum means you have achieved the best results possible within the range of options you have considered, but that better alternatives—that you *haven't* considered—exist outside of those options. You can tell you are in a local maximum when you are unable to drive additional improvements to your product-market fit or to your key metrics. At this point, you need to take a fresh perspective to make further progress. Shift your current thinking to a higher level and use divergent thinking to come up with new ideas worth exploring.

8. **Try out promising tools and techniques.** Team members often employ tools and techniques with which they have prior experience. Some product teams can be somewhat insular in this area, sticking to what they know instead of seeking out potentially better solutions. In contrast, many product teams proactively investigate new tools and techniques once enough people deem them better than the status quo. You don't want to constantly change based on the latest fad, but it's valuable to compare notes with others and stay relatively current on this front. You should give promising new ideas a try when they could significantly improve how your team accomplishes its work.

9. **Ensure your team has the right skills.** As you can see from the breadth of topics this book covers, creating a successful product requires a wide range of skills. For software products, the list of skills includes product management, user research, interaction design, visual design, copywriting, Agile development, front-end coding, back-end coding, QA, DevOps, and analytics. Different product teams will possess different levels of each important skill. You should assess where your team is strong and where it is weak. Identify which skill improvements will make the biggest difference in your situation and try to augment your team accordingly (e.g., through additional hires, contractors, advisors, or training).

10. **Cultivate your team's collaboration.** I like to say that building products is a team sport. Picture a basketball team of five players. The guards, forwards, and center each have their own role. To achieve their goal of scoring a basket, the five individuals need to coordinate their actions as a team, passing the ball to one another to execute the play. A product team creating a new feature is like a basketball team scoring a basket. The product manager drives the ball down the court by writing user stories and prioritizing the backlog. The product manager passes the ball to the interaction designer, who designs the flows and wireframes and then passes the ball to the visual designer. The visual designer creates the look and feel with high-fidelity mockups and passes the ball to the developer. The developer, who implements the product based on the user stories and mockups, shoots the ball and scores the basket. Strong skills alone don't make a great product team. Team members must each understand their role, the other roles on the team, and how the team works together to achieve its goals. You should take an occasional break from working to discuss *how* you work as a team and how you can do so better. It's fun being on a team that works well together, and strong collaboration increases your chances of building a successful product.

I encourage you to visit this book's companion website http:// leanproductplaybook.com. There you'll find new and updated information related to the topics I covered in the book. The website is also a place for us to share and discuss ideas with others who are passionate about building great products. You can also find me online at:

@danolsen on Twitter: http://twitter.com/danolsen
LinkedIn: http://linkedin.com/in/danolsen98
SlideShare: http://slideshare.net/dan_o
Lean Product Meetup: http://meetup.com/lean-product
Olsen Solutions consulting: http://olsensolutions.com

I would enjoy hearing about your experiences applying the ideas in this book as well as any questions or feedback you have. You can reach me at dan@leanproductplaybook.com. I hope you find my advice in this playbook useful and that it helps you achieve success with your products.

Acknowledgments

First and foremost, I give my deepest thanks to my wonderful wife, Vanessa. This book would not have been possible without her incredible support; our lives were already quite busy before I started working on this project. Thank you for selflessly shouldering such a large burden so that I could have time to pursue my goal of writing this book.

Thank you, Mom and Dad, for all the love, support, encouragement, and happiness you have given me.

Thank you, Sofia and Xavier. Every day you make me smile and inspire me to be my best.

Thank you, Diane, for always being there for us, and for everything you do to keep our lives sane.

I thank my editorial team at John Wiley & Sons for their hard work to make this book a reality: Richard Narramore, Christine Moore, Tiffany Colon, and Abirami Srikandan. Thank you, Richard, for sharing the vision of what this book could be. Christine, I sincerely appreciate your valuable contributions to my writing as well as your indispensable advice and encouragement.

I am very grateful to Dave McClure. Thank you for getting me started on the speaker circuit, for all your support, and for being the unique individual you are.

Thank you to my reviewers, Leon Barnard, Eli Beit-Zuri, Luca Candela, Anand Chandrasekaran, Greg Cohen, Steven Cohn, Sam Crisco, Mike Goos, Kaaren Hanson, Laura Klein, Thomas Kunjappu, Alexis Longinotti, SC Moatti, Michael Nolan, Christian Pirkner, Don Pitt, Hiten Shah, Sunil Sharma, and Christina Vaquera. Your feedback was incredibly valuable, and I really appreciate how you came through on short notice.

Thank you to Sean Ellis, Christine Liu, Dave McClure, Geoffrey Moore, Ben Norris, Jussi Pasanen, Christian Rohrer, Hiten Shah, Juanma Teixidó, Becca Tetzlaff, and Tony Ulwick for kindly allowing me to reference their great work.

I'm grateful to Marty Cagan, Jean-Christophe Curelop, Diana Kander, Ash Maurya, Brian O'Leary, David Vandagriff, Alexandra Watkins, and Bruce Williams for their helpful advice related to the book.

To Ken Fine, Mike Goos, Steve Grey, Chris Haase, Christian Pirkner, John Gatewood, Ivan Gatewood, Rich Shank, Guy Borda, Matt McPartlin, Ty Ahmad-Taylor, Marty Cagan, Chung Meng Cheong, Greg Cohen, Steven Cohn, Sam Crisco, Sean Ellis, Josh Elman, Kaaren Hanson, Laura Klein, Ranjith Kumaran, Tom Lee, Aaron Levie, Alexis Longinotti, Alex Lopes, Jack Lynch, Jeff Maggioncalda, Dan Martell, Dave McClure, Scott Mitic, SC Moatti, Michael Nolan, Ken Norton, Alberto Savoia, Jim Scheinman, Jeff Schulte, Hiten Shah, Jeff Tangney, Joe Wolf, and Kai Xu: I'm grateful for your friendship and support.

I'm fortunate to have learned a lot from working with talented people at some incredible places. At Naval Reactors, a one-of-a-kind organization that sets a high bar for rigorous thinking, I learned how to design and build highly complex products with cross-functional teams. I thank Jim Kearney, Steve Rodgers, Carl Oosterman, and Bill Shirley for their mentorship there.

I'm grateful to the Stanford Graduate School of Business for everything I learned during my two unforgettable years there and for connecting me with so many amazing classmates and alumni.

Thank you to all the great people I worked with at Intuit, where I learned so much. I am especially grateful to Steve Grey for his mentorship, for building such a strong team, and for so many fond memories.

I give my heartfelt appreciation to my YourVersion team for all your dedication and hard work. As a first-time CEO, I learned a lot from you and our experiences together. I'm proud of our accomplishments and how we pushed the envelope to build, test, and launch new product features so quickly.

Thanks to everyone who has attended or watched videos of my talks and workshops, viewed my SlideShares, and read my posts—for listening to what I had to say and helping to spread the ideas in this book.

To all the members, speakers, and sponsors of my Lean Product & Lean UX Silicon Valley Meetup: Thank you for your enthusiasm in sharing and discussing best practices together every month.

Finally, I extend my sincere gratitude to all of my clients for the opportunity to work with you, which helped me refine the ideas in this book. I've had the chance to meet and work with so many great CEOs, founders, product leaders, and team members. There are too many to list, but you know who you are, and I am grateful to each of you. I also want to extend a special thanks to the teams at Medallia and Financial Engines for all their support while I worked on this book.

References

Cooper, Alan. 1999. *The Inmates Are Running the Asylum*. Indianapolis: Sams.

Moore, Geoffrey. 2014. *Crossing the Chasm, 3rd ed.* New York: Harper Business.

Ries, Eric. 2011. *The Lean Startup*. New York: Crown Business.

Ulwick, Anthony. 2005. *What Customers Want*. New York: McGraw-Hill.

Resources

Here's a list of the tools I mention in the book, plus others that I've found useful. I also list valuable books, people, and blogs that I recommend checking out. They are all great sources of information related to the topics I've covered in this playbook. For an updated list of resources, visit http://leanproductplaybook.com.

TOOLS

UX Design

- Balsamiq: http://balsamiq.com
- Axure: http://axure.com
- UXPin: www.uxpin.com
- Sketch: http://bohemiancoding.com/sketch
- InVision: http://invisionapp.com
- Flinto: https://www.flinto.com
- Marvel: https://marvelapp.com
- POP: https://popapp.in
- Dapp: http://dapp.kerofrog.com.au
- OmniGraffle: https://www.omnigroup.com/omnigraffle
- Bootstrap: http://getbootstrap.com

User Research

- UserTesting: http://usertesting.com
- Validately: https://validately.com
- Ask Your Target Market: http://aytm.com
- Qualaroo: https://qualaroo.com
- SurveyMonkey: https://surveymonkey.com
- Join.me: https://www.join.me
- Screenleap: http://screenleap.com

Agile Development

- Trello: https://trello.com
- JIRA Agile: https://atlassian.com/software/jira/agile
- Pivotal Tracker: http://pivotaltracker.com
- Rally: https://rallydev.com
- VersionOne: http://versionone.com
- SwiftKanban: http://swiftkanban.com
- LeanKit: http://leankit.com

Analytics and A/B Testing

- Google Analytics: http://google.com/analytics
- KISSmetrics: https://www.kissmetrics.com
- Mixpanel: https://mixpanel.com
- Flurry: http://flurry.com
- Optimizely: https://www.optimizely.com
- Unbounce: http://unbounce.com
- Visual Website Optimizer: http://vwo.com

BOOKS

- *What Customers Want* by Anthony Ulwick
- *UX for Lean Startups* by Laura Klein
- *The Lean Startup* by Eric Ries
- *Running Lean* by Ash Maurya
- *Crossing the Chasm* and *Inside the Tornado* by Geoffrey Moore
- *Inspired* by Marty Cagan
- *The Inmates Are Running the Asylum* by Alan Cooper
- *Don't Make Me Think* and *Rocket Surgery Made Easy* by Steve Krug
- *The Non-Designer's Design Book* by Robin Williams
- *The Elements of User Experience* by Jesse James Garrett
- *Measuring the User Experience* by Tom Tullis and Bill Albert
- *Designing for Emotion* by Aaron Walter
- *Smart Choices* by John Hammond, Ralph Keeney, and Howard Raiffa
- *Prototype It* by Alberto Savoia
- *Information Visualization* by Colin Ware

PEOPLE AND BLOGS

Person/Website	Twitter	Website URL
Eric Ries	@ericries	http://startuplessonslearned.com
Steve Blank	@sgblank	http://steveblank.com
Ash Maurya	@ashmaurya	http://practicetrumpstheory.com
Dave McClure	@davemcclure	http://davemcclure.com
Hiten Shah	@hnshah	https://hitenism.com
KISSmetrics	@KISSmetrics	https://blog.kissmetrics.com
Sean Ellis	@SeanEllis	http://startup-marketing.com
GrowthHackers	@GrowthHackers	https://growthhackers.com
Andrew Chen	@andrewchen	http://andrewchen.co
Laura Klein	@lauraklein	http://usersknow.com
Dan Martell	@danmartell	http://danmartell.com/blog
David Skok	@BostonVC	http://forentrepreneurs.com
Luke Wroblewski	@lukew	http://lukew.com/ff/
A List Apart	@alistapart	http://alistapart.com
500 Startups	@500Startups	http://500.co/blog

Index

About the Author

Dan Olsen is an entrepreneur, consultant, and Lean product expert. At Olsen Solutions, he works with CEOs and product leaders to help them build great products and strong product teams, often as interim VP of Product.

Dan has worked with a range of businesses, from small, early-stage startups to large public companies, on a wide variety of web and mobile products. His clients include Facebook, Box, Microsoft YouSendIt (now Hightail), Epocrates, Medallia, Chartboost, XING, Financial Engines, and One Medical Group.

Prior to consulting, Dan worked at Intuit, where he led the Quicken product team to record sales and profit. He also led product management at social networking pioneer Friendster, and was the cofounder and CEO of TechCrunch award winner YourVersion, a personalized news startup.

Dan earned a BS in electrical engineering from Northwestern and an MBA from Stanford. He also earned a master's degree in industrial engineering from Virginia Tech, where he studied the Lean manufacturing principles that inspired the Lean Startup movement.

Dan lives in Silicon Valley, where he hosts the monthly Lean Product Meetup http://meetup.com/lean-product. He enjoys sharing and discussing his ideas with as many people as he can and gives talks and workshops frequently. Feel free to drop him a line anytime at dan@leanproductplaybook.com or @danolsen on Twitter.